Brandwashed

Also by Martin Lindstrom

buy·ology

Brandwashed

TRICKS COMPANIES USE to MANIPULATE OUR MINDS and PERSUADE US to BUY

Martin Lindstrom

CROWN
BUSINESS
NEW YORK

Published in the United States by Crown Business,
an imprint of the Crown Publishing Group,
a division of Random House, Inc., New York.
www.crownpublishing.com

CROWN BUSINESS is a trademark and CROWN and the Rising Sun
colophon are registered trademarks of Random House, Inc.

Crown Business books are available at special discounts for bulk purchases for
sales promotions or corporate use. Special editions, including personalized covers,
excerpts of existing books, or books with corporate logos, can be created in large
quantities for special needs. For more information, contact Premium Sales at
(212) 572-2232 or e-mail specialmarkets@randomhouse.com.

Library of Congress Cataloging-in-Publication Data
Lindstrom, Martin, 1970–
    Brandwashed : tricks companies use to manipulate our minds
and persuade us to buy / Martin Lindstrom.—1st ed.
        p.   cm.
    Includes bibliographical references and index.
    1. Consumer behavior. 2. Consumers—Psychology. 3. Brand
choice—Psychological aspects. 4. Marketing—Psychological
aspects. 5. Neuromarketing. I. Title.
HF5415.32.L557   2011
658.8'343—dc23   2011023484

ISBN 978-0-385-53173-3
eISBN 978-0-385-53174-0

Printed in the United States of America

JACKET DESIGN BY EVAN GAFFNEY

10 9 8 7 6 5 4 3 2

First Edition

Dorit, Tore, and Allan—

without you I would be nothing

CONTENTS

Foreword by Morgan Spurlock   ix

Introduction: A Brand Detox   1

CHAPTER 1

Buy Buy Baby

When companies start marketing to us in the womb   9

CHAPTER 2

Peddling Panic and Paranoia

Why fear sells   28

CHAPTER 3

I Can't Quit You

Brand addicts, shopaholics, and why we can't live
without our smart phones   54

CHAPTER 4

Buy It, Get Laid

The new face of sex (and the sexes) in advertising   79

CHAPTER 5

Under Pressure

The power of peers   104

CHAPTER 6

Oh, Sweet Memories

The new (but also old) face of nostalgia marketing   131

CHAPTER 7

Marketers' Royal Flush

The hidden powers of celebrity and fame   153

CHAPTER 8

Hope in a Jar

The price of health, happiness, and spiritual
enlightenment   181

CHAPTER 9

Every Breath You Take, They'll Be Watching You

The end of privacy   203

CONCLUSION

I'll Have What Mrs. Morgenson Is Having

The most powerful hidden persuader of them all: us   237

Acknowledgments   256

Notes   261

Index   285

MORGAN SPURLOCK PRESENTS THE GREATEST FOREWORD EVER WRITTEN

by Morgan Spurlock,

director of *Super Size Me* and *The Greatest Movie Ever Sold*

O ver the years, I've put myself in some of the most horrible situations and scenarios possible. I once traveled to a half dozen or so Middle Eastern war zones, including Pakistan and Afghanistan, in the hope of finding the exact coordinates of Osama bin Laden. I worked as a coal miner in West Virginia, and I spent nearly a month wearing a jumpsuit in a prison cell. I also wrote, directed, and starred in the movie *Super Size Me,* in which I gorged myself with McDonald's hamburgers, French fries, and sodas until my body was bloated, my liver was pâté, and my cholesterol was just this side of death.

But can I just go on record as saying that nothing—not jail, not black coal dust, not the Afghanistan mountains, not the awful mirror image of my own McTorso—prepared me for the world of advertising and marketing?

My latest film, *Pom Wonderful Presents: The Greatest Movie Ever Sold,* is a documentary about the insidious ways corporations manage to get their brands in our faces all the time—and incidentally, includes my own efforts to finance my film by precisely the same means. (In the end, I approached roughly six hundred brands in all. Most of them told me politely to get lost. In the end, twenty-two of them agreed to sponsor

my movie.) As is the case with all the movies I make, all I was looking for was a little honesty and transparency. This *is* the Information
Age, right? Aren't honesty and transparency supposed to be "the thing"
right now?

My goal in making *Pom Wonderful Presents: The Greatest Movie Ever
Sold* was to make you, me, and everybody else in the world aware of the
extent to which we are marketed to, and clubbed over the head with
brands, just about every second of our lives. After all, you can't even go
into the men's room at the mall without being obliged to pee on a urinal
cake that's advertising "Spiderman 6." Nor can you escape the brand
paradise that is your local shopping mall without climbing behind the
wheel of your Toyota Scion LC, turning up the volume on the Keb' Mo'
playing on your Apple iPod that connects to your car radio via a Griffin
iTrip FM transmitter, and sliding your Dockers-enclosed leg and Nike
Air Force 1 sneaker onto the gas, at which point you're assailed by one
highway billboard after another for Kenny Rogers Roasters, Taco Bell,
KFC, Papa Gino's, Holiday Inn, Comfort Inn, Marriott Courtyard Res-
idence, Shell Oil, and—are you getting some sense of why I wanted to
make my movie? In one scene, I asked consumer advocate Ralph Nader
where I should go to avoid all marketing and advertising entreaties. "To
sleep," he told me. It was a depressing moment.

Which brings me to Martin Lindstrom and the groundbreaking
book you're gripping in your hands.

I first met Martin when he agreed to appear in my film. I'd read
his last book, *Buyology,* which explores the hot spots in our brains that
compel humans to buy everything from Harley-Davidson motorbikes
to Corona beers, and I thought he'd be an interesting, innovative person
to talk to. As a global marketing guru who works with everyone from
Coca-Cola to Disney to Microsoft, as well as a consumer who detests
being manipulated by advertisers and corporations, Martin maintains a
very fine line between what he knows and (how else to put it?) what he
really knows. If you catch my drift.

In *Brandwashed,* Martin yanks back the curtains and serves up a
page-turning exposé of how advertisers and companies make us feel
we'll be bereft, stupid, and social outcasts unless we buy that new model
of iPad or that new brand of deodorant or that make of baby stroller

whose price is equal to the monthly rent of your average urban studio apartment. Just as I do in my documentary, he aims to expose all that goes on in the subterranean world of marketing and advertising. Only he has one distinct advantage. He's a true insider. Martin takes us into conference rooms across the world. He talks to advertising and marketing executives and industry insiders. He teases out some fantastic war stories, including some of his own.

Along the way he shows us the most underhanded ploys and tricks that marketers use to get us to part with our money. Such as scaring the crap out of us; reminding us of wonderfully fuzzy days gone by (which actually never existed); using peer pressure so we'll feel like wallflowers if we don't do, or buy, what the rest of the world is doing, or buying; using sex to sell us everything from perfume to men's underwear; paying celebrities a bajillion dollars to endorse bottled water, or just cross their skinny legs (clad in $300 jeans) in the front row of a fashion show; injecting what we eat and drink with this or that magical elixir that promises to give us a one-way ticket to Shangri-la and eternal life; and that's not even the half of what you'll learn inside *Brandwashed.*

In the course of these pages, Martin also rolls out a TV reality show called *The Morgensons,* where he implants a real-life family inside a Southern California neighborhood to test whether word-of-mouth recommendations work. (It's fascinating, and also pretty horrifying, to consider that that sweet young couple down the block could actually be paid marketing commandos.) With my film and his book, he and I share a goal: to let consumers—you and me—in on the game, so that we know when we're being conned or manipulated, and can fight back, or at least duck for cover, that is, assuming there's anyplace left to hide.

Now, because I'm all about transparency, you may very well be saying to yourself, *Hmm, Morgan seems to like this book a lot and he's never struck me as a bullshitter, so it must be worth reading, right?* Well, guess what. You've just been hooked by not just one but several of the marketing ploys you'll read about in this book.

Only, in this case, it happens to be true: *Brandwashed* and Martin Lindstrom will blow your mind. Don't just take my word for it. Read on and see for yourself.

INTRODUCTION

A Brand Detox

In the UK, there's an anticonsumerist movement called Enough. Its adherents believe that we as a society quite simply consume too much *stuff* and that our overconsuming culture is partly responsible for many of the social ills that plague our planet, from world poverty to environmental destruction to social alienation. Enough urges people to ask themselves, "How much is enough?" "How can we live more lightly, and with less?" and "How can we be less dependent on buying things to feel good about ourselves?"[1]

I couldn't agree more. I may be a professional marketer, but I'm a consumer, too. As someone who's been on the front lines of the branding wars for over twenty years, I've spent countless hours behind closed doors with CEOs, advertising executives, and marketing mavens at some of the biggest companies in the world. So I've seen—and at times been profoundly disturbed by—the full range of psychological tricks and schemes companies and their shrewd marketers and advertisers have concocted to prey on our most deeply rooted fears, dreams, and desires, all in the service of persuading us to buy their brands and products.

Yes, I've been a part of it. No, I'm not always proud of it. I've been part of some campaigns that I'm incredibly proud of. But I've also seen how far some marketing goes. Which is why, around the time I started writing this book—one in which I hope to pick up where Vance Packard's 1957 classic, *The Hidden Persuaders*, left off and expose the best-kept secrets of how today's companies and their marketers are manipulating us—I decided that as a consumer, I'd quite simply had *enough*.

So last year I decided I would go on a brand detox—a consumer fast of sorts. More specifically I decided that I would not buy any new brands for one solid year. I would allow myself to continue to use the possessions I already owned—my clothes, my cell phone, and so on. But I wouldn't buy a single new brand. How do I define "brand"? Well, in my line of work I look at life through a particular lens: one that sees virtually everything on earth—from the cell phones and computers we use to the watches and clothes we wear to the movies we watch and books we read to the foods we eat to the celebrities and sports teams we worship—as a brand. A form of ID. A statement to the world about who we are or who we wish to be. In short, in today's marketing- and advertising-saturated world, we cannot escape brands.

Nevertheless, I was determined to try to prove that it *was* possible to resist all the temptations our consumer culture throws at us.

Yes, I knew this would be a challenge, especially for a guy who is on the road over three hundred nights a year. It would mean no more Pepsi. No more Fiji water. No more glasses of good French wine. That new album I was hearing such good things about? Forget about it. The brand of American chewing gum I'm partial to? No dice.

How else did my lifestyle have to change? In the morning, since I couldn't eat any branded foods, like Cheerios or English muffins, I started eating an apple for breakfast. To shave, I use a battery-powered Gillette Power razor known as the Fusion; luckily I already owned that, but since I couldn't buy shaving cream, I had to start shaving in the shower. I traded my electric toothbrush and Colgate toothpaste for tiny travel ones the airlines offer for free, and I started using the other freebies that airlines and hotels provided.

Some habits I had to give up completely. Sometimes, in countries where eating the local cuisine can be dodgy, I bring along packs of ramen noodles. Well, sorry, but no ramen. I'd just have to take my chances. As any traveler knows, the air gets dry on long plane flights and in hotel rooms, so I typically use a face moisturizer by Clarins. Not anymore. I often pop a vitamin C if I feel a head cold in the wings. Now I'd have to make do with a glass of orange juice (the generic kind). Sometimes before TV appearances, if my hair looks crazy, I'll use a hair gel called Dax. For a year I'd have to run a comb through it and hope for the best.

If I didn't live the kind of life that I do, I might have been able to survive without brands for an eternity. But given my insane travel schedule, I knew I had to allow myself some exceptions, so before I kicked off my detox, I first set a few ground rules. As I said, I could still use the things I already owned. I was also permitted to buy plane tickets, lodging, transportation, and nonbranded food, of course (so I wouldn't starve). I just couldn't buy any new brands—or ask for any. Thus, in midflight, when the drinks cart came rolling around, I couldn't ask for Pepsi or Diet Coke. Instead, I asked for "some soda." I continued going to restaurants, but I made sure to order the "house wine," and if a dish claimed it came with "Provençal" potatoes or "Adirondack tomatoes," well, I'd just have to order something else.

For the first few months I did quite well, if I may say so myself. In some respects, not buying anything new came as a relief. But at the same time it wasn't easy. Have you ever tried shopping at the grocery store and not buying a single brand? In airports, for example, while I'm killing time between flights, I like to wander through duty-free shops. I enjoy buying gifts for friends or stocking up on chocolate. Then I'd remember—*Martin, you're in brand rehab*—and I'd turn around and leave. At the time of my detox, the world was struggling through the worst economic crisis since the Great Depression—one precipitated in part by out-of-control consumer spending. So like most people, I wasn't immune to the feeling that unless my purchases were essential and practical, I shouldn't buy anything. Yet knowing that so many people felt this way, companies and advertisers were doing everything in their power to get us to open our wallets. From London to Singapore to Dubai to New York, fantastic sales and bargains and special offers were *everywhere*; it seemed every store window was a sea of signs for 50 percent off this or two for the price of one of that screaming my name. Each time I walked down the street, I seemed to be assaulted by posters and billboards for some sexy new fragrance or shiny new brand of wristwatch—on sale, of course. Every time I turned on the TV, all that seemed to be on were commercials: svelte twentysomethings gathered poolside drinking a particular brand of beer; rosy-cheeked children gathered at the breakfast table on a sunny morning, happily scarfing down a bowl of a certain brand of cereal; Olympic gold medalists performing feats of impossible athleticism in a certain brand of sports gear and sneakers. Somehow, even the packages of mouthwash and fruit juice and potato chips and candy bars I'd never noticed before were calling to me from the aisles of the supermarket and drugstore and seemed oddly alluring.

But I took the high ground.

Under the terms of my detox, I wasn't even allowed to buy a book, a magazine, or a newspaper (yes, I think of all of these as brands that tell the world who you are or, in some cases, would like to be perceived as being), and let me tell you, those fourteen-hour transatlantic flights got pretty boring with nothing to read. Then there were the frustrating times a friend would tell me about a fascinating article or novel that had just come out. Under normal circumstances, I would have hunted down the thing. Now I couldn't. Instead I'd stand balefully at the magazine kiosk or inside a bookstore, scanning the newspaper or magazine or book in question until a clerk shot me the universal look for "Get out if you're not going to buy something."

Harder still was being around my friends. I couldn't buy a round of beers at a bar or a gift for someone's birthday—and I happen to *love* buying people presents. Instead, I made up one lame excuse after another. I feared my friends secretly thought I was being a tightwad, that my brand detox was just an excuse to be cheap. But I stuck with it anyway. I was determined to prove that with a little discipline and willpower, I could inure myself to all the persuasive marketeering, advertising, and branding that surrounded me.

Then, six months into it, it all came tumbling down. The fact that my brand fast lasted only six months, and the fact that a person who should have known better got punked by his own profession, says a whole lot about just how shrewd companies are at engineering desire. So does what happened to me immediately after I toppled off the wagon.

If I Fell

My relapse took place in Cyprus. The night it happened, I was scheduled to give a keynote presentation. But when my plane touched down at the airport, I discovered the airline had misplaced my suitcase. It was gone. Which meant I didn't have anything to wear for my speech. I had the pants I was wearing, but no shirt other than a sweaty, unfragrant black T-shirt that I had no time to wash. Here's something they don't teach you in Harvard Business School: *Never give a keynote presentation naked from the waist up.* This wasn't some drive-by, meet-and-greet appearance, either. It was an important presentation, and they were paying me well and expecting a good crowd. I admit it, I freaked out.

Half an hour after checking into my hotel, I found myself standing at the cash register of a local tourist trap, holding a white T-shirt in my hands. It was the only color the store had. The letters on the front spelled out "I ❤ CYPRUS."

I'd officially relapsed. And all for a crappy T-shirt, too. Not only did I break my detox, but for the first time in recent memory, I broke my all-in-black rule and gave my presentation wearing black pants and my ridiculous white T-shirt. Despite my questionable attire, the evening went well, but that wasn't the point. As they say in certain twelve-step programs, one drink is too much, and a thousand is too few. In other words, now that I'd given myself permission to end my brand fast, the dam had burst. I went a little nuts.

Twenty-four hours later, I was debarking in Milan, Italy, the fashion capital of the world. Let me tell you: this is not a place you want to be if you're trying to give up brands. Wouldn't you know it, but there happened to be a huge furniture sale in a store not far from my hotel! Fantastic handcrafted stuff, too! *Sold* to the little blond guy in the I ❤ CYPRUS T-shirt! From then on, I was buying San Pellegrino water, Wrigley's gum, and minibar M&Ms by the caseload. Then there was the black Cole Haan winter jacket I bought in New York, and . . . the list goes on. Over the next few weeks and months, I couldn't stop. You could have sold me roadkill so long as it had a label and a logo on it. All because of one lost suitcase and one cheap replacement T-shirt.

Yes, I make my living helping companies build and strengthen brands, and in the end, even I couldn't resist my own medicine.

That's when I realized I had been *brandwashed*.

The New Generation of Hidden Persuaders

When I was first approached to write this book as a follow-up to my previous book, *Buyology*, the world was still digging out from economic free fall. Did anyone really want to read a book about brands and products, I wondered, at a time when the vast majority of our wallets and handbags were either empty or zippered shut? Then it struck me: could there actually be a *better* time to write a book exposing how companies trick, seduce, and persuade us into buying more unnecessary stuff?

In 1957 a journalist named Vance Packard wrote *The Hidden Persuaders*, a book that pulled back the curtain on all the psychological tricks and tactics companies and their marketers and advertisers were using to manipulate people's minds and persuade them to buy. It was shocking. It was groundbreaking. It was controversial. And it's nothing compared to what's going on in the marketing and advertising worlds today.

Nearly six decades later, businesses, marketers, advertisers, and retailers have gotten far craftier, savvier, and more sinister. Today, thanks to all the sophisticated new tools and technologies they have at their disposal and all the new research in the fields of consumer behavior, cognitive psychology, and neuroscience, companies know more about what makes us tick than Vance Packard ever could have imagined. They scan our brains and uncover our deepest subconscious fears, dreams, vulnerabilities, and desires. They mine the digital footprints we leave behind each time we swipe a loyalty card at the drugstore, charge something with a credit card, or view a product online, and then they use that information to target us with offers tailored to our unique psychological profiles. They hijack information from our own computers, cell phones, and even Facebook profiles and run it through sophisticated algorithms to predict who we are and what we might buy.

They know more than they ever have before about what inspires us, scares us, soothes us, seduces us. What alleviates our guilt or makes us feel less alone, more connected to the scattered human tribe. What makes us feel more confident, more beloved, more secure, more nostalgic, more spiritually fulfilled. And they know far more about how to use all this information to obscure the truth, manipulate our minds, and persuade us to buy.

In the pages ahead, we'll learn all about what they know, how they know it, and how they turn around and use that knowledge to seduce us and take our dollars. We'll pull back the curtain on how specific companies have crafted the most successful ad campaigns, viral marketing plans, and product launches in recent memory, including how Axe probed the sexual fantasies of thousands of male consumers in preparation for rolling out its infamous body spray campaign, how Calvin Klein rolled out its best-selling fragrance, Euphoria, how a marketing campaign for a popular brand of vodka transformed an entire country's drinking habits, and more.

We'll look at the subtle yet powerful ways companies use peer pressure to persuade us. We'll see how they stealthily play on our fear, guilt, nostalgia, and celebrity worship, often in ways that hit us beneath our conscious awareness. We'll see examples of how some particularly devious companies have figured out how to physically and psychologically addict us to their products and how certain popular Web sites are actually rewiring our brains to hook us on the act of shopping and buying. We'll look at the new ways sex is being used to sell to us, including the results of an fMRI study that reveals something shocking about how heterosexual men *really* respond to sexually provocative images of attractive men and surprising findings about who marketers are *really* selling to when they "brand" the newest sixteen-year-old teen heartthrob.

We'll see all the underhanded ways companies are collecting information without our knowledge, not just about our buying habits but about everything about us—our race and sexual orientation; our address, phone number, and real-time location; our education level, approximate income, and family size; our favorite movies and books; our friends' favorite books and movies; and much more—then turning around and using this information to sell us even more stuff. We'll explore the techniques advertisers and marketers are using to reach and influence children at a younger and younger age and read about alarming research revealing that not only do these techniques work, but children's lifelong preferences for brands can be shaped and set and at a *much* younger age than ever imagined.

I'll also be revealing the results of a revolutionary guerrilla marketing experiment I carried out in service of this book. The inspiration for it was the 2009 David Duchovny and Demi Moore movie *The Joneses*, about a picture-perfect family that moves into a suburban neighborhood. As the movie unfolds, it turns out they're not a real family at all but a group of covert marketers who are attempting to persuade their neighbors to adapt new products. Intrigued by this premise, I decided to stage my own reality television show, *The Morgensons*. I picked a family, armed them with a bunch of brands and products, and let them loose on their neighbors in an upscale Southern California gated community. The questions going in were: How powerfully can word of mouth influence our buying habits? Can simply seeing another person drink a certain type of beer, apply a certain line of mascara, spray a certain brand of perfume, type on a certain make of computer, or use the latest environmentally conscious product persuade us to do the same?

You'll find out in the last chapter of this book. And should you pick up the enhanced e-book version of this book (and have a video-enabled reading device), you'll get to see the Morgensons in action; throughout the book you'll encounter countless video clips of actual footage from the experiment.

My goal is that by understanding just how today's *newest* hidden persuaders are conspiring to brandwash us, we as consumers can battle back. The purpose of this book is not to get you to stop buying—I've proved that is frankly impossible. The purpose is to educate and empower you to make smarter, sounder, more informed decisions about what we're buying and why. After all, enough is enough.

Martin Lindstrom
New York

CHAPTER 1

Buy Buy Baby

WHEN COMPANIES START MARKETING TO US IN THE WOMB

Located in Paris, CEW France, short for Cosmetic Executive Women, is a group of 270 female beauty-business professionals whose avowed mission is to show the world that beauty products not only are more than a trivial indulgence but can actually be used to improve people's lives. To that end, in 1996, CEW set up its first-ever Center of Beauty at one of Europe's most prestigious hospitals, with the goal of providing emotional and psychological support to patients afflicted by trauma or disease.

Many of the patients at the center suffer from dementia or from amnesia caused by brain traumas resulting from car, motorcycle, skiing, and other accidents. Some are comatose. Many are alert but can no longer speak. Most can't remember any details of their accidents, how they ended up in the hospital, or in many cases even their names.

Which is why the professionals at the Center of Beauty, led by former psychotherapist Marie-France Archambault, decided to enter their patients' pasts through their noses. Teaming up with the international fragrance company International Flavors and Fragrances, Archambault's team has bottled more than 150 distinct aromas, including the forest, grass, rain, the ocean, chocolate, and many others, and then run what they call olfactive workshops, in which they use these fragrances to help patients regain memories they've lost.

CEW works closely with hospital medical teams and language therapists and also brings in family members and close friends to create a portrait of the life a patient was leading before his or her accident took place. Where did he grow up? In the country? In the city? What were the smells of his childhood? What were his youthful passions, his hobbies? His favorite foods and drinks? What smells might be most familiar? Then they design fragrances to trigger those memories.

CEW worked with one former cosmetics company executive who had suffered a serious stroke. When probed by doctors, he remembered almost nothing about his past. Yet once the CEW team placed the smell of strawberry under his nose, the patient began speaking haltingly about his youth. For another severely impaired patient who had no recollection of his motorcycle accident, the mere smell of street pavement was enough to "unfreeze" his brain. Just murmuring the words "tar, motorcycle" after sniffing the scent helped him take his first cognitive steps toward recovery.

The team has also worked with geriatric and Alzheimer's patients who, after being exposed to fragrances from their childhoods, have shown radical improvements in recalling who they were and are.

What this goes to show is that certain associations and memories from our childhoods are resilient enough to survive even the most debilitating of brain traumas. When I first heard about this amazing CEW program, it confirmed a suspicion I'd had for a long time, namely, that most of our adult tastes and preferences—whether for food, drink, clothes, shoes, cosmetics, shampoos, or anything else—are actually rooted in our early childhoods. After all, if a childhood love for the smell of strawberry can survive a serious stroke, the preference must be pretty deeply ingrained, right?

Studies have indeed shown that a majority of our brand and product preferences (and in some cases the values that they represent) are pretty firmly embedded in us by the age of seven. But based on what I've seen in my line of work, I'd posit that, thanks in no small part to the tricks and manipulations of probing marketers, stealth advertisers, and profit-driven companies that you'll be reading about throughout this book, our brand preferences are set in stone even before that—by the age of four or five. In fact, based on some new research I've uncovered, I'd even go so far to suggest that some of the cleverest manufacturers in the world are at work trying to manipulate our taste preferences even earlier. Much earlier. Like before we're even born.

Born to Buy

When I was very young, my parents loved the sound of bossa nova. Stan Getz. Astrud Gilberto. "The Girl from Ipanema," "Corcovado," "So Danco Samba," and all the others. There was one long, dreary winter when they played bossa nova practically nonstop. So I suppose it's little wonder I grew up to be completely in love with its sound (as I still am today).

Only thing is, my mother was seven months pregnant with me that winter.

Scientists have known for years that maternal speech is audible in utero; in other words, a fetus can actually hear the mother's voice from inside the womb. But more recent research has found that a developing fetus can hear a far broader range of tones that come from *outside* the mother's body as well. It used to be assumed that the mother's internal bodily sounds (the beat of the heart, the swooshing of the amniotic fluid) drowned out all external noises—like music. But studies reveal this isn't quite true; in fact, not only can soon-to-be babies hear music from inside the womb, but the music they hear leaves a powerful and lasting impression that can actually shape their adult tastes. Says Minna Huotilainen, a research fellow at the Collegium for Advanced Studies, University of Helsinki, Finland, "Music is very powerful in producing fetal memories. When the mother frequently listens to music, the fetus will learn to recognize and prefer that same music compared to other music." What's more, she adds, "The fetus will build the same musical taste with his/her mother automatically, since all the hormones of the mother are shared by the fetus."[1] I guess that may explain why I still have so many bossa nova CDs in my collection. And on my iPod.

In and of itself, this seems pretty harmless, even kind of sweet.

After all, who wouldn't feel a little warm and fuzzy inside knowing that their adult love of the Beatles or Norah Jones may be rooted in the fact that Mom listened to *Abbey Road* and "Don't Know Why" over and over while she was pregnant? But when you think about how many tunes, sounds, and jingles are linked to brands and products, this all starts to seem a whole lot more sinister. And there is indeed evidence to indicate that hearing tunes and jingles in the womb favorably disposes us to those jingles—and possibly the brands with which they are associated—later on.

In one study, Professor Peter Hepper of the Queen's University, Belfast, found that newborn babies will actually show a preference for a TV theme song (the more basic and repetitive the better) that was heard frequently by their mothers during their pregnancies. When newborns—just two to four days old—whose mothers had watched the long-running Australian TV soap opera *Neighbours* during pregnancy were played that show's theme song, they became more alert and less agitated, stopped squirming, and had a decreased heart rate—signs that they were orienting well to their environment. And it wasn't just because music in general has soothing qualities; as Hepper reported, those same infants "showed no such reaction to other, unfamiliar tunes."[2]

How can we explain this striking finding? Says another globally recognized fetal researcher, who chooses to remain anonymous, "While it is very difficult to test newborn babies, and the studies to date have been done on small numbers of children, it is possible that fetuses could develop a response to sounds heard repeatedly while they were in the womb, especially if those sounds were associated with a change in the mother's emotional state. So if, for example, the mother heard a catchy jingle every day while pregnant and the mother had a pleasant or relaxing response to the jingle, the fetus, and later the newborn, could have a conditioned response to that sound pattern and attend to it differently than other unfamiliar sounds." In other words, the minute we're born, we may already be *biologically programmed* to like the sounds and music we were exposed to in utero.

Shrewd marketers have begun to cook up all kinds of ways to

capitalize on this. For one, a few years ago, a major Asian shopping mall chain realized that since pregnant mothers spent a great deal of time shopping, the potential for "priming" these women was significant. Pregnancy, after all, is among the most primal, emotional periods in women's lives. Between the hormonal changes and the nervous anticipation of bringing another life into the world, it's also one of the times when women are most vulnerable to suggestion. So the shopping mall chain began experimenting with the unconscious power of smells and sounds. First, it began spraying Johnson & Johnson's baby powder in every area of the mall where clothing was sold. Then it infused the fragrance of cherry across areas of the mall where one could buy food and beverages. Then it started playing soothing music from the era when these women were born (in order to evoke positive memories from their own childhoods, a popular tactic you'll read more about later on).

The mall executives were hoping this would boost sales among pregnant mothers (which it did). But to everyone's surprise, it also had another far more unexpected result. A year or so into the sensory experiment, the chain began to be inundated by letters from mothers attesting to the spellbinding effect the shopping center had on their now newborns. Turns out the moment they entered the mall, their babies calmed down. If they were fussing and crying, they simmered down at once, an effect that 60 percent of these women claimed they'd experienced nowhere else, not even places where they were exposed to equally pleasant smells and sounds. After analyzing these perplexing findings, the mall management finally concluded that the baby powder and cherry scents and the comforting, soothing sounds (including these mothers' own heartbeats, the sound of children giggling, and a carefully choreographed selection of instruments and repetitive rhythms) had infiltrated the womb. As a result, a whole new generation of Asian consumers were drawn—subconsciously, of course—to that shopping mall. And though management hasn't been able to measure the long-term effects of these "primed" baby shoppers, some evidence indicates that these shopping mall experiments may have a potent effect on the shopping habits of the next generation for years to come.

You Are What Mom Eats

Pregnant women the world over know that what they consume has a profound effect on their unborn child. The typical mother-to-be kicks off the pregnancy diet the moment the doctor gives her the joyous news. From now on, no more pinot grigio at dinner. If she snuck a cigarette every now and then, well, those days are over. But what many pregnant women don't know is that what they consume doesn't just affect the baby's development while it's in the womb; it actually *influences the baby's adult habits.*

It's been found that when mothers smoke during pregnancy, their children are more likely to become smokers by the age of twenty-two.[3] Similarly, when mothers consume a lot of junk food during pregnancy, children are more likely to later have a strong affinity for junk food. In a study published in 2007 in the *British Journal of Nutrition,* Stephanie Bayol and her team at the Royal Veterinary College in London fed groups of pregnant and lactating rats two different diets; one was a normal rat diet, and the other included copious amounts of junk food: jelly doughnuts, potato chips, muffins, marshmallows, you name it. It turned out that the baby rats whose mothers had consumed all that junk food were *95 percent* more likely to overeat than those whose mothers had eaten rat chow alone (and they later grew up to become 25 percent fatter than the other little fellows).

And this doesn't just happen in rats. A 2007 study of 1,044 mother-and-child pairs at Harvard Medical School found that the children of women who gained "excessive weight" during pregnancy were four times more likely to become overweight in early childhood than those born to mothers who "gained inadequate weight."[4] In other words, even controlling for genetic, dietary, and other behavioral factors, mothers who ate more gave birth to children more likely to eat more. "If [a mother] eats healthy food, the child will prefer healthy food," explains researcher Josephine Todrank, PhD. Todrank conducted a two-year study on pregnant mothers and fetuses at the University of Colorado School of Medicine that concluded that a pregnant mother's diet not only sensitizes a fetus to those fragrances and flavors but physically transforms the fetal brain, thereby affecting what the baby consumes in the future.[5]

It turns out that just as with music, we also develop preferences for specific tastes and flavors in the womb. There's real biological credence for this; it's been found that strong tastes and aromas—like garlic—pass through the mother's amniotic fluid and are actually "tasted" by the fetus. As Minna Huotilainen explains, "All olfaction and taste sensations are mediated through the amniotic fluid floating in the nasal cavity and the mouth. It has been known for a long time that the amniotic fluid is rich in the concentration of fragrances typical to the mother's diet."

This goes a long way in explaining why one study found that when a mother ate a lot of a food with the taste of garlic or vanilla during the last three months of pregnancy, the newborn chose milk that smells like garlic or vanilla over milk that didn't,[6] and a 2001 experiment found that babies whose mothers drank carrot juice during pregnancy later expressed preference for carrot-flavored cereal over the plain variety.[7] Says Julie Menella, a psychobiologist at the Monell Chemical Senses Center in Philadelphia, "Mothers are giving information to their offspring through what they consume during pregnancy and breast-feeding, telling them this is about what is good and safe for us to eat."[8]

Menella explains that because amniotic fluid retains the flavors and aromas of the foods, drinks, and spices consumed or inhaled by the mother, and because the unborn child's olfactory and taste systems are fully functional by the last two trimesters, as early as week twelve, the neonate can actually *detect* these flavors and aromas—and develop an affinity that will influence his or her preferences as a baby and beyond. "The sense of smell is created in the womb—in the embryo," says International Flavors and Fragrances' group president, Nicolas Mirzayantz. "Smell is the most powerful, the most primitive, the most directly hard-wired [sense] in our brains. And the first contact with the outside world are those smells we associate with our mothers. How many foods are successful because we are primed at a young age?" he asks hypothetically. "Many. I think the first four years are instrumental."

Believe it or not, companies are not only onto this but are using it to their advantage. How? Well, to give one example, Kopiko—a popular, successful Philippine candy brand that can be found in even the smallest mom-and-pop store in any Philippine town, has figured out a way to win over the taste buds of the unborn. During one visit to Manila, I discovered that Kopiko distributors were apparently supplying pediatricians and doctors with Kopiko candies to give away to pregnant mothers in the maternity wards. Intrigued as to why, I dug a little deeper. Turns out this may have not just been about treating soon-to-be moms to a tasty snack.

Around that time, Kopiko had been preparing to roll out a new product: coffee that happened to taste just like those candies. Interestingly, the second that the Kopiko coffee did hit the shelves, its success was phenomenal—particularly among children. Yes, kids, who would normally never go within a mile of the stuff, turned out to love the taste of Kopiko coffee. In focus groups, both parents and children spoke not just of the brand's round, smooth taste but of the feelings of nostalgia and belonging it evoked. What's more, when I polled mothers who'd sucked on Kopiko candies while pregnant, many told me that when they'd given their fussy, screaming newborns a small dose of Kopiko *coffee*, it had instantly, and magically, calmed these babies down (a parenting strategy I can't say I recommend). Today, a mere four years into its existence, Kopiko coffee is the third-largest brand in the Philippines.

Baby's First Brands

As a kid growing up in Denmark, by the time I was five I was already preoccupied with a handful of brands. LEGO. Bang & Olufsen (the supermodern Danish designer of everything from sound systems to telephones). James Bond, the pop group Abba (I hereby apologize). And the fact is, thirty-five years later, the brands I loved as a child *still* influence my tastes and buying choices. For one thing, I always (unconsciously) dress like James Bond (all in black) and wear a Rolex watch. When I'm on the road, which is approximately ten months out of the year, I almost always stay in hotels that recall the ultramodern Bang & Olufsen style. And while my clothes may be all black, I've always been drawn to colorful art. I could never quite figure out why, until a few years ago, when it struck me that every single painting in my house was made up of yellow, red, blue, black, and white—exactly those five basic LEGO colors I was so obsessed with as a kid.

All right, I confess it, I still listen to Abba every now and again. In my defense, I am Scandinavian.

I'm living proof that not only are very young children aware of brands, but we cling to the brands we liked as children well into our adult lives. But to find out just how common this phenomenon is, I enlisted SIS International Research, a New York–based global custom market research and strategic business research company, which has served over 70 percent of the Fortune 500 and many of the world's most influential organizations in the course of conducting research projects in over 120 countries, to conduct a study looking at how our childhood preferences shape our buying habits as adults. In surveying 2,035 children and adults, SIS found that 53 percent of adults and 56 percent of teens used brands they remembered from their childhoods, especially foods, beverages, and health-care and consumer/household goods—if you think companies and their marketers don't know this and aren't actively marketing to young children left and right, think again. As you'll see at various points throughout this book, marketers and advertisers have many clever tricks up their sleeves to brandwash those young (and impressionable) consumers—in an attempt to secure their loyalty for life.

This may help explain why children under the age of three years represent an approximately $20 billion market to advertisers. Yup, these are the very same children who watch roughly forty thousand television ads a year and who, as I've found in my studies over the years, know the names of more branded characters than of actual animals. What most parents probably don't notice, however, is the extent to which babies as young as eighteen months are picking up subtle (and not-so-subtle) cues in their environment about brands and products.

What's the first word recognized by most kids all over the world? No, it's not "Mom" or "Dad." It's "McDonald's" (or "Ronald"), according to Bryan Urbick, CEO of the Consumer Knowledge Centre in Middlesex, UK. True, most eighteen-month-old babies can't physically articulate the word "McDonald's," but what they *can* do is recognize the fast-food chain's red and yellow colors, roofline, golden arches, and logo. Then they can jab their chunky little fingers at a McDonald's from the backseat of a minivan, at which point Dad pulls into the parking lot and everyone eats and feels stuffed and happy. Thus, that baby's recognition of McDonald's becomes layered with emotional reward, familiarity, and, of course, taste, sound, and smell.

It gets worse. As early as two decades ago, the *Journal of the American Medical Association* found that "nearly all of America's six-year-olds could identify Joe Camel, who was just as familiar to them as Mickey Mouse." My guess is that today, kids as young as three or four can not only recognize Joe Camel but associate him with the brand.[9]

The main reason that eighteen-month-old babies can recognize brands like McDonald's and Camel is that in today's media-saturated culture, younger and younger children are being exposed to more media and advertising than ever before. By the age of three months, 40 percent of all infants are watching screen media regularly,[10] and by the time these same children are two, the number rises to 90 percent. And let's not forget the advertising these toddlers are now being bombarded with on the Internet, cell phones, video games, and billboards.

And all this makes a more powerful impression than you'd think. By the age of six months, babies are able to form "mental images" of corporate logos and mascots.[11] Which is no surprise given that these days, everything from bibs to strollers is adorned with licensed characters from Elmo to SpongeBob to Tigger to Buzz Lightyear—the very same iconic figures that will continue selling these kids food, toys, and more throughout their childhoods. According to Dr. Allen Kanner, a renowned child psychologist at the Wright Institute in Berkeley, California, "Recent studies have shown that by the time they are 36 months old, American children recognize an average of 100 brand logos."[12] In one 2007 experiment, when children aged three to five were shown a dozen flash cards with assorted corporate logos on each, most of the children screamed "Target!" with delight when they spotted the store's signature red bull's-eye.

Scarier still, babies are able to actually request brands by name as soon as they can speak. In one notable study, a twenty-three-month-old was heard to repeat the mantra "Coke is it, Coke is it, Coke is it," while a second twenty-three-month-old gestured to the bottle of beer his father was gripping, murmuring, "Diet Pepsi, one less calorie."[13] By the first grade, an average child can recite roughly two hundred brand names—a figure that makes sense, seeing as most children receive an average of seventy new toys and gadgets a year. By age ten, a Nickelodeon study found, the average child has committed anywhere between three hundred and four hundred brands to memory.

It's not just that these young kids are simply learning the names of brands, either. *They are actually beginning to form preferences for them.* According to a study published in a 2010 issue of *Pediatrics*, when forty preschoolers were given a choice between two versions of a particular food (in this case, graham crackers, fruit snacks, and carrots), the only difference being that one package had a licensed character on it and the other didn't, they not only chose the branded version, they actually reported that the food with the character *tasted* better, reports study author Christina Roberto, a doctoral student at the Rudd Center for Food Policy and Obesity at Yale University.[14] In another study, sixty-three preschoolers were asked to taste pairs of five completely identical foods: hamburgers, chicken nuggets, French fries, milk, and carrots. The first set was wrapped in plain old logo-free packaging. The second pair was packaged in a McDonald's wrapper. By a long shot, the children rated the tastes of the foods and drinks higher if they believed they were from McDonald's. This even went for the carrots[15] (and the last time I looked, McDonald's doesn't even sell carrots).

As Douglas Rushkoff writes in his book *Coercion: Why We Listen to What They Say*, "By seeding their products and images early, [the] marketers can do more than just develop brand recognition; they can literally cultivate a demographic's sensibilities as they are formed. A nine-year-old child who can recognize the Budweiser frogs and recite their slogan (*Bud-Weis-er*) is more likely to start drinking beer than one who can remember only Tony the Tiger yelling, 'They're great!'"[16]

According to Juliet Schor, author of *Born to Buy*, children who can recognize logos by age eighteen months not only grow up to prefer these brands but grow up to believe the brands correspond to their own personal qualities (or desired personal qualities), like being cutting-edge, strong, fast, or sophisticated.[17] What's even more frightening is that even three-year-olds already feel social pressure to use certain brands and already believe that wearing, owning, or consuming certain brands can help them make their way through life. In a 2009 study on the topic published in the journal *Psychology and Marketing*, when one preschooler was asked about LEGO, he said, "It's really fun and I have to have it. If I have it, everyone wants to come to my house and play. If you don't have it, they maybe don't like you." Said another, "McDonald's has a playground so you can play there and everyone likes you."[18]

Some food marketers in particular are using an especially pernicious strategy (and one we'll be talking about a lot more in chapter 3) to target young and impressionable children: ads disguised as entertainment. As a *New York Times* cover story recently reported, many food companies, "often selling sugar cereals and junk food, are using multimedia games, online quizzes, and cell phone apps to build deep ties with young consumers." More specifically, as a 2009 report from the Rudd Center for Food Policy and Obesity at Yale University found, three major food companies—General Mills, Kellogg's and Post—were using games to "hawk cereals ranked among the least nutritious," including Lucky Charms, Honey Nut Cheerios, Trix, Froot Loops, Apple Jacks, and Fruity and Cocoa Pebbles. As the article reports, a game on the Lucky Charms Web site invites kids on virtual adventures with Lucky the Leprechaun; Apple Jacks offers an iPhone app called Race to the Bowl Rally, a racing-car game in which kids collect Apple Jack Cereal Pieces for extra race points; and the Honey Nut Cheerios site lets kids create their own comic strip featuring BuzzBee, the cereal's iconic mascot.[19] In blurring the line between advertising and entertainment, these ads-as-games have several benefits for the companies in question. For one, they allow marketers to circumvent the regulations on advertising junk food on television. For another, they spread virally—as kids play or share these games with their friends, they unwittingly become guerrilla brand ambassadors. And third, as we'll talk more about in chapter 3, these games are inherently addictive in nature. In short, they employ not just one but several powerful yet hidden persuaders.

As we'll see throughout this book, food marketers are not alone in these tactics. Companies of all stripes know full well that advertisements also begin to shape children's lasting preferences at an alarmingly young age and that the younger we are when we begin using a product, the more likely we are to keep using it for the rest of our lives. Which is why makers of so many distinctly adult products are targeting their ads and marketing to inappropriately young customers. Let's look at how.

Unleashing the Sex Kitten Inside

Studies show that today, both boys and girls are reaching puberty on average a full year earlier than they did decades ago, a phenomenon known in marketing circles as "precocious puberty." So what? Well, puberty means products—razors, shaving cream, face wash, acne gel, deodorant, makeup, and more. And you better believe companies are taking advantage of that fact. Seattle-based manufacturer Dot Girl, for example, sells a "first period kit," a pink or robin's-egg-blue pack decorated with cartoon characters and youthful logos. Inside, your eleven-year-old daughter will find an assortment of feminine hygiene products, including a heating pad to alleviate cramps. According to Dot Girl cofounder Terri Goodwin, "We wanted to keep it on the young side." Says Toyna Chin, the San Francisco–based founder of Petite Amie, which carries the kits and sells them primarily to young teens, "Young girls are your first brand users. It's important for any company to try and get that target audience as young as possible." [20]

According to a report from the NPD Group, a consumer research company, "From 2007 to 2009, the percentage of girls ages 8 to 12 who regularly use mascara and eyeliner nearly doubled—to 18 percent from 10 percent for mascara, and to 15 percent from 9 percent for eyeliner." [21] As journalist Peggy Orenstein says in her recent book, *Cinderella Ate My Daughter*, close to half of six- to nine-year-old girls regularly use lipstick and lip gloss, and "tween girls now spend more than $40 million a month on beauty products." [22] That's why Dylan's Candy Bar, a high-end confectionery store on New York's Upper East Side, offers a beauty line that includes "cupcake body lotion" and strawberry licorice "lip saver" (according to the Web site, "Lips should always be candy-luscious and sweet to kiss"). [23] It's also why there's a Hannah Montana Makeover Set, Barbie makeup, and hair-straightening products that feature seven-year-olds on the box. It's also why Bonne Bell markets its cosmetics to girls as young as seven, the age at which it claims girls "become adept at using a lip gloss wand." Even Nair, the hair-removal brand, has released "Nair Pretty," a line aimed at ten- to fifteen-year-olds or, as it's put in the industry, "first-time hair removers."[24]

More appalling still, as the *Huffington Post* recently reported, Abercrombie and Fitch, the popular clothing retailer among the tween set, has begun marketing and selling padded bikini tops to girls as young as eight. As bloggers on Babble.com aptly pointed out, "The push-up bra is effectively a sex tool, designed to push the breasts up and out, putting them front and center where they're more accessible to the eye (and everything else). How is that okay for second graders?"

In my book, it isn't.

Still, nothing is as wildly age-inappropriate as a toy that Tesco, the UK retailer, released in 2006: the Peekaboo Pole Dancing Kit, a pole-dancing play set marketed to females under ten—as something that will help them "unleash the sex kitten inside." Not surprisingly, outraged parents lobbied to have the product removed from shelves, and I can't say I blame them.

And how do you create a lifelong drinker? Start him or her off early by rolling out sweet, flavored, colored, sodalike beverages (laden with alcohol), known in the industry as "alcopops." Though they are allegedly intended to be consumed by adults, an American Medical Association study found that alcopops are most popular among thirteen-year-old girls and that these kid-friendly, candylike cocktails make up 29 percent of the alcohol this group consumes.

So how do companies get their products talked about among the Miley Cyrus set? One technique is hiring the Girls Intelligence Agency, which recruits a stable of forty thousand girls from across the United States to act as guerrilla marketers. The agency gives these girls exclusive offers for products, events, and free online fashion consultations and then sends them into the world to talk up the products to their friends and classmates. The GIA even organizes events it calls "Slumber Parties in a Box," "innocent" overnight parties these tween brand ambassadors host for eleven friends. Naturally, the point is for the GIA to pass out assorted free items, including new DVDs and cosmetics. Moreover, "GIA instructs the girls to 'be slick and find out some sly scoop on your friends,' such as what they think is currently fashionable."[25]

Welcome to Adulthood

Marketers aren't just pulling these kinds of stunts on the girls, either. Though figures vary from company to company, my research shows larger and larger portions of marketing budgets are being devoted to brandwashing the next generation of male customers at as young an age as possible. You can hardly blame them; Gillette's internal "war team" (an internal research team whose main purpose is to keep a close eye on the company's key competitor, Wilkinson) found that once a boy has tried a Gillette shaver twice, there is a staggering 92 percent chance he will continue using the brand as an adult. Upon which Gillette began sending out special "Welcome to Adulthood" packs to young men on their birthday (the age varies according to state regulations) or high school graduation, according to one man I interviewed.

The upstart company Stinky Stink courts the tween boy set with a new body spray that mimics the distinctly adolescent scents of snowboard wax, rubber on skateboard wheels, the pine of skateboards themselves, and even the smell of a new PlayStation 3 or Wii gaming machine. "My happiest moment?" company founder Chris Sellers told me, "was when one thirteen-year-old boy told me, 'This smells like my life.'" And when Gatorade (owned by PepsiCo) rolled out its new "G series" of drinks, its marketers established a "Mission Control" team, which tweets words of encouragement to high school athletes before big games and maintains a presence on Facebook, "where it answers queries from body-conscious teenagers about things like when it's best to gulp down the new protein drink."[26] According to the *Wall Street Journal*, "Gatorade staffers monitor social-media posts 24 hours a day . . . hoping what they see and learn will help the company more effectively promote" its new line to Facebook- and Twitter-obsessed tweens and teens.[27]

Boy or girl, once your eighteenth birthday rolls around, you're likely to receive a present from a very unlikely sender: a tobacco company. Kool's birthday gift, for example, contains an expensive-looking silver box full of coupons and even vouchers for this popular brand of menthol cigarettes, CDs of several up-and-coming rock bands, and an invitation to go online and create your own playlist (cigarette companies have found music to be a potent inroad for hooking smokers, which is why they so heavily promote at clubs and concerts). Since you're not a smoker, you throw most of this stuff away. A month later, a second identical entreaty comes. Then another. If by the third or fourth attempt you don't bite, the cigarette company knows you're a lost cause—as studies have shown that by the third pack, a typical smoker is hooked—and moves on to the next victim.

Would you believe even gas companies and car manufacturers are starting to target kids? Shell gasoline's marketing department has a long-standing partnership with LEGO to affix the Shell brand to LEGO toys, and in one animated BP commercial, children pull up to the pump in a BP station wagon while singing a catchy jingle in unison.[28] In a TV advertisement for Porsche, a little boy sits in a classroom, daydreaming about adulthood, speed, and Porsches. In his daydream, he shows up at a Porsche dealership, asks to see Porsche's 911 model, perches in it for a significant moment, then asks for the salesman's business card. "I'll see you in about twenty years," the boy says. Cue the voice-over: "It's a funny thing about a Porsche. There's the moment you know you want one; there's the moment you first own one; and for the truly afflicted, there's the decade or two that passes in between."[29]

Porsche is hardly the only automaker with its eye on these future consumers. Car manufacturer Audi makes a line of teddy bears, as well as "Rob the gecko," a cartoon lizard featured in plush toys and baby items.[30] Nissan sponsors the American Youth Soccer Organization, while Chrysler doles out hundreds of thousands of pop-up promotional books via snail mail to appeal to children.

Even Starbucks has acknowledged that the younger set is a big part of its demographic. According to the *New York Times*, "Starbucks is considering whether to add new drinks or drink sizes that better meet the needs of kids or tweens. 'We need to be realistic about who comes into our stores, so if we have children who are coming into our stores on their own, we want to make sure we have products that are appropriate to that age group,' " Starbucks spokesman Brandon Borrman said.[31] The same article goes on to say that the baristas at one local Starbucks refer to steamed milk as a "babyccino."

The Chicken or the Egg

The younger we are when we start using a brand or product, the more likely we are to keep using it for years to come. But that's not the only reason companies are aiming their marketing and advertising younger and younger. Another is that children can be a marketing tool in and of themselves, thanks to what I call their "pester power"—meaning their ability to influence their parents' purchases. As James U. McNeal, a professor of marketing at Texas A&M University, puts it, "75 percent of spontaneous food purchases can be traced to a nagging child. And one out of two mothers will buy a food simply because her child requests it. To trigger desire in a child is to trigger desire in the whole family."[32] Kids "have power over spending in the household, they have power over the grandparents, they have power over the babysitter, and on and on and on," Professor McNeal recently told the *New York Times*.

I've found that children's "persuasion" techniques are universal: negotiation ("If you buy me that chocolate, I'll clean my room"); making a scene (which is self-explanatory); setting parents up against each other, which works especially well for children of divorce ("Dad got me Odwalla—why won't you?"); and sneaking into the supermarket basket a product Mom doesn't discover until she's at the cash register, at which point she'll let it go for fear of making a scene or appearing cheap or withholding.

At the same time, the persuasion also works in the other direction; parents are directly and indirectly responsible for influencing the lifelong tastes and preferences of their children. This increasingly common phenomenon is known in the industry as "hand-me-down influence," and it tends to happen extremely early in the child's life. Which raises the question: which comes first—the child's influence or the parent's? The short answer is both.

Here's what I mean: Most families have strong cultures, attitudes, beliefs, values, and habits that a child grows up believing are the norm, and this includes everything from what they wear, to what they eat, to what brands and products they buy.[33] To see how the cycle of influence works, take, for example, Tropicana orange juice, a staple of many children's households. The child who observes his parents buying bottle after bottle of the stuff grows up believing Tropicana is the only orange juice in the universe. So when that kid goes with Mom to the grocery store, guess what brand of juice he or she will pester Mom to put in her cart? So Mom keeps buying Tropicana, and by the time that kid is older and doing her own grocery shopping, she just grabs that brand out of sheer habit. Thus a lifelong preference is born (by the way, since it's usually the mother who takes the kid grocery shopping, mothers tend to influence adolescents' purchases more strongly than fathers do, particularly for household products like soaps, condiments, cleaners, and laundry detergents).[34]

Oftentimes, our adult preference for a brand we used as a child is about nostalgia—often planted in our brains by the subtle yet clever manipulations of marketers, as we'll read more about later on. Marketers see to it that we subconsciously link the brand with warm memories of home and family, so that using that brand becomes a way to reconnect both with our past and with our loved ones. I have a friend who insists on using Crest toothpaste and Crest toothpaste only. When I asked him why, he thought for a moment. "Because," he said, "I feel somehow as though I would be betraying my parents if I used another toothpaste."

Yet like most of the hidden persuaders we'll be talking about throughout the book, "hand-me-down" influence doesn't happen by accident. Far from it. Companies and retailers work hard to get us to pass on our brand preferences to our children; it's part of their strategy, in fact. This is why so many brands are creating mini versions of their adult products for children and even infants in the hopes that the brand will stick. This is the calculus behind babyGap and J.Crew's Crewcuts, and it's why there even exists a Harley-Davidson line of onesies (for that tiny motorcycle mama in your life).

Oh, and if you've dropped by an Apple store lately, did you happen to notice it resembled an international day care? That's because Apple, a favorite brand among children (as the *New York Times* pointed out in 2010, Apple's iPhone "has . . . become the most effective tool in human history to mollify a fussy toddler"), offers all kinds of baby-friendly apps, like Toddler Teasers, Baby Fun!, Infant Arcade, Peek-A-Boo, Pocket Zoo, and more. Sure, these apps are a godsend to many tired parents, keeping the kid busy so Mom and Dad can have a bit of peace and quiet, but they are also one of Apple's many stealth strategies (you'll read about others later on) for recruiting the next generation of customers. Apple's "back-to-school" offer of an iPod Touch free with your new laptop is another. Sounds generous, but what's really going on is slightly more calculated than that. I have no doubt that Apple's marketers know full well that once Mom or Dad passes along the iPod Touch to their child, the kid can't help but get hooked on the gizmo and will eventually be asking for a high-priced Apple computer of his or her own.[35] (And there's evidence to suggest children's obsessions with Apple products start much, much earlier. I once conducted an experiment in which I handed a group of one-year-old children BlackBerrys—only to watch each one of them immediately swipe their fingers over it as though it were an Apple touch screen.)

The point is that one of the main reasons all these strategies targeting children are so effective is that they pack a one-two punch: not only do our earliest preferences and impressions as children stay with us for life, but we're also drawn to products that capture and allow us to relive the feeling of being young. In fact, as you'll read later on, nostalgia is one of the most powerful hidden persuaders around, and it's being used in all kinds of ways to brandwash us.

CHAPTER 2

Peddling Panic and Paranoia

WHY FEAR SELLS

The most recent outbreak of the H1N1 influenza virus, better known as swine flu, was first detected in Veracruz, Mexico, in the spring of 2009. Both the World Health Organization and the U.S. Centers for Disease Control termed the outbreak a pandemic. Millions of people all over the world panicked, and although swine flu never became the kind of global catastrophe the 1918 flu did, it has been blamed for roughly fourteen thousand deaths.

Six years earlier, in 2003, another potentially fatal flu, severe acute respiratory syndrome, or SARS, caused a similar global panic. SARS originated in southern China but spread to infect citizens in roughly forty countries. By the time the virus was contained in 2006, it was thought to be responsible for nearly eight hundred deaths—and people all over the world were going to heroic lengths to protect themselves and their children from exposure.

For doctors, CDC workers, and other health officials, a well-publicized global contagion spells a nightmare scenario: stockpiling and administering gallons of vaccines, diagnosing and treating thousands of patients, and spending countless hours and dollars trying to allay widespread panic. For a number of companies and marketers, however, it spells something entirely different: a golden opportunity.

Can anyone say "hand gel"?

Thanks in large part to these two global health scares, today we've welcomed antibacterial hand sanitizers into our lives as a cheap, everyday, utterly essential staple. Expected to exceed $402 million in profits a mere five years from now (and that's just in the United States),[1] containers of the soaps and hand gels can now be found at virtually every airport, hotel, restaurant, public restroom, newspaper kiosk, grocery store, and kitchen and bathroom sink across the globe. Millions of women, men, teenagers, and children won't leave home without a small bottle or spritz canister in their purse or pocket. Bath & Body Works and Victoria's Secret have even devised hand sanitizers as fashion accessories. Recently, while I was on a layover in Chicago's O'Hare International Airport, a voice over the loudspeaker alerted me repeatedly to the presence of hallway soap dispensers. In short, our war on this unseen enemy—a terrorist cell of germs, so to speak—has become a global family affair.

Turns out, though, that neither swine flu nor SARS can be prevented by the use of antibacterial cleansing gels. Both viruses are spread via tiny droplets in the air that are sneezed or coughed by people who are already infected (or, though this is far less common, by making contact with an infected surface, then rubbing your eyes or your nose). Nevertheless, the idea of an unseen, potentially fatal contagion has driven us into nothing short of an antibacterial mania, one that has helped sales of Purell, the top-selling hand sanitizer, to jump by 50 percent[2] and Clorox disinfecting wipes 23 percent since the 2009 panic.[3]

But our near addiction to these overpriced germ killers isn't just a happy accident for the companies that make them. The advertisers and marketers at brands like Purell, Germ-X, Germ Out, and Lysol have worked extremely hard to make us believe that using their product is the only surefire way to stave off grave and deadly disease. How? Well, first they capitalized on the global panic during the swine flu scare by releasing an onslaught of new products and redoubling their efforts to stress the importance of hygiene in staving off disease. "We want to make sure that people understand that effective hand washing is the best way to keep yourself and your family healthy," echoed a spokesperson for Dial, the soap manufacturer. Purell then posted on their Web site: "According to the Centers for Disease Control and Prevention (CDC), one of the ways you can help protect yourself from Swine Flu is by practicing good hand hygiene. Specific CDC recommendations include keeping your hands clean by washing with soap and water, or using an alcohol-based hand sanitizer when soap and water may not be available." [4]

The disinfectant brand Lysol, too, updated its home page with information on swine flu, asserting that although it is not yet clear how the virus spreads, "following proper hygiene routines can help prevent the spread of illness." [5] Of course, what they are trying to insinuate is that their product is the key to good hygiene—and in turn instrumental in staying healthy. Only they can't *say* that because, well, it would be a lie; in fact, hand sanitizers have not been found, by the CDC or anyone else, to be effective in fighting airborne disease.

It wasn't just makers of soap and hygiene products who saw serious marketing opportunities in the swine flu panic. Kleenex very swiftly rolled out a line of "antiviral" tissues, which allegedly "have a specially treated middle layer that helps stop cold and flu viruses" and that "kills 99.9% of cold and flu viruses in the tissue within 15 minutes" and are "virucidal against Rhinoviruses Type 1A and 2; Influenza A and B; and Respiratory Syncytial Virus." [6]

Major online retailers such as Amazon.com and ReStockIt.com also got into the game, taking the opportunity to manufacture and market swine flu protection kits, swine flu safety DVDs, ionic air purifiers (ranging in price from fifty dollars to six hundred dollars) and hundred-dollar designer face masks. [7] "The spread of swine flu is of global concern and we want to do our part to help contain it," said Jennifer DiMotta, VP of marketing at ReStockIt.com. "These products really work to help curb the spread of germs and disease," she added. [8]

What's in a swine flu protection kit, you ask? Why, hand sanitizer and bacterial wipes, among other useless items designed to give us the illusion of protection and safety. None of these kits, some of which came with surgical masks and a light blue garment that looks uncannily like a hospital gown, were endorsed or distributed by the World Health Organization or any other health organization. But it was no coincidence that they were designed and packaged to have a decidedly clinical, medical feel.

Even some of the food companies tossed their hat into the ring of paranoia. A few months after those first swine flu cases began to appear in the headlines, Kellogg's, in an attempt to tap into the growing misconception (fed largely by the opportunity to profit off it, of course) that a healthy immune system was the key to staying swine flu free, introduced a new variant of Rice Krispies and Cocoa Krispies loaded with "antioxidants and nutrients that help the body's immune system." Too bad it was also loaded with 40 percent sugar. Just a few months later, the company's health claims were so widely criticized for being bogus that it decided to pull the words "helps support your child's immunity" from all boxes. (The word "immunity," it should be noted, appeared in giant, boldfaced letters that could practically be seen from Jupiter.)[9]

Kellogg's denied preying on swine flu fear, claiming that it had begun work on its revamped Rice Krispies a year before the H1N1 virus peaked. Still, one has to question the company's motives, given that in November 2009 it bowed to the negative publicity, announcing that "given the public attention on H1N1," it would no longer sell the antioxidant-enriched cereal, though "we will continue to respond to the desire for improved nutrition."[10]

Companies are equally quick to prey on public panic over food contamination scares. For example, in 2010, when over half a billion eggs were recalled due to reports of salmonella, the marketers of brands like Egg Beaters and Davidson's sprang into action, adding sections to their Web sites boasting that their products were uncontaminated. Davidson's even bought the Google adwords for the searches "pasteurized eggs" and "safe eggs," so that panicked egg lovers looking online for information on the recall would most likely find themselves on the Davidson's Web site, where they were immediately assured, "Our pasteurized eggs eliminate the risk of food borne illness and cross-contamination of your kitchen from shell eggs."[11]

Fearmongering is also a tactic favored by big-box retailers like Walmart, Kohl's, and Target, which employ a company called Weather

Trends International to help them adjust their inventory to capitalize on the anxiety generated by predictions of hurricanes, fires, ice storms, and other extreme weather events.[12] It's true that in the case of an *actual* disaster like Hurricane Katrina, this can be a genuine public service (as one journalist reported, "unlike local, state and the federal government, which didn't react until days after the hurricane hit, Walmart was at work around the clock before Katrina even hit to have the stores fully stocked with full pallet positions of water, flashlights, batteries, canned soup and canned meat").[13] But it's also true that if there's even a remote possibility of extreme weather, these retailers are lightning quick to erect huge front-of-store displays of everything from bottled water to power generators to shovels to mosquito nets, pulling in a tidy profit in the process.

Why "Thrillers" Thrill

Fear is an interesting, complex, and not altogether unpleasant emotion. Do you remember the delicious thrill you felt as a kid when you watched your first horror movie—whether it was *The Blair Witch Project* or *The Shining* or *The Exorcist*? Your pulse probably raced, your heart likely beat wildly in your chest, and you may have found yourself involuntarily holding your breath as you waited for that ax-wielding killer to jump out of the shadows. You were scared out of your mind, and you loved every minute of it. It's not just horror movies and scary urban legends that deliver this delicious thrill. Ever wonder why Stephen King has sold more than five hundred million copies of his books over the years, or why on *Publishers Weekly*'s list of best-selling books in 2009, a staggering thirteen of the top fifteen fell under the category of thriller?[14] As the popular media gossip blog Gawker.com noted sarcastically, American readers love being scared—of everything from Freemasons to lawyers to murderers to aliens to lawyers to pirates to even our northern neighbor, Canada. And what do you think is behind the enormous popularity of scary TV shows like *Bones* or *CSI* or even the Discovery Channel's "Shark Week"? I read once that a human being's chances of being eaten by a shark are smaller than his chances of being hit by a coconut falling from a palm tree, but if you look at how many movies and TV shows feature shark attacks, you'd think otherwise.

Counterintuitive though it sounds, there's a real biological basis behind our attraction to fear. Fear raises our adrenaline, creating that primal, instinctual fight-or-flight response. This in turn releases epinephrine, a hormone and neurotransmitter that produces, as many "adrenaline junkies" will attest, a deeply satisfying sensation. There's a substantial overlap between those brain areas involved in processing fear and pleasure," said Allan Kalueff, a neuroscientist at the University of Tampere in Finland. Adds Yerkes National Primate Research Center neuroscientist Kerry Ressler, the amygdala, our brain's "fear center," "gets just as activated by fear as it would in the real world, but because your cortex knows you're not in danger, that spillover is rewarding and not frightening." [15]

By uniting us against a common enemy, fear also brings humans together. It has a perverse yet delicious binding quality. It's for this reason that we love to spread fearful rumors, sometimes blowing them out of all proportion just to heighten the sense of danger. Nothing travels as quickly as a frightening rumor—think of those ubiquitous urban legends about highway murder gangs and escaped convicts. Says Michael Lewis, director of the Institute for the Study of Child Development at Robert Wood Johnson Medical School in New Brunswick, New Jersey, "Fear has a certain contagious feature to it, so the fear in others can elicit fear in ourselves. It's conditioning, like Pavlov and the salivating dog." [16]

According to Harjot Singh, the senior vice president and director of planning at the marketing communications firm Grey Canada, our brains are hardwired to fear potential threats.[17] Professor Joseph LeDoux of the Center for the Neuroscience of Fear and Anxiety at New York University concurs, explaining that "we come into the world knowing how to be afraid, because our brains have evolved to deal with nature." [18]

What's more, as anyone can attest who's ever had the bejesus scared out of them by the sound of a branch scratching on a windowpane on a windy night, fear is far more potent than our facility for reason. Explains *Newsweek*, "The amygdala sprouts a profusion of connections to higher brain regions—neurons that carry one-way traffic from amygdala to neocortex. Few connections run from the cortex to the amygdala, however. That allows the amygdala to override the products of the logical, thoughtful cortex, but not vice versa."[19] Adds UCLA neurobiologist Michael Fanselow, fear is "far, far more powerful than reason. . . . It evolved as a mechanism to protect us from life-threatening situations, and from an evolutionary standpoint there's nothing more important than that."[20]

Says an article on political fearmongering that appeared on the left-leaning political Web site Daily Kos, "When a threat is perceived, the body goes into automatic mode, redirecting blood to certain parts of the body and away from the brain. The respiratory response also decreases the blood supply to the brain, literally making a person unable to think clearly. In other words, the loss of blood to a person's brain can make him or her stupid, literally."[21] What's more, an academic study entitled "The Extended Parallel Process Model" explains that people who are exposed to fear appeals think carefully about the responses proposed in these messages, then follow the advice of the persuasive message in an attempt to neutralize the danger."[22]

Clearly, fear is a powerful persuader, and you'd better believe that marketers and advertisers know it and aren't afraid to exploit it to the fullest.

Which is why the marketing world uses scare tactics to sell us everything from antidepressants to condoms, dental floss to laundry detergent, burglar alarms to cell phones, bottled water to pizza dough, as well as countless other brands and products you'll read about in this chapter. I recall once seeing a vintage 1950s ad for lunchbox thermoses that bore the unforgettable tagline "A Fly in the Milk May Mean a Baby in the Grave." As you're about to read, advertisers have since gotten a lot more subtle and creative in the ways they use fear to persuade us.

But really, I don't mean to scare you.

Nothing to Fear but Future Selves

Perhaps you recall a 1994 TV advertisement for an Aquafresh toothbrush. In one hand a woman is holding up a toothbrush, in the other, a ripe tomato. "With this tomato, I'm going to make an important point about your toothbrush," she says, pressing the bristles into the poor tomato, creating a gash that resembles a bleeding gum. "Only Aquafresh Flex Brush has a unique, pressure-sensitive neck that bends and flexes if you press too hard," the woman continues, "so you can prevent damaging your gums, while still giving your teeth a thorough cleaning." [23] On the face of it, Aquafresh was just using a simple prop to show how great its product was. But in fact something a little bit more subtle and sneaky was going on. After all, a prop resembling a bleeding gum calls to mind only one thing: a trip to the dentist. What else could be more universally terrifying?

So besides dentists and germs, what other kinds of fears do companies play on in marketing us their products? For one, the fear of failure. In a surprising 2008 study, researchers at the University of Bath, UK, found that the fear of failure drives consumers far more than the promise of success; the latter oddly tends to paralyze us, while the former spurs us on (and pries open our wallets). In fact, as the study found, the most powerful persuader of all was giving consumers a glimpse of some future "feared self." [24]

We all have some version of a future self we'd take great pains to avoid. Do most of us go to the gym because we want to be healthy, or because we're scared of getting flabby or out of shape? Do we bathe, shampoo, and brush and floss our teeth out of reverence for the rules of hygiene, or are we imagining the "feared self" we might resemble if we smelled bad, our hair were scraggly and unwashed, and our teeth were rotted and yellow? I can't help but think back to a classic L'Oréal ad in which an older man is walking down the street. To our eyes, he looks great—dapper and distinguished. The camera then cuts to a beautiful younger woman passing him by. And through her eyes we see him as old, decrepit, and repulsive—his worst-feared self realized.

Sometimes, advertisers prey on our fears of our worst selves by activating insecurities that we didn't even know we had—like about the appearance of our armpits. This is exactly what Dove's recent "Go Sleeveless" ad campaign was doing; by claiming that their new special moisturizing formula will make our underarms "not only odor free but prettier," Dove was subconsciously planting the fear that our armpits might be not only smelly but also hideous. As *Slate* aptly pointed out, "Dove's empowerment-via-shame marketing approach for Go Sleeveless has its roots in advertising techniques that gained popularity in the 1920s: a) pinpoint a problem, perhaps one consumers didn't even know they had; b) exacerbate anxiety around the problem; c) sell the cure." Among the many "feared selves" that have been historically planted by marketers, the article cites such concerns as "bad breath," "smelly underarms," and "the many troubles down there."[25]

What else frightens us nowadays? A lot. Most of us are scared about the economy, of losing our jobs, and of defaulting on our mortgages. We're scared that our spouse or partner might leave us. We're scared of loneliness and having no friends. We're afraid of sexual inadequacy. Of getting cancer. Of getting old and breaking a hip. Of death. We're scared of driving and we're scared of flying. We're scared of terrorists and of global warming. We're scared of the bright sun and the dark night. We're afraid of *E. coli* bacteria in our beef, hormones in our milk, and mercury in our fish. We're scared of viruses infecting our computers and our water supplies. We're scared of earthquakes quite literally shifting the ground beneath our feet and of our children being abducted by strangers in cars. We're scared that we talk too much or too little, that we dress badly, that our nails are unclean and our hair wayward. Or that no one will tell us about the piece of kale in our teeth, or that while we strive to be charming and amusing, we're actually fatally unfunny . . . and everyone knows it but us. According to Gavin Johnston, a behavioral science–based branding consultant, many brands prey on what anthropologists dub "panoramic fear"—namely, "an overwhelming sense that control has been lost, prompting consumers to scramble to find any kind of comfort they can."[26]

It's these seemingly infinite fears—some planted in our minds by marketers and advertisers, others merely amplified by them—that drive us to buy triple-moisturizing creams and heat-safe leave-in conditioners, teeth-whitening strips and multivitamins. Not to mention gym memberships and organic food and bottled water and humidifiers (and dehumidifiers) and designer clothing and Viagra and earthquake insurance and water-filtration systems and plastic surgery and bike locks and . . . burglar alarms.

"If You're a Lady, Most Men Want to Kill You"

Picture this: You're a single, twentysomething female in a skimpy T-shirt and sweats, ready to work out at home to a yoga DVD when you hear suspicious noises coming from outside. Or you're a teenage girl home alone at night, convinced you hear the sound of keys jiggling in the downstairs lock. Or you're a mother preparing dinner while your kids play in the yard, and you've failed to notice the suspicious-looking fellow lurking near the garage. Or perhaps you're a recent divorcée who's just been flirting with a charming hunk at your house party and are startled, once the house has emptied out, to see this same hunk punching in your back door.

These are all scenes from widely viewed commercials for Brink's Home Security, now known as Broadview Security. When they aired in 2008, many media observers and consumer advocates decried them as sensationalistic, salacious, and sexist. Not to mention transparently obvious in their intent to terrify. Airing a few months into the global recession—for many Americans, one of the scariest times in recent memory—the ads worked like a charm, especially among their target audience: women. Thanks to this unabashed fearmongering, alarm sales rose by an unprecedented 10 percent in a single year—a year during which crime rates actually *decreased.*[27]

"Are you a single woman who lives alone in a large, five-person house? Studies show that if you're a lady, most men want to kill you," went the hilarious parody of these ads that ran on *Saturday Night Live.*[28] But what's not funny is the fact that Broadview and burglar alarm companies are hardly alone in identifying our most deeply held fears and then playing them back to us in the most nightmarish scenarios possible. In one ad sponsored by the Insurance Corporation of British Columbia (it was billed as a drunk-driving ad, although I'm willing to bet it sold more insurance policies than it saved lives), an adolescent boy is pictured flying through a car windshield because he's forgotten to secure his seat belt. In a TV commercial for American Express traveler's checks, a vacationing couple suddenly victimized by theft is shown huddled, helpless, and broke—before the credit card company, like a white knight, comes obligingly to the rescue. Prudential life insurance's

"Don't wait until it's too late" ad campaign featured a pitiful-looking family barely managing to carry on because a deceased patriarch had failed to sign up for life insurance.

And of course there's GM's OnStar, a subscription-based "vehicle security, safety and communication service," whose manipulative but riveting radio commercials are recordings of actual distress calls from customers—from a panicked woman reporting she's just been involved in a collision to a terrified child calling for help because his mother is having trouble breathing.

I'm not proud of it, but I once helped create an ad like this. It was a TV commercial featuring a father and his young daughter. The father was about to leave on a business trip, and the daughter was dejected. The camera cut to the father in a black limousine as it pulled away from his visibly unhappy daughter. Next, the screen showed Dad on an airplane. Then the daughter again, looking up longingly into the sky. Next we see Dad striding into a meeting overseas, his daughter back at home. At last the phone rings. The daughter picks it up, almost tearily. It's Dad. He told her he would call her, didn't he?

The commercial was for Allianz, a well-known life insurance company. Yes, we were using fear to remind fathers to look out for the families they love. Without saying so, the ad asked, *If something were to happen to you, would your family be financially protected?* Later, we scanned people's brains as they viewed it to see which shot was the most affecting (and persuasive). The hands-down winner was the shot of the little girl gazing up at the sky.

Yet this was nothing compared to another ad I saw once. "I Want More Time," which is available on YouTube, is dubbed the "saddest commercial ever," but I think a more proper description is the "most emotionally manipulative commercial ever." In it, a middle-aged man driving a car along a highway speaks in voice-over about his teenage son. "I want time to understand him," we hear, as we see flashbacks of the father berating the young man. "I want to listen to his songs," the father's voice-over resumes, and "tell him I'm sorry," and "I want time to do what I've never done: take better care of him. Love him more."

At which point a highly realistic-looking commuter bus rams his car head-on. He's dead.

Cue the words "Thai Life Insurance."[29]

The reason ads like these work so well is because they hit us in two powerful places. Fear and its close cousin, guilt. I consider guilt to be a global virus. And no one is better at spreading that virus than marketers and advertisers. As an article that appeared in the *Journal of Consumer Research* in 2006 explained, fear mixed with a high level of blame, regret, guilt, or even a dare tends to translate emotion into action.[30] This instinctively makes sense; after all, isn't it the combination of fear and guilt that makes you reach for the nicotine gum instead of the cigarettes or baked Cheetos over the fried ones? (I might add that the packaging of these baked snacks is designed with the "feared self" of today's health-conscious woman in mind. Note the matte, unshiny bags they come in, compared to the slippery, gleaming bags enclosing regular Cheetos, which subconsciously remind us of oily, greasy skin.) In short, fear and guilt are marketers' one-two punch.

The Mother of All Fear

You may have noticed that many of the tactics we've been talking about so far seem to be aimed at women. That's because studies have shown that women are more prone to fear and guilt than men are. When psychologists in Spain recently questioned three hundred men and women between the ages of fifteen and fifty about the kinds of daily situations that engendered feelings of guilt—whether failing to make the time to visit a sick relative in the hospital, forgetting a friend's birthday, or losing patience with a friend—in each and every case women felt significantly higher levels of guilt than their male counterparts (and were also more likely to feel angry with themselves if they felt they had hurt another person).[31]

No one is more vulnerable to fear and guilt than mothers, particularly new mothers. Now that you're responsible for this fragile little person, the entire world has suddenly become one giant death trap. And you haven't seen germophobia until you've seen a new mother. No matter where I am in the world, when I ask new mothers what they do when the baby finally arrives, 90 percent tell me that they begin to clean as if there's no tomorrow; they're absolutely terrified of anything that could possibly harm or even contaminate their new arrivals. If Purell and other body and home sanitizers don't yet play a major part in their lives, they will now. But those aren't the only products out there marketed to paranoid mothers and fathers. Not even close. Among the many other health- and safety-related items there are: ointments, humidifiers, car seats that make Alcatraz look easy to escape, baby gates, cabinet locks, three-hundred-dollar digital color video baby monitors, "safety bath-time thermometers," "safety bath-time faucet covers," and more. This stuff doesn't necessarily make the little ones any safer, either. For example, across Japan physicians are finding that Japanese babies' immune systems are actually breaking down as an unfortunate consequence of their parents' preoccupation with germs.

Still, marketers and advertisers are very skilled at playing to new mothers' inherent fears, which I believe to be evolutionarily wired, that if they *don't* buy all this stuff, they're "not a good enough mother." And in fact these are the first words that pop out of mothers' mouths when their infant gets an infection or catches a cold—even though the chances of this happening at some point in the first few years of the child's life are nearly 100 percent. Nonetheless, an insecure, hormonal, frequently isolated new mother believes it's *her* fault. She messed up. She didn't protect her child—a false impression she gleaned from one televised image after another of plump-cheeked, airbrushed babies who look as though they've never caught a cold, had an ear infection, or had a scrape on them.

I don't know any new mother who doesn't feel guilty about something. Maybe she's worried she doesn't buy her child enough educational toys. Or that she's not preparing every meal from scratch, or that if she is, she isn't using fresh or high-quality-enough ingredients. Is she a good mother compared to other mothers? There are so many ways for her to feel she isn't living up to society's standards. Naturally, there are an endless array of products out there—from LeapFrog computers for young children to organic baby food to postnatal exercise videos to LED lightbulbs to Priuses—to alleviate all that guilt.

In our time-starved society, how many mothers have time to drive to the supermarket, buy fresh ingredients, lug them home, then spend hours peeling, chopping, simmering, sautéing, baking, and broiling them to perfection? Yet most moms (and dads) feel incredibly guilty about bringing home a prepackaged meal—or worse yet, getting takeout. No matter how convenient that frozen lasagna looks, if it comes in a cardboard box, most mothers feel guilty about serving it, as if doing so would be saying she doesn't really care. That's why food marketers came up with the ruse known as the finishing touch.

A few years ago, supermarkets began selling pizza. Not just in the frozen-food section; now a busy mom can buy raw pizza dough, a bag of mozzarella, and a jar of sauce, bring it home, roll out the crust herself, and voilà—feel as though she's cooked homemade pizza (in the real world they may call it "cooking," but behind the scenes, marketers dub creating a meal of any kind "assembling"). This was a brilliant marketing ploy, not just on the part of the supermarkets for shelving these existing products together but also on the part of brands like Pillsbury for rolling out a new "pizza dough" (not so different from its regular crescent roll dough) and Ragú for expanding its offerings to include "pizza sauce" (not very different from its regular tomato sauce). These canny companies learned that they could make a killing by selling us products that look "finished" but in fact require a little effort—the finishing touch—on our part.

Thus, a guilt-ridden mother can now provide a well-rounded, nutritious, home-cooked meal for her family. In the time it takes to mix in a packet of spices, gone is the fear that she's served her family a premade, manufactured, subpar product.

Now you understand what Hamburger Helper or Duncan Hines brownie mix (add an egg and half a cup of water) are all about.

There's a Pill for That

"Your dad wants you to have things he never had. Like hair," reads the ad for Rogaine. Immediately the male viewer thinks about his hardworking, self-sacrificing father—before terror of losing more inches of his own rapidly retreating hairline sets in. Notice the sly combination of guilt and fear at work here?

An ad for the much maligned pain reliever Vioxx shows the famous figure skater Dorothy Hamill perched on a bench, lacing up her skates, with the voice-over "Along with all the great memories has come something I thought I'd never experience—the pain of osteoarthritis." Our reaction? *Oh no! If an Olympic ice skater can come down with arthritis, so can I! But look—thanks to Vioxx, she's skating again!* Fear, followed by hope and renewal. The classic one-two punch.

Do you suffer from allergies? The woman pictured in the ad for Flonase allergy spray sure does. In a series of photos, we see her unhappily rubbing and wiping her runny, red nose and finally clutching her nostrils in agony. She looks miserable, at the end of her rope. Then we see her after two squirts of Flonase spray. She's now outdoors, laughing while her hunky husband rakes the lawn. Her teeth quite miraculously have suddenly become blindingly white. A beautiful blond child stands nearby, beaming. There's a wheelbarrow and a watering can and probably more pollen and dander and grass than anyone can imagine, and guess what? It doesn't bother her one bit. Flonase has transformed our sneezy, hacking worst nightmare into a sexy, feminine, outdoors-loving, allergy-free object of our envy and desire.

Sure, pharmaceutical ads play on our fear of death and disease and aging to get us to buy their products. But I believe that's not the only fear tactic at work. Pharmaceutical companies also play on one of the most subtle yet powerful of psychological tricks: our fear of social isolation, of being outsiders. Countless studies show that humans have a universal need to belong (dating way back to our early ancestors, for whom survival depended on being a member of a band or tribe); for most of us, the thought of being left out or alone is terrifying.

How exactly do the drug companies play—and prey—on this fear? Believe it or not, they use a formula that, according to a research study carried out at Stanford University, is more or less standard for this kind of fear-based advertising. They begin with solitary shots of our worst "feared" self—a balding man, an overweight woman, or an unhappy or distracted child—whose gaze is conspicuously averted. Once the person in the ad has taken whatever it is that is designed to improve their appearance, steady their mood, or alleviate their symptoms, not only do they look brighter, happier, and sexier, but they face straight ahead at the camera. This accomplishes two things. First, as any psychologist will tell you, averted gazes are generally associated with shame and social isolation, while a straight-ahead gaze is a sign of confidence and connectedness. So the straight-ahead gaze implies that taking the drug or medication has magically made the person in the advertisement not just healthier but more popular, loved, and accepted. Second, it invites you, the viewer, into the person's life. In the advertising industry, this "after" picture is termed a "demand" photo, because the newly slimmed down/refocused/cured model "demands" a connection from the viewer. *Recognize me*, the photograph says. *Meet my gaze. You know me. This brand works. If you want to be as happy as I am, use it.*[32]

Big Pharma has plenty of critics. And while I'll concede that pharmaceutical executives don't actually sit around in boardrooms rubbing their hands together, concocting new ways to terrorize the public, given that the very nature of their products is to cure or treat things that most people find universally scary, like serious disease, it's inevitable that fear finds a way into their marketing and advertising strategies.

Pharmaceutical companies don't just remind us of all the horrible conditions we might one day come down with, like an embarrassing skin disease, sexual dysfunction, cancer, and so on. They also spend millions of dollars a year stirring up fear in our hearts over conditions we never even knew to be afraid of. Restless leg syndrome? Fibromyalgia? Premenstrual dysphoric disorder? Who knew such things even existed? Well, thanks to the psychologically manipulative and oft-aired commercials, we all do now.

Do you suffer from shyness? Apparently shyness isn't just a personality trait but an actual pathology, and one that only Paxil can cure. What about acid reflux disease, formerly known as heartburn? Today there are over a dozen drugs, from Nexium to Prilosec to Zantac, available to treat it. Who knew that irritable bowels weren't just the unfortunate repercussions of a spicy Mexican dinner and were actually a "syndrome"? PMDD, or "premenstrual dysphoric disorder," is a relatively recent condition, though it bears much in common with the monthly hormonal changes fertile women have been experiencing for centuries. LBL, which stands for "light bladder leakage," is an even newer one, pharmacologically speaking. Anyone who's ever gone swimming in a public pool has probably encountered a young child who suffers from this.

These days, we're being persuaded to ask our doctors for medications to address what were once considered nothing more than everyday inconveniences. A recent study by two York University researchers found that Big Pharma spends nearly twice as much on promotion and advertising as it does on research and development. No wonder Americans are the most overmedicated people on earth, with overall domestic sales of prescription drugs totaling $235.4 billion.[33]

Germophobia

I'll bet that if you're in the habit of buying the morning paper, you bypass the one directly on top of the stack. Instead, you lift up the top newspaper and pull out the one directly underneath it. Did you know that consciously or not, 72 percent of people do the same? Why? Because we imagine that the second one from the top hasn't been manhandled by countless germy fingertips and is therefore somehow cleaner than the one above it. (Ironically, though, after scanning the headlines, many of that same 72 percent of consumers replace that paper right where they found it, under the top one, so they all end up thumbing through the same finger-smudged newspaper over and over.) It's the same phenomenon that explains why when women visit the ladies' rooms of hotels, stores, and restaurants, only 5 percent of them will enter the first stall. Why? Because they believe it's less clean than the second or third one. Go figure!

The point is that the illusion of cleanliness or freshness is a subtle but powerful persuader—and marketers know it. I believe this is tied into our nearly universal fear of germs, which ties in to our innate fear of disease, illness, and even death. Think of all the lengths we go to in order to avoid "contaminants" in our lives. We slather on epic amounts of hand sanitizer. We pay exorbitant prices for fruit and produce grown without pesticides. We shell out extra for household cleaning products labeled "nontoxic" (so persuasive is this messaging that the company Method, which claims its products are "a cleaner clean," is now the seventh-fastest-growing private company in the United States).[34] Does any of this actually make us any healthier? No, not really. But it does make us less afraid of getting sick.

Global contagions aside, our fear of germs pervades a whole host of buying decisions we make in our everyday lives, from which newspaper we pull off the stack to which groceries we buy. On a recent (NBC) *Today* segment, when my team and I scanned the brain of a female volunteer named Kelly as she made her way down the supermarket aisle so we could analyze her thought patterns as she made her selections, one of the most interesting things we found was that perceptions of cleanliness had a big impact on her decisions—without her even realizing it.

Over the length of the segment, store executives, the film crew, the producer, and even TV viewers failed to notice one thing that our brain scanners were able to pick up. Every time Kelly picked a product off the shelf, the scientists were able to detect a slight pause or increase in reaction time before she put the object either in her basket or back on the shelf. This in itself isn't all that surprising; it takes most of us a second or two to decide whether or not to buy something. But what was really interesting was that every time Kelly held a product in her hand, the brain scans revealed strong activity in her brain's amygdala region—the region responsible for fear, dread, danger, and discomfort (it also serves as a memory storage unit). Literally every product she touched during her shopping excursion sparked a fear response in Kelly's brain.

What was going on here? After watching the tapes again, we noticed that generally, if Kelly liked a product enough to touch it, study it, and ponder it, she'd buy it, *but not the one she'd picked up.* Instead, just like those newspaper buyers, she'd put that "tainted" bottle of shampoo or can of coffee or bag of tortilla chips back on the shelf before selecting an identical one stashed one or two items behind it. And on one occasion, when the product Kelly wanted was the lone one remaining on the shelf, the fear response in her brain was so pronounced she ended up choosing another brand altogether—though if you had asked her, she would have had no idea why she had done so.

It makes sense that our fear of germs or contamination would be particularly pronounced when it comes to food products. But how do we explain the fact that Kelly's fear response was just as strong for, say, paper towels as it was for a carton of milk? I chalk it up to clever marketing that plants seeds in our brains—subconsciously, of course—that maybe a product is or isn't as "clean" as we believe. To see what I mean, picture, say, a marmalade display. Marmalade, as most people know, is a fruit preserve with a thick, peely texture and a syrupy taste. From the beginning of time, marmalade, which originated in Scotland, has been marketed and sold in jars with tartan-plaid screw tops, to cultivate that exotic suggestion of its being "imported" (even though most is manufactured in the United States). Still, because most Americans believe jars of this "exotic" product have traveled thousands of miles in who knows what conditions and been manhandled by who knows how many grimy mitts, the average consumer, before buying a jar of marmalade, will carefully inspect it, hoping to confirm that what he or she is buying is safe, fresh, and uncontaminated.

Yet there is no way on earth a marmalade manufacturer can guarantee freshness. Marmalade is simply *not* a fresh product. It's not meant to be. Those glass jars have been sitting on this supermarket shelf for upwards of eight months. But marketers don't want us to know that! So what do they do? They try to create the *illusion* of freshness by attaching the top of the marmalade lid to the glass jar with a narrow white strip of adhesive paper. When the strip is unbroken, it means that no one has twisted the top of the can open (and done who knows what to it). It signals to consumers, *Hey, don't worry, you've got a fresh jar!*

Hotels, incidentally, employ a similar tactic by placing a paper seal on the seats of their toilets and a paper lid on glasses you'll find in the bathroom or near the minibar. I've always been astonished by the fact that a single, flimsy sheet of paper is enough to create the illusion that no other person has ever used that toilet or drank out of that glass, but somehow it does. (And in fact one hotel employee once admitted to me that the glasses are not actually washed—merely dried with a towel—before being used again and again. Yet that paper lid gives us the illusion of cleanliness.)

Marketers call this the "fresh strip." Along with its close relative, the plastic seal, the fresh strip is today standard in many food and product categories including, among others, yogurt, peanut butter, coffee,

ketchup, iced tea, mustard, juice, vitamins, and over-the-counter medicines. It conveys the (in many cases false) impression that what's inside
this jar, bag, or container is unsullied by germs, untouched by another
human being. Moreover, many of these jars and containers are deliberately engineered so that when we unscrew that marmalade at home,
we'll hear that comforting *smack* sound, further reassurance that what
we've bought is fresh, clean, and safe—never mind that the smacking
sound was created and patented in a sound lab to manipulate us into
believing that the marmalade was flown in from Edinburgh just this
morning.

Don't be fooled. The reality is that this jar of marmalade has likely
been sitting on this shelf unbothered for months. Occasionally, a clerk
will come by and dust it.

When a Banana Is Not Just a Banana

To truly see all the tricks marketers have for creating the illusion of
freshness, there's no place better to go than Whole Foods, the world's
largest purveyor of natural and organic edibles. What passes through
your mind when I say the word "fresh"? Free-roaming cows and chick-
ens? Handpicked fruit and flowers? Homegrown tomatoes, still on the
vine?

As we enter Whole Foods, symbols, or what advertisers call "symbolics," of freshness just like these overwhelm us. No matter what
Whole Foods you visit in any city in America, the first thing you see is
flowers. Geraniums. Daffodils. Jonquils. Behind the display of flowers
cascades a stream of clear water against a coppery backdrop (another
"symbolic," suggestive of calm and serenity). Flowers, as everyone
knows, are among the freshest, most perishable objects on earth. Which
is why fresh flowers are placed right up front: to "prime" us to think of
freshness the moment we enter the store. (Consider the opposite: what
if we entered the store and were greeted with stacks of canned tuna and
plastic flowers?) Now that we're primed, we proceed to carry that association, albeit subconsciously, with us as we shop.

The prices for the flowers, as for all the fresh fruits and vegetables, are scrawled in chalk on fragments of black slate, which is a tradition of outdoor European marketplaces. It's as if, or so we are meant to believe, the farmer or grower pulled up in front of Whole Foods just this morning, unloaded his produce (chalk and primitive slate boards in hand), then hopped back in his flatbed truck and motored back upstate to his country farm. The dashed-off scrawl also suggests the price changes daily or even throughout the day, just as it might at a roadside farm stand or local market. But in fact, most of the produce was shipped in by plane days ago, its price set and fixed at the Whole Foods corporate headquarters. Not only does the price not change daily, but what may *look* like chalk on the board is actually indelible; the signs have been mass-produced in a factory. In industry parlance, marketers use the term "Farmgate" to refer to this strategy of planting a (false) image of a real, all-natural working farm in our minds, and "Factorygate" to refer to the fact that most everything we see before us is actually manufactured by a large corporation.

These same "Farmgate" tactics are behind the coolers of chipped ice planted everywhere you look. Ever notice that there's ice everywhere in this store? Why? Does hummus really need to be kept ice-cold? What about cucumber-and-yogurt dip? No and no. This ice is another "symbolic"—an unconscious suggestion that what's before us is bursting with freshness. To our irrational, germ-fearing minds, tortillas, hot dogs, pickles, and other nonperishables must be fresher—and thus safer to eat—when they're sitting on a bed of ice, especially when the soda or juice perspires a little, a phenomenon the industry dubs "sweat" (the refrigerators in most juice and milk aisles are deliberately kept at the exact temperature needed for this "sweating" to occur). Similarly, for years now supermarkets have been sprinkling select vegetables with regular dew drops of water—a trend that came out of Denmark. Why? Like ice displays, those sprinklerlike drops serve as a symbolic, albeit a bogus one, of freshness and purity. (Ironically, that same dewy mist makes the vegetables rot more quickly than they would otherwise. So much for perception versus reality.)

When carrying out experiments on consumer behavior across the world, I often ask people a truly obnoxious question: would they mind emptying the contents of their fridge and freezer onto the kitchen table, then, one by one, ranking and replacing the items depending on how "fresh" they perceive the products as being?

You would be surprised at how the extraordinarily persuasive effects of advertising play into people's perceptions of freshness. The one product consistently at the top of people's lists? Heinz ketchup. That's right, consumers rank bottled ketchup as being fresher than lettuce, tomatoes, onions, and so on. "Why Heinz?" I always ask, noting that the expiration date on the bottle isn't for another six months. "You're right," the majority reply after a moment. "I have no idea why I put that there."

So what's behind this bizarre impression that ketchup is fresh? It's all in the way it's marketed. Heinz subtly plays up the "tomato-ness" of ketchup, with its deep red color—the shade of a picked-right-off-the-vine beefsteak tomato—even though it's actually made from tomato concentrate. Moreover, Heinz does not, in fact, have to be refrigerated once the seal is broken, as we are led to believe. That's yet another illusion meant to trick us into thinking the product is fresh.

My extensive work for McDonald's shows that symbolics like these can alter our perception of everything from freshness to value or even quality. I once helped McDonald's incorporate symbolics of freshness in its restaurants throughout Europe. We painted green leaves on the insides of the lamps and even went so far as to display fresh tomatoes and vegetables behind glass displays. In France, McDonald's went so far as to transform its fabled logo from yellow to a dark, leafy green. And trust me, it worked.

Another powerful "symbolic" of purity and freshness? Fruit. In the juice world, it's a general rule of thumb that the more fruit a manufacturer displays on the side of the juice carton, the greater will be our perception of freshness. Note the spill of kiwis, oranges, mangoes, strawberries, and raspberries that blanket most juice cartons. Would it surprise you to find out that many of these blends contain only the tiniest trace amounts of the more expensive, exotic fruits like kiwi and mango, and are typically more water and sugar than actual fruit juice? (By the way, even though you might think of brands like Dole, Minute Maid, Just Juice, and Odwalla as "natural" brands, in fact they are owned by Coca-Cola, while Pepsi owns Tropicana. And guess who has a true monopoly on the entire category of fruit juices, not to mention milk, buttermilk, and lemonade? A Swedish conglomerate called Tetra Pak, the global manufacturer of those rectangular plastic containers in which our juices and milks are packaged.)

This reminds me of the time a couple of decades ago when I was asked to develop a "cheese ball" snack—a round version of Cheetos. On my preliminary package design, I placed five cheese balls in a minimalist, Stonehenge-like pattern. The person who hired me had a fit. "Who would buy only five cheese balls?" he asked. "We need to see tons of cheese balls on that package!" Over the years I've realized how right he was, and across all categories, too. I redesigned the package to show seemingly hundreds of those cheese balls. Why? Because it seduces us into thinking we are getting that much more in the package. This may have nothing to do with freshness (after all, even the smartest marketers out there would be hard-pressed to fool any consumer into thinking that Cheetos are remotely fresh), but it goes to show why, despite the minimal amount of actual fruit inside most fruit juices, their containers picture a veritable cornucopia of kiwis, mangoes, and so on.

Speaking of fruit, you may think a banana is just a banana, but it's not. Dole and other banana growers have made the creation of a banana into a mini science, in part to manipulate perceptions of freshness. In fact, they've issued a "banana guide" to greengrocers, illustrating the various color stages a banana can attain during its life cycle. Each color represents the sales potential for the banana in question. For example, sales records show that bananas with Pantone color 13-0858 (otherwise known as Vibrant Yellow) are less likely to sell than bananas with Pantone color 12-0752 (also called Buttercup), which is one grade warmer, visually, and seems to imply a riper, fresher fruit. Companies like Dole have analyzed the sales effects of all varieties of color and, as a result, plant their crops under conditions most ideal to creating the right "color." And as for apples? Believe it or not, my research found that while it may *look* fresh, the average apple you see in the supermarket is actually fourteen months old.

Knowing that even just the suggestion of fruit evokes such powerful associations of health, freshness, and cleanliness, brands across all category lines have gone fruity on us, infusing everything from shampoos to hair conditioners to baby soaps to bottled waters to nicotine chewing gum to lip balm to teas to vitamins to cosmetics and even to furniture polish with pineapple, oranges, peaches, passion fruit, and banana fragrances, engineered in a chemist's laboratory, of course. Mango-papaya conditioner, anyone? Lemon lip gloss? Orange-scented Pine-Sol? Will these products get your hair or your floors any cleaner than the regular versions? Of course not. But the scent of fruit evokes strong associations of cleanliness for germophobic consumers, and that's really all that matters. We've reached a point where our shampoos are so fruity we almost want to guzzle them down.

Shampoo companies also realize that the sheer volume of bubbles a shampoo generates can evoke associations of freshness and cleanliness—bubbles signal that the shampoo is strong and invigorating (just as the "sting" of an aftershave or the bubbles hitting our throat when we down sparkling water "inform" us that the product is fresh and uncontaminated). Some companies I know have even gone so far as to create a chemical that accelerates the appearance and quality of bubbles, to make unwitting bathers feel as though their hair is getting cleaner faster. I call this a "perceived justification symbol"—a moment designed to reassure us that we made the right purchase (and, of course, ensure that we'll stay loyal to that product in the future).

Similarly, ever wonder why Aquafresh toothpaste looks the way it does? There's a good reason each squirt is a rainbow of colors. The white is meant to be a symbolic for whiter teeth, the red a symbolic for protecting the gums, and the blue a symbolic for fresh breath. And it works. In one experiment, I asked two groups of consumers to try two different versions of the toothpaste—one the regular version and one that had been dyed just one color. Sure enough, the group using the paste with the three colors not only reported that the toothpaste worked 73 percent better, they even claimed they believed that their teeth looked whiter.

Back at Whole Foods, as I round the corner, a decidedly nonfruity smell hits me. Seafood! There are whole fish, eyes, scales, and all, laid out on yet another cold bed of "symbolic" ice, again suggesting that the fish in this store were reeled in just this morning. But the fish you actually buy sit behind a glass counter in individual plastic containers and have already been beheaded, deboned, and pared down to a more manageable size—you'll never actually take home one of those four whole fish lying balefully across their ice coffin. In fact, these are probably the only four intact fish in the entire store, and they probably aren't even fresh at all, as they've been lying out there in the open all day, if not longer. Yet again, our brains have been tricked into believing that everything in the store was fished, trucked in, and hand-delivered just this morning.

I was once called in to advise the owner of a Dubai fish market who had attempted to sell frozen fish. At first, very few customers showed any interest. Then the manager decided to place the store's supply of frozen fish atop coolers of ice cubes. Suddenly (and irrationally), sales of the fish—the *frozen* fish, remember—rose by 74 percent. Why? It was perceived as fresher simply because it was displayed on blocks of ice. Interestingly, in France consumers actually believe frozen foods are "fresher" than fresh fruits and vegetables. I credit an ingenious frozen-food industry for stressing in its marketing and advertising how long it takes fresh produce to make its way from the farm to the production facility to the supermarket to a consumer's refrigerator. Why, that fresh bunch of spinach could easily be weeks old! Whereas, they inform consumers, frozen food is conserved and preserved on the spot!

A final fish story. A friend of mine once worked on the small island of Tenerife, largest of the Canary Islands off the coast of Spain. He was a fisherman, and his very best customer was a popular local restaurant known as Los Abrigos. But the restaurant owners had specific instructions. Once my friend and the other fishermen had caught their day's supply of seafood, Los Abrigos's management asked them to deliver the fish to a small nearby port, where it was then transferred onto a traditional-looking fisherman's boat (the kind no one, including my friend, uses anymore). When customers would arrive for lunch between noon and 3:00 p.m., the fisherman's boat would putter into the harbor, and everyone would look on as a grizzled old Spanish fisherman would step out and hand over the fish, ostensibly reeled in just moments earlier, to the waiting restaurant staff. It was all completely staged, but people fell for it, and soon the restaurant had to turn away a daily overflow of customers.

So whether it's germs or disease or some feared version of a future self, marketers are amazingly adept at identifying a fear out of the zeit-geist, activating it, amplifying it, and preying on it in ways that hit us at the deepest subconscious level.

As you read on, you'll learn that fear is far from the only psycho-logical tool companies and marketers are surreptitiously using to per-suade us.

Which may be the scariest thing of all.

CHAPTER 3

I Can't Quit You

BRAND ADDICTS, SHOPAHOLICS, AND WHY WE CAN'T LIVE WITHOUT OUR SMART PHONES

Your cell phone's ringing! Is it a colleague checking in? News of a canceled meeting? A sick child? A death, a birth, an emergency? Without this lifeline in your hand, where would you be? Lost. Distracted. Cut off. Alone.

I know a man whose iPhone sits in a bedside dock beside him at night. Most nights, he wakes up involuntarily at 1:00 a.m. to check his e-mail. Then again at three. Then again at five. In the morning, his phone awakens him with a soft but audible rendition of Louis Armstrong and Ella Fitzgerald's "Can't We Be Friends." By the time he's kissed his wife good morning or roused his kids, he's already sent three text messages, checked his three e-mail accounts, scanned the headlines of the *New York Times*, and watched a highlight reel from last night's Knicks game on ESPN.com. As he gets ready for the day, his phone goes with him everywhere. To the bathroom while he takes his morning shower. Outside when he takes the dog out for a quick walk. While driving to work, he recharges it in the passenger seat, lest the battery run out before he makes it to his office (where he has a backup). As he drives, his GPS app tells him which route has the least traffic. He checks the day's weather on it, not to mention the temperatures in Paris,

New York, and five other cities. At work, he plugs it into his computer. In idle moments, he plays Angry Birds, Tetris, and Super Mario Kart on it. Sometimes he squints to read a book on the Kindle app. He uses his smart phone as a stopwatch, a flashlight, a calculator, a calendar, a camera, a stock checker, a note taker, and more.

More than once he's misplaced it. At those times he felt as though his very identity had been stripped from him. The feeling, he tells me, was similar to that of a smoker who knows there's got to be one more cigarette around here somewhere, or a junkie who knows there's one more fix stashed in a drawer, if only he could find it. And in this behavior he is far from alone. A recent study of two hundred students at Stanford University revealed that 34 percent rated themselves as addicted to their phones, while 32 percent worried they someday would be addicted. The way things are trending, I suspect this number is only going to grow. Think about how many times *you* check your phone throughout the course of the day. Twenty-five? Fifty? Two hundred? Now think about that sick, uneasy feeling you get when you discover that not a soul has called, texted, e-mailed, or written on your Facebook wall (at least not since you last checked five minutes ago). Let me ask you another question: Where do you keep your cell phone when you go to sleep at night? On your nightstand, within arm's reach? In bed with you, tucked away soundly, inches from your snoring spouse's pillow? You wouldn't be alone; as a recent *New York Times* article put it, "After six to eight hours of network deprivation—also known as sleep—people are increasingly waking up and lunging for cell phones and laptops, sometimes even before swinging their legs to the floor and tending to more biologically urgent activities."[1]

I was once dining at an elegant restaurant in Paris. Two tables away sat an American couple. It was lunchtime. I glanced over as the familiar digital choreography—what I call the "cell phone dance"—got under way. Lowering his head, the man drew his hand to his pants pocket, surreptitiously slid out his phone, and cocked his eyes down at the small, glowing screen. A moment passed. Then the man excused himself and went to the bathroom. I followed him in, simply because I wanted to prove he was there for no other reason than to check his e-mails and texts. I was right. The moment he returned to the table, the woman, who had undoubtedly taken his absence as an opportunity to check her own phone, rose to use the bathroom herself. I imagine the same routine took place in the ladies' room (a female executive once told me about a time when she was having lunch with her boss and excused herself to use the bathroom—where she found herself trading text messages with her seated boss).

These days, we're tapping away at our phones and handhelds while eating breakfast with our families, during our kids' soccer games, and apparently from the bathrooms of fancy Parisian bistros. Tucking our recharged cell phones into our purses or pockets before leaving the house in the morning has become a ritualized step of arming ourselves against the day. A poll conducted by *USA Today* asked WiFi users how long they could last before they started getting "antsy" about checking their e-mail in-box, instant messages, or social-networking sites. Forty-seven percent replied, "One hour or less."

I recently conducted an experiment in conjunction with global audio identity experts Elias Arts to identify the fifty most powerful and addictive sounds in the world. The third-place winner? The sound of a vibrating phone. Be it an iPhone, a BlackBerry, or an Android, there's no question that the vast majority of us are extremely attached to our phones. But addicted? Really? Isn't that a bit much?[2]

Not really. While it's true that most of us wouldn't meet the American Psychological Association's definition of an addict, some psychologists have argued that smart phones may tap into the same associative learning pathways in the brain that make other compulsive behaviors—like gambling—so addictive."[3] In other words, when we use our phones, our brains create a powerfully positive associative memory—in effect conditioning us to crave that activity again. Just as with addiction to drugs or cigarettes or food, the chemical driver of this process is dopamine, that feel-good neurotransmitter. Some psychologists have asserted that when we receive a new e-mail or text, our brains release a shot of dopamine, and thus we learn to associate that pleasurable feeling with the act of checking our phones. So like an alcoholic who craves that euphoric feeling he gets from drinking, we're left craving that rush we get from seeing that text message pop up.

Still, the theory that behavior like that of my iPhone-obsessed friend is driven by the same neurological processes as drug or alcohol addiction remains unproven and controversial. So I decided to conduct an fMRI study to find out whether smart phones—iPhones and BlackBerrys—are really, truly addictive.

With the help of MindSign, a neuromarketing firm based in San Diego, California, whose brain-activating methodology shows companies what consumers are thinking when they're using products and viewing ads, we enlisted eight males and eight females between the ages of eighteen and twenty-five. As the study got under way, researchers screened both audio and video of a ringing and a vibrating iPhone. Researchers then screened these audiovisual images to our volunteers three times in a row.

Were iPhones really, truly addictive, no less so than alcohol, cocaine, shopping, or video games?

Two weeks later, the MindSign research team rang me up with the results. First, a straightforward observation: The audio and the video of the iPhone both ringing and vibrating activated both the audio and visual cortices of our study subjects—in other words their brains had visual, not just auditory, associations with the sound of the ring tone. What was more surprising, though, was that there was also a flurry of activation in the brain's insula—which is connected to feelings of love and compassion.

In short, these participants didn't demonstrate the classic brain-based signs of addiction to their iPhones. What the sights and sounds of a ringing or vibrating cell phone did reveal, however, was that our study subjects *loved* their iPhones; their brains responded to the sound of the phones the same way they would respond to their boyfriend, girlfriend, niece, nephew, or family pet. In short, it may not be addiction in the medical sense, but it is true love.

When You Shop and Can't Stop

Brand and shopping addictions may not be as life-threatening as addictions like alcoholism or drug dependency, but they are very real and, when taken to the extreme, can be very debilitating. Take the case of

Carolyn Longmead, a middle-aged shopaholic secretary from the UK who stole roughly $225,000 over a two-year period from the small electronics store where she worked. Did she use this money for a down payment on a house or to send her kid to college? Nope, she used it to fund her Louis Vuitton, Prada, and Gucci habits (when she was caught, the brand-name clothes, handbags, and shoes bought with the stolen money were enough to fill twenty-seven garbage bags).[4] Or the case of Amy Gagner, whose shopping compulsion, says CBS News, caused her to empty out IRAs, stock options, and 401(k)s, all to pay off a $200,000 shopping debt—and who, after spending thirty days at a residential addiction center, now lives for her own safety without a credit card, a checking account, or even a computer.[5]

A true addiction can be defined as a persistent, uncontrolled reliance on either a behavior or a substance, whether it's alcohol, a particular food, chocolate, prescription pills, smoking, gambling, shopping, or even sex. Most psychologists would agree that addictions result from a combination of genetic predisposition and environmental factors, though the relative influence of each varies and isn't precisely known. Today most experts also agree that regardless of its cause or what shape it takes, addiction is, biologically speaking, a brain disease. In other words, it's "caused by persistent changes in brain structure and function"[6]—which goes a long way toward explaining why many addicts are unable to give up their particular poison by sheer willpower alone.

The *Annals of General Psychiatry* defines shopping addiction, or "compulsive or pathological buying (or oniomania)," as "frequent preoccupation with buying or impulses to buy that are experienced as irresistible, intrusive, and/or senseless," and goes on to say that in order to qualify as a true addiction, "the buying behavior causes marked distress, interferes with social functioning, and often results in financial problems."[7] Based on this widely accepted definition, a Stanford University study estimates that roughly 6 percent of the population, or seventeen million Americans, suffers from a shopping addiction,[8] a condition that, according to the authors of the study, typically coincides with other disorders ranging from mood and anxiety to eating disorders to substance abuse.[9] A more recent study published in the *Journal of Consumer Research* put the prevalence of shopping addiction at a startlingly high 8.9 percent.[10]

Shopping addictions tend to follow the same general patterns as any other addiction, according to experts in the field. First comes anticipation of shopping or buying something, followed by the shopping or buying experience itself, "often described as pleasurable, ecstatic even, and as providing relief from negative feelings," according to a study carried out by researchers at the University of Richmond and the University of Illinois at Urbana-Champaign and published in the *Journal of Consumer Research*.[11] But the relief is fleeting, and ultimately the high wears off and the shopper crashes. Then, like an alcoholic after a binge, he or she is overcome with guilt and remorse before the cycle starts all over again. While psychiatrists aren't in complete agreement about whether shopping addiction qualifies as a clinical addiction (at the time of writing, the American Psychiatric Association is debating whether to include compulsive shopping in the fifth edition of its mental-health bible, the *Diagnostic and Statistical Manual of Mental Disorders*), they do agree that compulsive shoppers "use shopping as a way of escaping negative feelings, such as depression, anxiety, boredom, self-critical thoughts, and anger,"[12] and many are prescribing an antidepressant known generically as citalopram and sold in the United States as Celexa to curb uncontrollable shopping urges.

As we saw in the last chapter, marketing and advertising entreaties that play on emotions like fear, insecurity, and the universal need for acceptance are incredibly persuasive. Well, it turns out that if we're already predisposed to compulsively shop or buy, their seductive powers become that much more magnified. One four-year-long German study has even found that a critical factor in shopping addiction is the boost of self-esteem shoppers get from interacting with store clerks! "We discovered that shopping addicts get a real kick out of the interaction they have with store personnel. Their fragile egos are given a tremendous boost by sales people who fawn over them and smile and treat them like royalty," says Astrid Mueller, who wrote the study findings. "Their conscious minds know, of course, that these people only want to make a commission on a sale. But their subconscious minds enjoy being treated as a special somebody."[13]

So how does shopping addiction—or any addiction, for that matter—start? Again, it all goes back to dopamine, that feel-good neurotransmitter our brain's limbic system spurts out to give us a "high" or "rush" so pleasurable that we can't help but repeat the behavior as soon as the dopamine drops back to normal levels. The catch is, the more we experience the object or behavior of our addiction—whether it's cigarettes, a drink, a drug, or new Manolo Blahnik pumps—the greater a tolerance we build up, meaning we need more and more of the substance or the behavior to get back that dopamine high.

Dr. Peter Kalivas, chair of physiology and neuroscience at the Medical University of South Carolina, explains that over time, our persistent pursuit of that rush of dopamine can actually change our brains' DNA (specifically the proteins that control a neurotransmitter known as glutamate) in a way that triggers an uncontrollable urge to secure the drug, the drink, or the item of clothing. "You will not let things stand in your way," Kalivas says. "The brain has been altered permanently." [14]

The Thin Line Between Obsession and Addiction

Brand addiction, and its slightly less severe cousin, brand obsession, are subsets of shopping addiction, and while they may not be recognized as psychiatric disorders, I've found them to be alarmingly common. In fact, I'm guessing that whether it's the coworker who has to have her Starbucks in the morning before she can function (not just any coffee; it has to be Starbucks) or the brother-in-law who mopes around depressed for days because the Yankees lost or the little cousin who stands in line all night in minus-ten-degree weather because she just *has* to have tickets to the Miley Cyrus concert (sports teams and celebrities are brands, and highly addictive ones, too), you too know plenty of people who suffer from it. There are so many brand obsessives out there, there's even an online community called MyBrandz, where the afflicted can swap stories about their obsessions. Over the years, I've met people addicted to all kinds of brands and products, from a man who owned ten Harley-Davidsons to a woman who drank twenty-five Diet Cokes a day. And while there's certainly a difference between brand fanaticism and true addiction, I've found that line to be rather thin.

Still, do companies and advertisers have a hand in creating these addictions to their products? Obviously, they can't penetrate our brains and alter the DNA. But while they may not be able to directly manufacture addiction, based on what I've seen in boardrooms and back rooms over my two decades of work with some of the most successful brands on the planet, you better believe that they do have a lot of clever tricks and tools for nudging us in that direction and spurring addictions along. Sometimes they use subconscious emotional or psychological cues, like when cigarette companies imbue their ads and packaging with subtle imagery meant to induce craving. Other times they actually make their products physically addictive, the way cigarette companies manufacture tobacco products to be chemically addictive and potato chip companies use recipes that ensure we won't be able to stop until we've eaten the whole bag. And other times they persuade us to engage in behaviors that actually rewire our brains to become hooked on the act of shopping and buying.

To find out exactly how these addictions form, I spoke with a former senior executive at Philip Morris (seemed like the logical place to start my research on addiction) about how mere consumer habits and preferences can cross the line into addictions—and the role companies play in pushing us over it. He told me that his company has identified a model of how we get hooked on brands. It happens in two stages. The first is known as the "routine stage." This is when we simply use certain brands or products as part of our daily habits and rituals—when we brush our teeth with Crest, use Dove soap in the shower, drive our Toyota to work, etc. These are all products we buy regularly and replace or replenish whenever they break or run out. They are essential to our everyday functioning. The second stage, known as the "dream stage," however, is when we buy things—a new dress, a new pair of earphones, a new bottle of perfume—not because we need them but because we've allowed *emotional* signals about them to penetrate our brains. When do we slip into the dream stage? According to this executive, who asked that he not be named, it's usually when we've let our guard down, when we're relaxed. During the summer, over the weekend, on vacation. Think about it. Beyond the essentials, how many times do you open your wallet during the workweek? Typically not often, because you're in work mode, not shopping mode. But as the weekend approaches, we shed our routines like an unwanted skin and become susceptible to the dream stage.

According to the former Philip Morris executive, *that's* when a real attachment to a brand tends to take root. Here's how it happens. During a brief respite from the routine stage, or "work mode," we feel more relaxed, less inhibited, and more open to trying new drinks, new clothes, new cosmetics, new foods. Pretty soon, we've subconsciously linked the good memories or pleasant emotions of the dream stage with the taste of that new cocktail or the feel of that new face cream against our skin or the fragrance of that new lemon-scented candle. So once Monday rolls around again, or autumn gets under way, we try to "reactivate" this feeling by integrating those brands and products into our daily routines. And once something is part of our routine, it becomes almost impossible to shake.

In sum, a habit is formed during the dream stage, then the habit is reinforced and permanently embedded during the routine stage, at which time we are unconsciously longing for the dream-stage feelings we left behind at the beach or at the spa or at that outdoor concert. This, in fact, is why most beverage brands are so ubiquitously present at summertime music festivals and concerts; those companies know this is one of the best windows to hook new customers on their products. Red Bull, for example, got its start by distributing free caseloads of the stuff at cool "hangouts" like malls and surfing shops, where teenagers and college kids tend to gather to escape the mundane routines of their everyday lives (by the way, it's no coincidence that malls and certain kinds of stores become the "cool" hangout location—that's another happy "accident" engineered largely by marketers, who often hire sexy, good-looking kids to stand casually in front of the entrance. Miraculously, the area is soon packed with other kids; mission accomplished). The company knew that if it caught these kids in their dream stage, once Monday rolled around and they went back to their classes, chores, and homework, they'd associate Red Bull with the carefree feeling of hanging out at the surf shop—and pretty soon they'd be hooked (though in the case of Red Bull there are other reasons, as you'll soon be reading).

Of course, this doesn't work every time. In order for a product to truly take root, its makers have to imbue it with some addictive—whether physically or psychologically—qualities. So what exactly do companies and advertisers do to engineer our desire and make their brand or product so impossible to resist? Let me give you one example from the front lines.

The Power of Craving

A couple of years ago, one of the largest beverage companies in the world hired me to help solve a problem. The sales of its top soft drink had been declining over the past three years, and despite rolling out every trick in its playbook, nothing (including more TV ads and a viral campaign) was working. It looked hopeless, until I realized something the marketing executives had overlooked. Though it seemed like a small detail, psychologically speaking it was anything but.

Now I'm going to let you in on the secret ingredient behind some of the most successful food, beverage, and cosmetics brands out there: the element of *craving*. It's a word that the industry finds hard to admit that it strives for, yet most hit brands and products would be nothing without it.

Face it: all of us experience cravings at some point or another, whether they're for fast food after a long day at work, a bar of chocolate on our way home from the gym, or a cigarette with our morning coffee. Craving is why we're drawn at 2:00 a.m. to the quiet glow of our refrigerator, why the munchy allure of those Doritos or Cheetos refuses to fade until we've polished off the whole bag, and why we fight an internal battle each time we walk by the candy aisle in the drugstore or supermarket. But while cravings may seem to come out of nowhere, in reality they are often triggered by some physical and emotional cues in our surroundings, whether we realize it or not.

The truth is, no matter how much we believe we're in control, when it comes to craving, we are often powerless in the face of these triggers. Companies know this, which is why they deliberately imbue their packaging and advertising with "unconscious signals"—cues that lie just beneath our conscious awareness, right at those very moments when cravings are liable to strike. At Coca-Cola, for example, marketing executives spend hours discussing how many bubbles they should feature in their print ads and on in-store refrigerators. Realizing how much craving bubbles generate—they make us think of that cool, refreshing feeling of carbonation hitting our palates—some executives I spoke with told me they've actually come up with a confidential model for how many bubbles they need to trigger our cravings.

These kinds of craving-inducing "unconscious symbols" were precisely what the big beverage company that hired me had been overlooking. In this case, it was one type of symbol in particular. Think about the countless ads or signs you've seen for Coca-Cola, Pepsi, or any other soft drink displayed in front of kiosks, restaurants, or street cafés. Ever notice that the glass or can or bottle in the photo has water drops—what beverage executives dub "sweat"—trickling down the side? Maybe you didn't notice them consciously. But what those little drops of sweat signal to us *sub*consciously is that the beverage is not just cold but *ice*-cold, which, as everyone knows, makes soda a million times more tasty and refreshing.

Believe it or not, these little sweat drops, which beverage companies have been using in their advertising for decades, kick-start our brains' craving impulses. Yet the company I was helping had decided that those sweat drops—in short, the seeds of craving—looked chaotic and over-complicated, so it had left them out of its ads, and that's why its beverage was tanking. This wasn't just my theory; when we went back and looked at the data, it became clear that the decision to eliminate these unconscious symbols had coincided with the drink's decrease in sales.

It was clear to me that if it was to revive the brand, the company would have to come up with a new unconscious symbol—something even more powerful, more seductive, more crave-worthy than the sweat drops. The only question was what. So I began touring the country, going so far as to spend the night in the homes of soda drinkers of all ages and races. I ate with them. I talked with them. I partied with them. And, of course, I drank a lot of sodas with them. Along the way, something clicked . . . literally.

A few years ago, I conducted a study about the powerful role that sound plays in our subconscious minds. By scanning the brains of fifty consumers from around the world, I was able to isolate the ten most evocative and addictive sounds. The most powerful sound was a baby laughing. But interestingly, also rounding out the top-ten list were the sizzle of a broiling steak and the crackle and fizz of a beverage being poured into a glass filled with ice cubes.

Point is, sounds are incredibly effective triggering cravings. So if I wanted to help that soft drink company revive its brand, the key would be to find out exactly what sounds would trigger the most powerful cravings for its product. So when I sat down with all those soda drinkers around the country, I played them a long list of soft drink–related sounds: the snap and hiss of a cap being opened; the click of a bottle cap careening off a glass bottle; the gurgle and crackle of soda being poured into an ice-filled glass; that unmistakable slurp when a straw sucks the last drop out of a plastic cup; and so forth, to see which triggered the strongest craving for the beverage.

What I found was that not everyone responded the same way to the sound of a can opening or a beverage being poured. These sounds didn't sound the same to every consumer. Believe it or not, people who drink a lot of soda can actually *hear* the difference between the click of one brand and the click of another. From my research on how cigarette companies trigger cravings (something I wrote a lot about in *Buyology*), I knew that depending on the person, certain unconscious signals trigger cravings for certain brands and not others. (I found in my earlier fMRI research that Camel smokers experienced more cravings when they saw illustrations of Camels and Camel logos, and Marlboro smokers experienced more cravings when they saw illustrations of the iconic Marlboro Man.)

True fans of a brand can discern a subtle, distinct difference (which you and I most likely can't hear) when they snap open *their* favorite soft drink. And whether or not they're aware of it, that one-of-a-kind sound subtly activates their brains' unconscious craving centers. Bizarrely enough, if soft drink engineers tweaked that familiar sound even slightly, the drink aficionado would feel no craving sensation whatsoever. The sound is *that* subtle. So if a company wants to trigger a craving for its brand, it needs to "own" a symbol that people associate with its brand and no other.

Which is why I helped this brand create a *snap* sound that was just slightly, subtly different from that of other soft drink cans. First we altered the can design in a lab. Then, once we had achieved the sound we wanted, we recorded it in sound studios, then incorporated it into the soundtrack of the soft drink's TV commercials, radio spots, and even online ads. The manufacturer even played its new and improved sound at major concerts or sports events it was sponsoring.

That was two years ago, and to this day whenever the sound is played at sponsored events, the manufacturer witnesses an instantaneous uptick in sales. Yet when I ask people why they "suddenly" choose that beverage over another, their answer is invariably "I haven't the faintest idea—I just fell for it."

Bet You Can't Eat (or Drink) Just One

Chocolate. Cheese puffs. Cookies. It doesn't take a marketing genius to know that fatty foods are some of the most addictive products out there (perhaps second only to booze and cigarettes). But what you probably didn't know is that this is no happy accident for the companies that sell these foods. Quite the contrary. The reason these products are so addictive is because the companies that sell them deliberately spike their recipes to include addictive quantities of habit-forming substances like MSG, caffeine, corn syrup, and sugar (and by the way, it's also no coincidence that the cigarette company formerly known as Philip Morris and today known as the Altria Group is currently invading the processed-foods industry).

According to a recent study published in *Nature Neuroscience*, high-fat, high-calorie foods affect the brain in a way that is nearly identical to cocaine and heroin. When two researchers from Florida's Scripps Research Institute fed rats high-fat-content foods, including cheesecake, candy bars, and even bacon, every single one of the foods activated a release of dopamine, just as the drugs do. Scarier still, over time the rats needed bigger and bigger quantities of junk food to get that same amount of dopamine, just as drug addicts need more and more of their drug of choice to maintain the same "high." Researchers concluded that when the rats ate enough of these foods, and in big enough quantities, "it leads to compulsive eating habits that resemble drug addiction."[15] The most unsettling finding of all? When the researchers compared the brains of the junk-food-addicted rats to the brains of rats hooked on heroin and cocaine, they found that the addictive effects of the junk food actually *lasted seven times longer.* "While it took only two days for the depleted dopamine receptors in rats addicted to cocaine or heroin to return to baseline levels, it took two weeks for the obese rats to return to their normal dopamine levels," the study reported.[16]

Clearly, fatty foods aren't just psychologically addictive; they are chemically addictive as well. But what about the latest food villain of the twenty-first century—salt? Everyone knows that salt is bad for us; it causes high blood pressure, which is linked to heart disease, and so on. But were you aware that, thanks to the obscene amounts of MSG, or monosodium glutamate—a well-known flavor enhancer widely used in both Eastern and Western cuisines—that companies are dumping into our foods, the human body is developing a very real addiction to salt? Indeed, by several accounts, the amount of MSG in processed, pack-aged, and even some restaurant-prepared foods is doubling every year, not surprisingly given that it's not only much cheaper than any "real" flavor-enhancing ingredient like spices or grains or even oil—it also keeps us coming back for more. As a result, our bodies are building up an unhealthy tolerance, just as with any other addictive substance. Studies reveal that adding MSG to foods not only makes us want to eat more of those foods in the moment but also increases our cravings for salty foods later. One study reported in the *Annals of the New York Academy of Sciences* found that young adults are more likely to acquire a taste for a new food if MSG is added; another study found that when elderly or diabetic patients are given an item of food prepared with extra MSG, they'll not only eat more of it, but they'll also eat less of a non-MSG-laden food later (presumably because they've lost their taste for it).[17]

If all this talk of salt is making you thirsty, now might be a good time to look at what it is in that can of Red Bull that makes you keep coming back for more. Some actually believe it to be cocaine, which German authorities claim to have found traces of in the popular energy drink (which they subsequently banned in six states across Germany.)[18]

But this hasn't been proven in the United States. The real culprit in Red Bull is actually another white powdery substance, which may be legal but can be almost as addictive: sugar. A single six-ounce can of Red Bull contains twenty-seven grams of sugar—approximately six teaspoons, or the amount found in a chocolate bar. Like most drugs, sugar stimulates the release of our old friend, the feel-good neurotransmitter dopamine (among others). In one Princeton University study, Professor Bart Hoebel deprived rats of food and drink for hours each day, before giving them a heavy dose of sugary fluids. The research team noted that after consuming the sugar meal, the rats experienced a torrent of dopamine. Not only that, but their opioid receptors—the ones that respond to the highly addictive drug morphine—were also stimulated. A few days later, not only did the rats crave more and more of the sugar water, but their brains actually created more dopamine receptors. Then, when the researchers took away the sugar, the rats exhibited withdrawal symptoms to the point that their teeth were audibly chattering. While Hoebel confirmed that it's too early to know how this finding might apply to humans and admits that sugar addiction is milder than drug addiction, he concludes that sugar can and does take on addiction-like properties.[19] "In certain models," Hoebel says, "sugar-bingeing causes long-lasting effects in the brain and increases the inclination to take other drugs of abuse, such as alcohol."[20]

And what about caffeine? Is it simply a habit or an actual addiction? Scientists agree that caffeine activates the pleasure centers of the brain by slowing down the rate of dopamine reabsorption, thus making us feel peppy and good (cocaine and heroin do the same thing, but obviously to a much greater degree). Caffeine also provides a shot of adrenaline, so we feel charged up, while blocking reception of adenosine, another neurotransmitter believed to play a part in promoting sleep, making us feel sharp and awake. Now, once the adrenaline wears off, what's next? Well, as any coffee drinker knows, we feel tired, in the dumps, irritated, and jumpy, and our heads hurt, too, since caffeine restricts the blood vessels in our brains, and we need a coffee to get our adrenaline levels back to the levels to which our bodies have grown accustomed.

So those unsubstantiated rumors about cocaine in Red Bull aside, this would all seem to be good evidence that its makers deliberately design the stuff to be addictive; a glance at the Red Bull label tells us that a single can of the stuff contains two hundred milligrams of sodium, eighty milligrams of caffeine (nearly twice as much as a can of Diet Coke), twenty-seven grams of sugar (about five teaspoons per can), and some synthetic taurine, calcium pantothenate, acesulfame-K, and aspartame. This could explain why one New Zealand woman was so addicted to Red Bull that she suffered classic withdrawal symptoms ranging from sweating to nausea to shaking to stomach pain and cramping to anxiety attacks.

Almost makes you want to quit cold turkey, doesn't it!

A "Balming" Influence

Okay, sure, anyone who's ever polished off an entire bag of Doritos knows that salty, fatty foods are hard to put down. But if you think prepackaged junk foods are the only products out there deliberately infused with addictive ingredients, I suggest you reach into your pocket for your lip balm.

"Wait a sec," I can hear you saying, "Lip balm?" You mean that cute little tin or tube of strawberry-flavored goop rolling around in my purse? If the idea that lip balm could be addictive seems far-fetched, stop and think for a minute about how many times a day you apply the sticky stuff. Five? Ten? Twenty-five? Unless you live in the Arctic, there's no way your lips are getting so chapped that you need to reapply every hour. People are so hooked on lip balm there's even a support Web site, http://www.lipbalmanonymous.com, for people who "feel mild to moderate withdrawal on having to stop."[21] True, some experts argue that lip balm's addictive quality isn't in the substance itself but in the soothing, repetitive ritual of putting it on, but others are convinced we do get an actual "buzz" from applying lip balm, especially those brands that contain menthol.[22]

Menthol, a nonessential ingredient added to many a brand of lip gloss, while not dangerous by itself, can be habit-forming. When it shows up in cigarettes, some antitobacco groups claim that it makes them "more addictive, more dangerous and more likely to hook teenagers than unflavored cigarettes," and in 2009 the FDA even considered banning it from cigarettes.

But menthol isn't the only ingredient some lip balm makers add to their formulas to make their products more addictive. Many include "fragrances, preservatives, lanolin and colorings [that] can cause sensitivity and irritation"[23] as well as phenol, a carbolic acid, which can actually *dry out* our lips by interfering with our skin cells' natural ability to produce their own moisture. So with repeated use, guess what happens? It takes our lips longer to replenish their natural moisture, which means our lips feel drier faster and we need to use more lip balm to get the same effect. In other words, the more lip balm you use, the more you need to use. Which to me sounds a whole lot like an addict who's built up a tolerance.

In the case of the best-selling lip balm Carmex, it's even more sinister than that, according to Dr. W. Steven Pray, Bernhardt Professor at the College of Pharmacy at Southwestern Oklahoma State University. An international authority on nonprescription products and devices, Dr. Pray has spent decades on what he's the first to admit has been a fruitless attempt to get Carmex to own up to what he maintains is the *real* reason it uses certain ingredients. Back in the early 1990s, one of Dr. Pray's students raised her hand in class and asked him if lip balm might be addictive. Upon examining the product's ingredients, Dr. Pray was taken aback to find not only phenol but also salicylic acid, a substance that is generally used to eat away at dead tissue like corns, calluses, and warts. Phenol, Dr. Pray told me, is a deadening agent that literally anesthetizes our lips, at which point "the salicylic acid begins eating away at *living* tissue, namely our lips."

In 1993, Dr. Pray contacted Carmex's manufacturer in an attempt to find out just how much phenol and salicylic acid its product contained, only to be told it was a "trade secret." (The manufacturer has since revealed the concentration of phenol as 0.4 percent and that of salicylic acid as less than 1 percent.) So how can Carmex, which Dr. Pray calls "the black sheep of lip balms," get away with including an ingredient that actually exfoliates the dead skin cells, effectively *eroding* our lips? By listing salicylic acid as an "inactive" ingredient—meaning an ingredient that's there simply to make a product more palatable, like a sweetener in cough syrup, rather than an "active" ingredient, which is what it actually is, says Pray.

Trade secret, Carmex? Guess what, the secret's out.

The Name of the Game

Zach Richardson is seventeen years old and lives in Fareham Hants, UK, with his mother, Louise. He doesn't attend school and has no job. So instead of spending his time doing homework or flipping burgers, he sits in his room all day, every day, playing fifteen straight hours of video games on a small TV set (and sometimes simultaneously playing an online football game on his laptop). Zach turns on the Xbox at 9:00 a.m., plays through lunch, then finally lays down his controls sometime after midnight. He often doesn't leave the house for days. His mother says, "There is nothing I can do to stop him playing." His physicians attribute the headaches and blackouts from which he's been suffering entirely to his video game addiction. Yet he keeps playing.

"I left school more than a year ago and I had nothing to do," says Zach, "so I turned to video games to fill the days while I searched for a job. . . . It started off slowly. I only spent two or three hours a day playing. It was just for a bit of fun. Now it has got out of control, and I know I have an addiction."[24]

Nearly nine thousand miles away, in Perth, Australia, a fifteen-year-old boy sits by himself in a dark room, playing a game called RuneScape, one of the most popular fantasy online games in the world, for up to sixteen hours a day. A community college student, bright and formerly (before he discovered video games, that is) outdoorsy and sports-mad, the boy hasn't attended classes in over two months, fooling his parents by dressing each morning in his school uniform, then changing back into his bathrobe after his mother leaves for work.

"He displays all the characteristics of a heroin addict," his father later said. "You haven't got someone putting a needle in their arm and having a high, but you've got all the telltale collateral damage of a heroin addict: withdrawal from his family, withdrawal from his friends, lies to cover his addiction. He'll do anything."[25]

While these are extreme cases, the point is that games can be extraordinarily addictive. Whether we're playing against our friends, a stranger in Tokyo, or even ourselves, and whether the objective is to beat the high score, unlock the most "badges," or build the biggest virtual farm, games are deliberately designed to be hard to quit; according to *Gamer Segmentation Report 2010*, a trade publication, "extreme gamers" spend roughly two full days a week playing video games,[26] and according to a recent Harris Interactive survey, the average eight- to twelve-year-old plays fourteen hours of video games per week, while 8.5 percent of gamers between the ages of eight and eighteen can be classified as "pathological, or clinically 'addicted' to video games."[27]

So I suppose it shouldn't come as a huge shock that marketers and advertisers have picked up on this and, taking a page from the gaming playbook, are using games and gamelike tactics to persuade us to buy.

Before we look at how they do this, we should first ask, Are games truly addictive, in the strictest sense of the word? After all, as we've seen, a true addiction is physiological, rewiring our brain in such a way that we need more and more of that substance or behavior to release the amount of dopamine needed to satisfy our craving or deliver that "high." Does playing a video or online game really qualify? Well, according to a 1999 study, our brains do respond to game playing in much the same way they do to drugs, alcohol, and fatty foods—by releasing more pleasure-inducing dopamine.[28] In fact, the study found that any kind of repetitive activity that becomes increasingly more difficult to carry out—which is, as any gamer knows, the key to a successful game—increases the amount of dopamine in our brains. A new study in the *Journal of Neuroscience* shows that we actually get a surge of dopamine from playing games that we feel we've almost won but have lost by a small margin. When we play games (or enter online auctions, something we'll read more about in a minute), the authors of the study explain, near-miss outcomes stimulate the brain's reward system, particularly those regions known as the ventral striatum and the anterior insula—the same thing happens when we gamble. "These brain regions are also linked to learning, meaning our brains may be duped into believing we're gathering new information with each near miss."[29] And according to another study, games such as World of Warcraft "are designed to be filled with challenges that deliver powerfully articulated rewards, and seem to be engineered specifically to get players' dopaminergic pathways (pathways that mediate interest, focus and reward) activated and resonating."[30]

But this means a lot more for companies and marketers than spiking sales of PlayStations and Wiis. Because as clever marketers have discovered, when games are designed the right way, repeated playing doesn't only hook us on that game itself; it can actually rewire our brains to addict us to *the act of buying and shopping.*

Our Brains Just Want to Keep on Playing

That's right, marketers are using games to make shopping addicts out of us, and like any brandwashing strategy, it starts at a very tender young age. According to one study, "When habitual gaming teaches the brain to rewire its reward mechanism, the brain changes its motivation stimulus. The brain releases dopamine to reward the individual for a beneficial activity—such as natural habits like eating [or] sex . . . or habits like injecting a chemical substance, or participating in a stimulating behavior like gambling or Internet shopping."[31]

Take Club Penguin, a multiplayer online virtual world that uses cute and cuddly penguins as avatars and is designed for children aged six to fourteen (though most of its users are on the younger end). Club Penguin advertises itself to parents as a "safe space"—a way to keep kids away from the seedy underbelly of the Internet (the site is password protected, there are online moderators, and any inappropriate language is blocked via a sophisticated filtration system). What's more, joining is free! In fact, Club Penguin actually *gives* its mini-shopaholics what more or less amounts to their very first credit card: "virtual coins" they are encouraged to spend freely on virtual things.

The "free money" lasts until the moment the children realize their penguins have to eat. And that they need an igloo over their heads. And that their igloos need furniture and decorations! That their penguins need clothing! And toys! And that penguins sometimes get lonely and need their own pets (known on the site as "puffles"). And so on. Once these kids get going, you'd be amazed at how many things they realize their virtual penguins (i.e., *they*) need. But wait, it turns out children can't spend their virtual coins unless they're full-fledged members of the club.

No big deal; Club Penguin costs only $5.95 a month! If you're a parent, that's not so bad, right? A small price to keep your children away from online pornography and YouTube (and get some peace and quiet). But hold on, what happens when the free coins run out? Your child can earn more . . . by playing. The more you earn, the more you can buy. The more you buy, the more you want to earn. The site may be keeping kids relatively safe, but it's also schooling them in the pain and pleasures of compulsive shopping.

Of course, there are games like this for grown-ups, too, like the highly addictive Facebook game Mafia Wars, which has so far grossed over $100 million and, as of August 2010, had 45.5 million active monthly accounts. Here, completing missions and "jobs"—like "icing" an enemy or unseating a "boss" or pulling off a successful heist—wins you cash and "experience points." The more points you win, the more levels magically unlock, keeping you in the never-ending pursuit of higher and higher highs and bigger and better rewards.

Then, of course, there's Mafia Wars' equally addictive cousin, Farm-Ville, another virtual-world phenomenon that, as of June 2010, was the most popular game on Facebook, with over 61.6 million active users and over 24.1 million fans. At time of writing, 20 million players checked into the game daily, according to the *New York Times*.[32] The structure of the game is more or less the same, only here, you win cash and unlock levels through activities like planting pumpkins, picking apples, and harvesting chicken eggs (though of course, as with Mafia Wars, you can also purchase virtual currency with real dollars). And the more levels you unlock, the bigger and better things you can buy; one self-proclaimed FarmVille addict once told me (and I swear, I saw stars in her eyes) that it was her "dream in life" to someday be able to afford what is apparently the most coveted purchase in this virtual world: the FarmVille Villa (priced at, in case you're wondering, one million FarmVille coins). Sure, it may sound monumentally tedious, but it is in fact utterly mesmerizing. So much so that today, according to Carnegie Mellon professor and game designer Jesse Schell, at the time of writing there were far more Farm-Ville members on Facebook than there were Twitter accounts,[33] and according to a new Nielsen report, social networks and online games eat up roughly a third of our Internet time.[34]

Of course, in addition to sending us shots of dopamine every time we buy a new tractor or renovate our barn, these games are also hard at work persuading us to buy real-world things. Let's not forget that while we're racking up all those "experience" points in pursuit of that dopamine high, we're also being exposed to a whole lot of targeted advertising. In fact, Zynga, the parent company that publishes both Mafia Wars and FarmVille, got into hot water in 2009 for its direct-marketing program that invited users to amass virtual currency in exchange for clicking on various offers, filling out surveys, and downloading applications (a Mother's Day ad campaign in which FarmVille players could earn virtual currency if they clicked on an offer promising that they would send someone real flowers).[35] And in 2010, a scandal erupted when it was discovered that ten popular Facebook applications, including FarmVille, may have been passing on users' personal information to marketing companies.[36]

It probably won't surprise you to learn that Facebook itself can be just as addictive as the games people play on it. I've spoken to teenagers and college-aged men and women who have attempted to go off the site, or rather, tried to take a break from it during, say, final exams. They can't. For most users, particularly adolescents, it's all or nothing. Like alcoholics who can trust themselves not to drink only by emptying the liquor cabinet, they find they can trust themselves not to log on only if they deactivate their accounts. Believe it or not, part of the reason the whole Facebook experience is so addictive is that it's deliberately designed to be that way. According to *Time* magazine, Facebook has intentionally created what it calls "aha moments," which reporter Dan Fletcher describes as "an observable emotional connection, like stumbling on the profile of a long-lost friend from grade school, seeing a picture of a newborn niece for the first time, or catching up with an ex-boyfriend."

And the company knows exactly how many of these moments users must have before they are good and truly hooked (though the site will not divulge the magic number, at least publicly). How do they know? "Because they've videotaped the expressions of test users as they navigate the site for the first time," says Fletcher.[37]

Last but not least there's Foursquare, in which users earn points and badges by "checking in" at bars, stores, and restaurants and compete viciously for "mayorship" of their most-frequented establishments (giving those establishments free advertising in the process). Foursquare is hailed as the next big thing in social media (at the time of writing, there were some 2.5 million users), and I've spoken to aficionados who describe it as being "like a drug" and admit to feeling uneasy and on edge if they go somewhere and fail to "check in." A recent *New York Times* article reveals the extent of players' obsession with the game, describing one Philadelphia man who was competing with his girlfriend over mayorship of *her own home* and another man who became so obsessed with gaining mayorship of an alley (yes, an alley) that he developed a computer program that helped him cheat by automatically checking him in to the alley every day at 1:23 p.m. To explain this baffling phenomenon, the article quotes Alexander R. Galloway, an associate professor in the Department of Media, Culture, and Communication at New York University, who noted that "Foursquare taps into our urge to win when placed in a competitive environment, especially in front of our peers" and that "Foursquare turns spaces into a game, and part of its allure is the gamelike aspect."[38]

A similar game is SCVNGR, an app you can download to your iPhone or BlackBerry (and some five hundred thousand users already have). As with Foursquare, you earn points and unlock badges by telling friends where you are and what you're up to. But taking the game one step further, you also earn points for completing bizarre challenges. Want four points? Fold the aluminum in which your burrito was served into an origami bird! According to *FastCompany*, SCVNGR is even testing out a partnership with Citibank to roll out a card that is "a game itself, with two buttons and tiny lights that allow users to choose at checkout whether to pay with credit or rewards points."[39]

Lately, Web sites that make a game out of real-life shopping are cropping up all over. I'm talking about social "flash shopping" sites like Gilt, HauteLook, Rue La La, Woot, and ideeli, which hold "limited time only" sales of items from top luxury designers. If you visit one of these sites in the next twenty minutes, the breathless e-mail in your in-box might say that you'll get 75 percent off a Coach handbag or a pair of Tom Ford sunglasses. The thrill of the hunt! The joy of discovery! The satisfaction of scoring a deal! How could that not be addicting? These sites are increasingly gaining traction, too. At the time of writing, Gilt had two million members,[40] and according to Hitwise data tracker, HauteLook's online market share grew 750 percent in 2010, while Gilt Groupe and Rue La La grew their shares by 200 percent and 160 percent respectively.[41] So how can a computer game or gambling addiction migrate over into a shopping addiction? Very simple: Once we shut down one dopamine supply, we desperately, and unconsciously, seek another source of the feel-good chemical. In short, once we've activated addiction in our brains, it stays with us forever.

Groupon (an amalgam of "group" and "coupon") is a similar and equally ingenious gamelike site that is catching on fast, with, at time of writing, a staggering four million members and a rumored market value of $15 billion.[42] As most people know, Groupon delivers daily specials in your city via an e-mail offering, for example, an 82 percent discount for a one-month membership at Gymboree. But hurry. The deal will take place only if, say, 150 members take advantage of it before time runs out.

When I spoke to Paul Hurley, the CEO of ideeli, he admitted that his remarkably successful site has both a "social component" and a "game structure." When you think about it, ideeli, Groupon, and these other social flash shopping sites really do have everything an addictive game could want. A prize. A ticking clock. A challenge. Other players. An "invitation only" exclusivity. Not to mention it's, well, *fun*. One study, which looked at an online auction site known as Swoopo, confirmed that although consumers aren't pleased when they lose out on a deal, near misses "increased the desire to play the game."[43] Win or lose, our brains just want to keep on playing.

Jesse Schell predicts that in the future the convergence between gaming and buying, especially online, will only continue to intensify. And what's more, games will increasingly migrate over from "dream stage" to the "routine stage" and become more and more integrated in our daily lives. To some extent, this is happening already, from the bargain hunter who checks her daily Groupon and Gilt offers first thing every morning to the Foursquare user for whom checking in at Starbucks is as routine as drinking his morning coffee.

So where does it all end? Time will tell. One thing, though, is for sure. Whether by engineering cravings, imbuing products with chemically addictive properties, or turning shopping and spending into a game we can't stop playing, companies and their marketers will only get better and better at manipulating our psyches and our desires to hook us on their brands and products.

CHAPTER 4

Buy It, Get Laid

THE NEW FACE OF SEX (AND THE SEXES) IN ADVERTISING

Guess how many times a day men across the world think about sex? Two? Five? Twenty? Try thirty-two times a day—which adds up to 224 times a week.

In my last book, I explored everyone's favorite subject: sex. Specifically, the question "Does sex sell?"

My research found that men and women reacted to sexually provocative advertising—suggestive commercials, ads featuring scantily clad models, that sort of thing—in much the same way they respond to sexual suggestion in real life. In general, women tend to be more easily persuaded by ads that are more romantic than sexual, ones that emphasize commitment, devotion, and partnership. Not surprisingly, men, on the other hand, responded to sexual innuendo and women in bikinis, especially when the ads or commercials were leavened with a heaping dose of adolescent humor.

That said, my research revealed that when it comes to persuading us to buy, sexy ads can sometimes backfire. In one study, I showed two separate groups of men identical ads. The first group watched sexually suggestive ads, while the other group saw the same ads, only without the sexual content. Turned out, the men who saw the sexually suggestive commercials were no better at remembering the names of the brands and products they'd seen advertised than the men who'd seen the unerotic ads. In other words, while the male volunteers may have enjoyed the whiff of sexuality, ultimately it had no effect on their memory or impression of the actual product.

Yet sexually suggestive advertising isn't going anywhere anytime soon, mostly because when we see attractive, scantily clad young people advertising an energy drink or a brand of underwear or a new line of cosmetics, the mirror neurons in our brain allow us to imagine ourselves as being equally attractive and sexually desirable. And after all, what is advertising about if not planting hopes and dreams inside our brains?

Sure enough, sex in advertising is still everywhere we look. Abercrombie & Fitch has recently reinstated its soft-porn in-store catalog, American Apparel still showcases its pouty, scantily clad models in giant store windows, footballer David Beckham still sprawls across a Times Square billboard in his skivvies (at the time of writing, at least), and the 420 million Web sites spawned by the $4.9 billion global pornography industry still carry ads for everything from "sexual enhancement" products to escort services to, well, more pornography (by the way, in case you're wondering, the average age a child stumbles across a porn site? I hate to say it, but it's eleven).[1] And though it may not work all the time, there is evidence to suggest that a sexed-up ad campaign can be persuasive, if it's done in the right way; as Dr. Geoffrey Miller, an evolutionary psychologist at the University of New Mexico, found, people are more likely to expend money and effort on products and activities if they're first primed with photographs of the opposite sex or stories about dating.[2]

To give you one example of how sex can still sell, a few years ago one of the world's biggest car manufacturers contacted me to help it turn around declining sales of one of its most iconic brands.

Throughout my years as a branding consultant, I've sought to explore the personality of the target customer so that I could help import that personality into the brand. This time around, though, I took a new-fangled approach to connecting with consumers' psyches. I created a rather unusual deck of cards—each of the two hundred cards picturing a different animal. Then I asked a group of middle-aged men (the target customers) to identify five different animals they believed best represented the brand.

Next, I used fMRI neuroimaging to narrow the findings. When my team showed the men pictures of the first four animals they'd named, it was pretty much business as usual in their brains. But to everyone's surprise, the final animal we showed them lit up those brain regions associated with sexual attraction and mating. When we then showed the same men photos and images of their dream cars (cars they either could ill afford or felt they were too old to drive), bingo: these same randy brain regions lit up.

Turns out that subconsciously, these nicely dressed businessmen, who had been married an average of twenty-three years and were the fathers of an average of 2.5 children, associated their dream cars—and that particular animal—with one thing, and one thing only. Sex. Bingo, we had our answer.

From that point forward, the animal—code-named "Asterix"— informed every single detail of the car's design, engineering, and appearance. The animal in question was and is black, sleek, and rare, with smooth lines and long curves mixed with a "feminine" smoothness. The goal was to give the car smooth, shapely curves and motions: to make the male driver feel as if he were saddling up, riding, and conquering a fast, powerful, supple, beautiful animal. The engineers at the auto company imported these sensuous qualities to the car's dashboard, gear stick, interior leather, and even door handles. In short, the car was sex on four wheels, and four years later, when it finally hit the road, the company enjoyed one of the greatest sales turnarounds in its history. (P.S. For the record, it was an Arabian horse, renowned, among other things, for, uh, the size of its penis.)

If You Spray It, They Will Come

So how do I know that men think about sex thirty-two times a day? Because I talked to David Cousino, a highly regarded Unilever executive and an expert in consumer and market insight, who shared this, as well as the many other surprising findings Unilever's internal re-search team uncovered when preparing to roll out what would become a multimillion-dollar brand: Axe.

Axe is a line of men's personal-care products that includes deodor-ant body sprays, sticks, and roll-ons; shampoos; and body washes with names like Apollo, Kilo, Phoenix, Tsunami, and Voodoo. Introduced in the United States in 2002, Axe is renowned in marketing circles for how it craftily positioned is products as bottled pheromones—magical potions that could transform the greasiest, scrawniest, most acne-prone schlub into a confident, gorgeous, chiseled sex magnet. The behind-the-scenes story of how Unilever created this now-legendary Axe campaign isn't just another demonstration of the power of sex in advertising; it's also a fascinating example of just how deeply compa-nies and marketers probe the depths of our inner psyches—our hopes, dreams, and daydreams—in the service of crafting the kinds of provoc-ative, scandalously sexual, and smashingly successful campaigns that push the very limits of advertising as we know it.

First, the Unilever team conducted an extensive, in-depth online survey of twelve thousand boys and men aged fifteen to fifty around the world—from the United States to the UK to Mexico to South Africa to Turkey to Japan. But it wasn't your average survey. This sur-vey asked these twelve thousand males a series of highly personal, somewhat embarrassing questions, such as: "What is your strategy when you want to pick up a girl?" "When do you feel really insecure?" "When were you rejected by a girl?" "What is your ideal sexual fan-tasy?" and the aforementioned "How many times do you think about sex a day?" Why was Unilever asking these questions? "We wanted to identify male human truths," recalls Cousino, whose team then ana-lyzed the research country by country. "The things that make men tick, that are the same no matter where you go, no matter where you were born or who you are."

The results were, to say the least, revealing (there's nothing like on-line anonymity to get a guy to spill his guts). It may sound like a cliché or a scene from a bad porno flick, but as it turns out, the number one fantasy among men is this: A boy or a man is lounging in a hot tub or spa. He's surrounded by three or four naked women. A corked bottle of champagne stands nearby, with its foam bubbling over into the hot tub. Based on these responses and others, the Axe team realized something. The ultimate male fantasy isn't just to be found irresistible by a sexy woman. It's to be found irresistible by *several* sexy women! This was the groundbreaking revelation that was soon to become the crux of Axe's campaign. Says Cousino, "We realized—or rather, had it confirmed . . . that if the campaign was to be successful, it would have to emphasize the pheromone aspects of the brand." But wait, these marketers weren't done probing yet.

Next, in a spirit of male camaraderie, Cousino and his Unilever colleagues accompanied roughly a hundred males (identical studies were later carried out across other European countries, North America, and Latin America) aged fifteen to fifty to the pubs until three or four in the morning and (soberly, while secretly taking copious notes) watched them in action. Their goal was to see how these men would pick women out of the crowd and ultimately approach them (to analyze their "game," as it were). After poring over their pages and pages of notes, in the end, and via a process known in the industry as "segmentation," the Unilever team isolated six psychological profiles of the male animal—and the potential Axe user.

The breakdown:

The Predator, as Cousino describes him, conceals his insecurity under a facade of swaggering bluster. He drives a brand-name car, adorns himself with high-end fashion brands, and is constantly on the prowl. He has little if any respect for women and is markedly deceptive—he's liable to lie to a woman about his job (when he's in fact unemployed), where he lives (typically with his parents), and so on. The Predator tends to target women who are out alone, preferably drunk ones he can take easy advantage of. In sum, the Predator is any woman's—and her father's—worst nightmare.

Natural Talent. This is the intelligent, athletic, achieving, magnetic, naturally confident male; the kind of guy other guys like to be around and women find inherently appealing. Natural Talent usually gets the woman he's after, though never deceptively (interestingly, when the Axe researchers polled all the men, they found that nearly everyone not only *wanted* to be the Natural Talent guy; the vast majority believed they *were* the Natural Talent guy. It was like a sexed-up version of the Lake Wobegon effect).

The Marriage Material Guy is exactly that: gentle, respectful, and self-confident. The kind of guy you want to bring home to Mom (despite what single women might tell you, according to Unilever's research, Marriage Material men make up a pretty large segment in the young male population).

Always the Friend. Is there a greater kiss of death for an amorous young man than to hear the words "Sorry, but . . . I like you more like a brother. Can we be just good friends?" Cousino remarks, not unkindly, "You watch them deflate right in front of you." Not surprisingly, quite a few gay men (and closeted gay men) turned up in this category.

The Insecure Novice. These poor young fellows haven't the slightest idea *what* they are doing around women. Along with Marriage Material and Natural Talent, the United States boasts quite a few Insecure Novices. Ironically, they outwardly resemble the Predator in that they will simply step up and behave in ways that make most women uncomfortable, but their motives are pure and not deceptive.

The Enthusiastic Novice. These young men have no idea what they are doing, either, but they come across as eager rather than creepy. They might not score, but darn it, no one is going to tell them they aren't doing their best.

So now that the Axe researchers had isolated these six segments, what did they do with the information? Well, the first step was to figure out which of these six types of men was their best target. Ultimately, they decided the most obvious choice would be the Insecure Novice, followed by the Enthusiastic Novice, followed by the Natural Talent. Why? Well, the first two segments, the marketers reasoned, with their lack of self-esteem and experience, could be easily persuaded that Axe would be the key to enhanced success with women—they would spray it on to ramp up their self-confidence. The Natural Talent guys, on the other hand, didn't need a shot of self-confidence, but they could probably be convinced to use Axe as a finishing touch before going out for a night on the town. This was unlike, say, the Predator, who the marketers knew would never feel he needed the product, or anything other than his own sexy self, to score with women.

So with the Insecure Novice as their primary target, Axe came up with a series of thirty-second TV commercials that preyed on what its research had revealed to be the ultimate male fantasy: to be irresistible to not just one but *several* sexy women. These ads were nothing short of marketing genius. In one thirty-second spot, an army of bikini-clad female Amazons, drawn by the irresistible scent, storms an empty beach to surround and seduce a helpless, scrawny young male Axe user. In another, a naked, soapy young man is showering when suddenly the bathroom floor cracks and he tumbles (still naked and dripping with suds) into a basement filled with scantily clad young women who proceed to bump and grind lasciviously enough to make a porn star break out in hives.

"No one wants to play with dirty equipment," intones a woman in another less-than-subtle Axe ad, before proceeding, with the help of an assistant—"Monica, can you help me with these dirty balls?" she asks—to clean and fondle two white golf balls in her manicured hand. "If you spray it, they will come," is the suggestive promise of another ad, in which a pair of college-aged women bodily drag another college-aged geek into what is, presumably, a waiting boudoir. In others, a gaggle of young women need only take a deep inhale of a nearby Axe man before they are immediately compelled to surrender their cell phone numbers, while in yet another, a man sprays on Axe's Dark Temptation body spray, which immediately transforms him into a life-sized piece of chocolate—which a bevy of hot women off the street nibble at suggestively for the remainder of the thirty-second spot. The message of each of these couldn't be clearer: use Axe and get laid. Repeatedly, by different women.

The campaign was an instant hit, and Axe quickly became the number one male brand in the total antiperspirant/deodorant category,[3] earning Unilever $71 million in sales in 2006 ($50 million more than its closest rival, Tag)[4] and $186 million (excluding Walmart sales) in 2007, an increase of 14 percent from a year earlier—which was leagues ahead of its nearest rival. What's more, sales of the brand's other products shot up as well, because body sprays are often used as a "training fragrance," and if a young male cottons to a brand, he's more likely to buy other products from the same company (what we in the industry call "the halo effect"). Moreover, Axe had achieved global fame for its envelope-pushing ads, which were variously termed funny, brilliant, offensive, or outrageously sexist. Either way, it was free publicity, and it worked.

However, the brand's early success soon began to backfire. The problem was, the ads had worked *too* well in persuading the Insecure Novices and Enthusiastic Novices to buy the product. Geeks and dorks everywhere were now buying Axe by the caseload, and it was hurting the brand's image. Eventually (in the United States, at least), to most high school and college-aged males, Axe had essentially become the brand for pathetic losers, and not surprisingly, sales took a huge hit.

Then Axe faced another big problem. Insecure high school students had been so convincingly persuaded that Axe would make them sexually appealing that they began completely dousing themselves in it. After all, if Axe = sex, then more Axe = more sex, right? According to CBC News, "Some boys have been dousing themselves in Axe, apparently believing commercials that show a young man applying the deodorant and being immediately hit on by beautiful women." It got to the point where the students were reeking so heavily of it that it was becoming a distraction at school. So much so that in Minnesota, school district officials attempted to ban it, claiming that "the man spray has been abused, and the aerosol stench is a hazard for students and faculty."[5] The principal of one Canadian school started actually confiscating bottles of Axe. "They spray it all over their heads and their necks," one teacher said. "They don't realize how powerful the odor is. . . . They have no idea how much it takes to be a walking stink bomb [which is] basically what they are."[6]

Today, Unilever is reinvigorating the brand with a series of viral videos focused more on showing men just where to spray Axe. Naturally, these too are charged with sexual innuendo; after spraying a mannequin, the spokeswoman tears off the man's right arm and begins paddling herself while crying, "I have been naughty!"[7]

Despite its few stumbles, the wild success of Axe's ad campaign just goes to show what can happen when a brand and its clever marketers probe and plug into our most private and deeply rooted sexual fantasies and desires. And it goes to show that these days, as ever, our most deeply seeded sexual fantasies and desires can be some of the most powerful persuaders there are.

And although some entrenched marketing techniques, like the one you just read about, remain in place, what most people don't know is that companies and advertisers are using sex in a host of sneaky new ways. In this chapter, we'll take a look at the provocative results of some experiments I recently did on sex in advertising, including shocking revelations of what heterosexual men *really* think about when they see naked male bodies in advertising (hint: it isn't their girlfriends) and what type of man some women won't admit to daydreaming about (hint: check out the posters on their tween daughters' walls). We'll also take a look at how changing gender roles in our society are shaping the way companies are using sex appeal and beauty to brandwash the twenty-first-century man.

Who Loves Ya, Baby?

The ads stretch across countless Abercrombie & Fitch storefronts and billboards from Times Square to London to Paris: doe-eyed, shirtless men with broad, smooth shoulders and six-pack abs jutting majestically out of a pair of bulging, tight-fitting jeans, arrayed in various supine poses, like wrestling in the woods or lounging languidly on a summer beach.

It's all very, very sexy. But when you stop and think about it for a minute, something doesn't add up. The jeans being advertised here are for *men*, and the majority of Abercrombie's customers (and target customers) are straight. If these billboards are trying to seduce customers with hot, near-naked bodies, shouldn't they be *women's* bodies? In other words, why are sexy men being used to sell jeans and underwear to heterosexual men? To begin to answer that question, we have to go back a couple of decades.

Back in the early nineties, when Madonna Badger (then senior art director at Calvin Klein's in-house agency and today the proprietor of Badger & Winters, her own successful New York boutique ad agency) and photographer Herb Ritts created two ads for Calvin Klein underwear, they couldn't possibly have predicted what effect they would have. I'm sure you've seen these now-iconic ads. The one for men's briefs pictured well-muscled actor and stud muffin Mark Wahlberg (back then known as rapper Marky Mark) clutching his crotch and grinning. The one for women's skivvies featured the waifish Kate Moss hugging her bony arms to her bony chest. These homoerotic ads boosted sales of Calvin Klein underwear—both men's and women's—by roughly 35 percent, instantly broadcasting to the advertising world that yes, you *can* use male sex appeal to sell to men, and female sex appeal (albeit a boyish female) to sell to women. And for the next two decades, use it they did.

More than twenty years later, American Apparel's billboard ads, so racy they've been accused of being downright pornographic, show young men in their underwear with their legs splayed open, while the male models in Dolce & Gabbana's cologne ads bare their glistening, rippling, tanned chests (in one controversial ad, a shirtless man leans suggestively over a woman in a skimpy black dress while other men in varying states of dress look on). Adidas advertises its sneakers with posters showing Canadian model Tym Roders baring his perfectly toned, athletic body while clutching a pair of sneakers in front of his crotch. And it's worth noting that *Men's Health*, with its monthly cover photos of shirtless men with six-packs, is among the most popular magazines in the United States. Point is, thanks in no small part to the barriers broken by those envelope-pushing late-nineties Calvin Klein ads, it's not uncommon for advertisers to use provocative images of male sexuality to sell *men* on everything from clothing to cologne to sporting equipment.

Yet most straight males would be loath to admit that these sexually charged images of attractive men with their V-shaped physiques, broad pectorals, rippling upper bodies, and bulging crotches have any effect on their buying behavior whatsoever. In the United States, at least, it's still not considered okay for a straight man to admire another male, and in fact men are used to averting their gaze when any hint of the naked male form is present—which could explain why when a man is standing at the urinal in a public restroom, a second man who enters the bathroom will set up shop ten miles away from him, for fear of being unwittingly perceived as on the prowl.

Yet the data doesn't lie. These homoerotic ads do work. They work incredibly well. So what's going on here? Dr. Belisa Vranich (a *Today* show psychologist who also serves as the psychologist for Gold's Gym and is on the advisory board for *Shape* magazine) conjectures that men rationalize ogling these ads by telling themselves they are simply looking at a single, isolated body part—say, to see how the jeans fit around the hips or how the T-shirt stretches across the chest—as opposed to the body itself. It's called *Playgirl* marketing, Dr. Vranich tells me, referring to the monthly magazine featuring male nudes founded in 1973. "It says it's for men trying to impress women, but it's really men for men."

Based on what I've seen in all my years in the advertising industry, I'd long suspected that these ads of chiseled males strike a chord in heterosexual men—why else would they be so ubiquitous? When I've asked young men about the models in the Abercrombie ads, they'll cheerfully admit, "Those girls are fit." But when I ask, "What about the guys?" the discomfort in the room is palpable. Then, quite often, I get a chorus of "I didn't really notice them" or "Why do you want to know?" as if I'm challenging their sexuality (which I'm not). But whether they cop to it or not, I believe that these ads and images that evoke male sexuality or the male body are powerful persuaders for men and influence their buying decisions more than they'd care to admit, even to themselves.

So I decided to carry out an fMRI research study to see how the male brain was affected by this sexually stimulating imagery. I wasn't trying to make some kind of social statement or prove some kind of point, like "All men are secretly gay." As someone who studies branding and advertising for a living, I simply was curious as to what effect photographic imagery of the near-naked male *really* has on the heterosexual male consumer.

So again with the help of San Diego–based MindSign Neuromarketing, we were ready for our research experiment to kick off. Our "underwear" study subjects consisted of sixteen males between the ages of eighteen and twenty-five—eight heterosexual and eight homosexual men. The MindSign neuromarketing team scanned the volunteers' brains under an fMRI as they viewed five images of male models stripped down to their tight white skivvies and boxer briefs. A couple of weeks later, some very provocative results came in.

Turns out that both groups of men showed significant activation in their visual cortex—to be expected, given the visual nature of the stimulus. But far more revealing was the fact that both groups also showed activity in the area of the brain (known as the inferior lateral prefrontal gyrus) that is involved in working memory and that most often comes alive when a person is attempting to lie, manipulate a fact, or somehow convince themselves of something not quite true. As a matter of fact, you could easily dub this brain region "the deception area." All of which indicated to the MindSign study researchers that our study subjects didn't *want* to be attracted to our skivvy-clad male models . . . but in fact, they *were*. And more telling still, the heterosexual men's brains' responses to the male underwear ads—denial, followed by varying degrees of interest—were extremely similar to those of homosexual men. All strong evidence, according to the team of experts who analyzed the results, that some of the heterosexual men were equally stimulated by the ads—their brains were just working harder at denying it.

Scent of a Woman

In December 2004, when the global fragrance firm International Flavors & Fragrances was bidding to win the account for Calvin Klein's new fragrance, Euphoria, it called on Erika Smyth and her then colleague Alex Moskvin, who ran IFF's internal BrandEmotions unit. The way it works in the fragrance world is that the manufacturer—in this case Calvin Klein, then owned by Unilever—tells the fragrance companies what it wants the scent to evoke and sends them off to create it. Then, once a fragrance is submitted, the company runs focus groups to see whether it succeeds in summoning the desired associations and emotions. So Unilever first submitted to the perfumeries what's known in the industry as a "mood-edit"—a montage of short, almost sub-liminal, and sexually suggestive clips from various films (like a scene in which a woman was willingly blindfolded and tied up, though in a very seductive way). Why does the industry use a film instead of simply explaining what it wants in the fragrance? Because, as David Cousino notes, "Language has a way of dulling things."

"Create a fragrance that takes a woman to *this* [emotional] space," Unilever's team told IFF (and the other bidders). Then, once the fragrance was ready, Unilever assembled a focus group of women and dabbed "juice" (the widespread name for perfume across the fragrance industry) on each woman's skin. Then the team asked the women to close their eyes and tell the first story that came to mind that expressed what the fragrance evoked for them. Without exception, the stories the women told were romantic, sexual, and passionate. Interestingly, without exception, the fragrance seemed to evoke in every woman the same gently clashing associations: innocence alongside passion; free-dom as well as capture; love that was soft and sweet while carnal and sexual at the same time. Bingo. IFF's juice would be Calvin Klein's new fragrance.

But the process was just getting started. Unilever loved what IFF had come up with but wanted to refine it further. To ensure they got it just right, the Unilever team decided to carry out additional research around the same question: *Where does this fragrance take you emotionally?* But then they realized something: there was no way to know whether the fragrance had taken the women to that dark, sensual place until they fig-ured out where, for these specific women, that place might be. So they decided to probe a little more deeply. This time they led each woman through a maze of corridors into various dark rooms (the rooms were dark to eliminate sensory distractions), each suffused with a different variation of the IFF fragrance. The women closed their eyes. What did they see, hear, feel? Afterward, the Unilever team pored over their re-sponses, trying to decode "where" and to what "space" the fragrance "took" each woman. The Unilever team knew where it *wanted* the scent to take them—to a "dark, sexual place," as one of the team members put it. But Unilever executives weren't sure which of the three or four different variations of the scent, then dubbed "Alchemy," had hit the spot.

So they showed the women the same "mood-edit" they'd submitted to the fragrance houses and asked the women to jot down what they thought of when they contemplated visiting this dark, seductive "space" evoked by both the film and the fragrance. The responses ranged from "dark" to "sinister" to "scary," yet one underlying reaction kept re-emerging. The women were all *drawn* to the sensation of losing control sexually. It seemed the emotional response the Unilever team was after was a kind of imprisoned lust—"We wanted there to be a sense that they might lose a little bit of themselves, but at the same time, they were happy to give it up," David Cousino recalls. But by now Unilever was torn between IFF's Alchemy and a submission from another house. So it hired a company called Scent Analysis to conduct a sophisticated test to figure out which fragrance hit every single note the women had described—and identify the best fit between the "emotional space" and the juice. Then Unilever hired a semiotician to help it come up with a word to describe the new fragrance—an adjective that would help advertise and position the brand. That word turned out to be "melancholic." Thus, in 2004 a sensual yet slightly mournful scent, Euphoria, was born. With the help of an ad company, Unilever rolled out a series of dark, shadowy, sensual, and—naturally—melancholic thirty-second ads, and the new Calvin Klein fragrance proceeded to fly off the shelves. In fact, even today Euphoria is the only fragrance launched in the past decade that remains in the top ten fragrances globally.

So what does sex appeal *really* smell like? Turns out it smells like money.

Robbing the Cradle

In his book *Why We Buy*, retail anthropologist Paco Underhill refers to adults who pay for their children's (or spouse's) purchases as "the Wallet Carriers" because tweens and teens generally depend on their parents to pay for their provisions and goodies, whether they're school supplies, clothes, cosmetics, or music downloads for their iPods. As the holder of the purse strings, the wallet-carrying adult has at least some say in what the child is buying, which, from a marketer's point of view, poses a bit of a challenge. How to craft a marketing or advertising strategy that will persuade an adult when you're selling a product meant for children? Very sneakily, as you'll read in a minute.

Today, thanks to technology, never before in the history of our species have contemporary parents had more in common with their teenage or even tween-age children. Mom, Dad, and the children all have cell phones, Facebook accounts, and a roughly similar cultural sensibility. They go to the same movies, they listen to much of the same music, they watch the same shows on TV (or iTunes or TiVo or Hulu). The result being that Hollywood and the music industry have had to find ways to develop adult content that will still be suitable for young audiences. How do they do it? By cleverly crafting semiambiguous lyrics and dialogue that have an adult—which more often than not means sexual—meaning to grown-ups but say something completely different and innocuous to an eight-year-old. Take, for example, a tune like the Black Eyed Peas' "Pump It!" or Fergie's solo hit "London Bridge," with its lyrics, "How come every time you come around, my London/ London bridge wanna go down" (makes you long for the innocent days of Peter, Paul & Mary's "Puff, the Magic Dragon," doesn't it?).

To see what I mean, try watching an episode of *The Simpsons* with an eight-year-old. You'll both be enjoying yourselves, but the kid will likely be guffawing at the toilet humor or "Homer Simpson is a klutz" type scenes, while you'll be chuckling inwardly at the homoerotic tension between Smithers and Mr. Burns. (In one 2000 *Simpsons* episode, "A Tale of Two Springfields," after the residents of Old Springfield find gold in a nearby river, one woman exclaims, "Thanks, Mayor Simpson! From now on, we'll all be taking golden showers!")

Movie franchises like *Shrek* and *Toy Story* employ this strategy as well; consider that the king in *Shrek* is named Farquaad, pronounced "Fuckwad," while in *Toy Story 2*, Buzz's love-struck reaction to a cowgirl named Jessie makes his wings spring rigidly erect. These scenes give a wink and nod to the wallet-carrying parents but aren't so overtly sexual that their children will pick up on it. As the BBC points out,

"Hollywood moguls didn't get where they are without being aware that the ultimate film is one that audiences of every age and type can sit through."[8]

So successful is this strategy in the entertainment industry (behind closed doors they in fact call this the *Simpsons* or *Shrek* strategy) that companies have begun to take a page from Hollywood's playbook, and marketers of all stripes are now employing the strategy across their brands. For example, the sandwich chain Quiznos recently came out with a new sub called the Toasty Torpedo. It's "12 inches of flavor," ads proclaim, just before a smoky-voiced toaster asks a chef to "say it sexy" and "put it in me."[9] Here's hoping the eight-year-olds didn't pick up on that one.

But no brand (and yes, he is a brand) has enjoyed so much success from the *Shrek* strategy as contemporary pop singing sensation Justin Bieber.

As anyone with a teenage daughter knows, Justin Bieber is a cherubic seventeen-year-old musician who got his start in 2007, when his mother uploaded videos of him singing in his bedroom onto You-Tube. Weeks later Bieber's videos had been viewed a hundred times, then a thousand, then ten thousand, then a million, and two years later, Bieber's album *My World 2.0* debuted at number one on Billboard. With fifty million subscribers to his YouTube channel, *Time* magazine dubbed Bieber "the first real teen idol of the digital age, a star whose fame can be attributed entirely to the Internet."[10] Aside from this distinction, though, Bieber merely is the latest in a long tradition of moppy-haired teenage boys whose perfect, boyish features adorn the walls of countless besotted tween and teenage girls' bedrooms. Plump lips. Dark, soulful eyes. Smooth skin. A disarmingly sweet smile. And let's not forget the hair flip! Incidentally, if you glance at a photo of 1970s tween idol Donny Osmond, who sang "Hey, There, Lonely Girl," followed by a photo of Justin Bieber, one of whose hits is "One Less Lonely Girl," you'll be struck by the spooky similarity not just of their songs' content but also of their facial features. No doubt about it: to girls aged ten to seventeen, the pure and innocent look is hot.

But wait a minute. Turns out not all the millions of adoring Bieber fans are teens and tweens at all. Many are, of course, but not all. Not by a long shot. So who are they, then? Believe it or not, a significant percentage of this boyish seventeen-year-old's most fervent admirers are actually women in their thirties and forties. That's right, women old enough to be his mother. Now, over the years I've spoken to many middle-aged women who will admit to an occasional crush on a young male celebrity. Understand that I'm not referring here to anything nefarious, illegal, or perverse; I have yet to hear of any middle-aged Bieber fans ever acting on their crush (at the same time, I recognize that if a forty-seven-year-old father acknowledged lusting after a teenage girl, he would be remanded to therapy or, in the worst-case scenario, led away in shackles). Still, these women can be scary in their own way; it's not unusual at a Bieber appearance to see eager mothers pushing their way through clusters of screaming tweens, literally shoving the young girls out of their path to the adolescent heartthrob.[11]

As a marketer fascinated by the celebrity brand, I couldn't help but wonder what this was all about. Bieber-mania among teenagers made perfect sense. After all, the teen idol phenomenon does go back decades, and Bieber *is* objectively cute, in a seventeen-year-old kind of way. But what was his appeal to these women twice his age? Were they sexually attracted to him? Was he simply some kind of projection of an old fantasy from their own teen years? I decided to find out. So I teamed up with Murray Hill Associates, a nationwide recruitment group, and together we assembled a focus group composed of women and mothers who, in their own teenage years, had been besotted by a teen idol—whether it was Leif Garrett or David Cassidy or Davy Jones. But before asking these women some admittedly personal questions, I first sought the insight of a female psychologist (and mother) who herself had admitted to similar crushes now and again on good-looking, underage young men. My question intrigued and amused her.

She paused. "It's not necessarily sexual, Martin," she said. Then she paused. "But it's not *unsexual*, either." Of course I had to know more.

Which is how, on a rainy night in Chicago, I found myself sitting in a focus group with a dozen forty-five-year-old mothers gazing at me from around an oval table. "So, ladies," I said, "I want to ask you what may seem like a strange question." I hesitated. "As an adult, have you ever had a crush on a really, really young guy?"

At this point I expected looks of utter outrage—maybe even a few pens or cups of coffee hurled in my face. But amazingly, no one in the room took any offense at my suggestion whatsoever! Quite the opposite. Every female beamed back at me with recognition and what could only be described as release. Clearly, I'd hit a major artery. Ever see the *Saturday Night Live* sketch where Tina Fey, playing Bieber's high school teacher, mutters to herself, "I don't know whether I want to marry him or put him in a stroller and push him around the mall"? Based on what I learned that night, this was apparently a widespread yet seldom-discussed sentiment.

The women in the room made sport of their crushes, all the while being careful to stress that of course they never *acted* on them. But the sense of pent-up desire in the room was palpable. I could barely hear all the women as they all tried to speak over one another, throwing out name after name of some alluring adolescent boy or another. One woman described taking her daughter to see *Eclipse*, the second of the two films based on Stephenie Meyer's *Twilight* books. "I literally had to contain myself in my seat when [then eighteen-year-old] Taylor Lautner came on-screen," she said. "Oh my God, he's gorgeous! Though of course I couldn't say a word, since I know my daughter would *die* if she heard that."

And so it went for the next ten minutes. Finally, one woman at the end of the table raised her hand. As a teenager she'd been a huge fan of the singer formerly known as Prince (well, back then I guess he was just Prince), she told me. Just as I began to question her taste, she said something extraordinarily insightful: "I think that women are much more attuned to beauty, and to beautiful things, than men are. And that includes boys."

Once the focus group wrapped up, I realized that *both* my theories had been partially correct. These maternal "crushes" *were* sexual in that they served as a way to relive the women's own teenage sexuality, but at the same time they were more about the nostalgia than the sex, a way to recapture the heat and thrill of longing for the Paul McCartneys and

David Cassidys of the women's youth. I sensed that more than anything these women were trying to prove, perhaps to their daughters as well as to themselves, that beneath the armor of motherhood, they were still the girls they'd once been.

More important, I'm convinced that certain marketers are acutely aware of this Bieber phenomenon, and that when they sell the next teen sensation they are deliberately if stealthily targeting the *mothers* of the teens they more transparently court. In fact, I'm quite certain that when marketers use sex appeal to sell wallet-carrying adults on a teenage celebrity—or any other brand ostensibly meant for children or teens, for that matter—they know *exactly* what they are doing. Media firms are fully aware that a middle-aged mother is liable to be watching TV shows with her daughter or listening to the daughter's music in the car. "When you have a Millennial target" (referring to someone born between 1980 and 2000), says Jack MacKenzie, president of the Millennial Strategy Program at Frank N. Magid Associates, a consulting firm), "you necessarily have a secondary target of her mother. That's the way it is today. Exploiting that is smart business."[12]

So husbands: Beware. Your wife, who you may *think* is buying that new Justin Bieber CD for your daughter, just may be concealing a shocking yet common secret that companies and marketers have known for years: gay, straight, young, or old, sex appeal comes in all shapes and sizes; and it's a mighty powerful persuader, whether we can admit it to ourselves or not.

I Shop Like a Woman

What it means to be a male consumer in America today is changing.

Historically, in our culture, women have been freer to play around with the boundaries of their gender than men; for example, for many years it's been acceptable for women to wear jeans or slacks, spray on a musky scent, or sport a masculine-looking watch, whereas most men wouldn't have been caught dead in a pink, flowery shirt or wearing perfume or makeup. But this is changing fast. In the United States, at least, more and more boys (and men) are giving themselves permission to

wear and adapt totems from the "feminine" world—whether it's an ear-
ring, skinny jeans, cosmetics, or a fragrance (in Europe, more men wear
fragrance than American females do). In fact, men today are more concerned about looking good than they've ever been—and more willing
to shell out the dollars to do it. The global men's grooming industry is
already valued at roughly $27 billion worldwide, and fashion experts an-
ticipate it will grow to $31 billion by 2014. And in 2009 the number of
men who went so far as to undergo plastic surgery procedures increased
by nine hundred thousand in the United States alone.[13]

Companies and marketers are well aware of this shift, which
is why they are going to new lengths to target the appearance- and
beauty-conscious male. Take the recent rollout of "Dove Men + Care,"
the first male-only line from a brand that's always catered to and been
associated with females. "Now that you are comfortable with who you
are, isn't it time for comfortable skin?" one ad asks.[14]

This migration of the male consumer into a traditional female arena
is overturning the rules of marketing and advertising for all kinds of
unexpected products. Take body wash, for example. According to research data from Deutsche Bank and Information Resources, Inc., in
2009 body wash outsold bar soap ($756.3 million versus $754.2 million) for the first time in the United States. And believe it or not, this is
largely due to the fact that the marketers of this historically "feminine"
product are more actively going after the male customer. So why are so
many boys and men amenable to using body wash all of a sudden?

A few reasons. The first is that our worldwide preoccupation with
hygiene, which I talked about in an earlier chapter, is starting to take
hold among more and more men. Fearmongering marketers have managed to convince many male consumers (females generally need less
convincing) that bar soap is slimy, germy, even downright *dirty*. A second reason is that the makers of liquid hand soaps are beginning to
hook new generations of men at an early age by strategically placing
dispensers in elementary school boys' restrooms, high school and college gym shower stalls, and coed college dormitories. As a result, by the
time these men are out on their own and purchasing their own hygiene
products, applying a liquid soap to their hands and body feels normal,
even ordinary.

Some years ago, one maker of body wash noticed that men were resisting the product because they felt that the way it was applied—by touching one's own body—was too feminine. So what did the company do? It invented a new type of loofah, providing men with a physical barrier of sorts between their hands and their bodies. It then distributed hundreds of thousands across the United States, and lo and behold, use of bar soap went down and sales of body wash went up.

The third reason more men are using body wash is one even I can't attribute to marketers: the rise in single motherhood. Today, many sons raised by single mothers have grown used to using *Mom's* body wash—and as we learned in chapter 1, the products we grow accustomed to using as children tend to stick with us as adults. All of which, of course, is a boon for companies like Unilever and Procter & Gamble, since selling body wash is far more lucrative than selling bar soap.

Seeking perspective on all this, I spoke with Rose Cameron, the chief marketing officer of EuroRSCG Chicago and a widely acknowledged expert on the male consumer. Cameron points out that as the first "Axe generation," as she calls it (the guys who were tweens in the early noughties), is coming of age, there's no question that the wants and needs of the male consumer—and in turn, how he is being targeted by marketers—are changing. "They were the first male generation to have scented products that early," she explains.

"So what's next, Rose?" I asked. "Where are we going with all this?"

"The new trends I'm seeing are tattooing and the removal of body hair. Have you ever heard of 'smoothies'?"

"Just the drink, Rose."

"I'm talking about people. Men in particular." Apparently, getting rid of all (and I mean all) of one's body hair is a trend that started in the gay community and then caught on, albeit for a different reason, in the world of professional sports. "In some sports, body hair slows you down—at least that's the rational justification," Rose tells me. "It could also come from the pornography industry, since more and more men shave themselves down there, and pornography, as everyone knows, is a huge industry."

It's a rather extraordinary truth, I found out from a source who works for a large consumer product company: 15 percent of all U.S.

males shave their private parts (I kid you not), and it's a growing trend. One that Gillette was quick to capitalize on by posting a video on its Web site instructing men on how to shave their groin area. It was entitled "Trim-the-Bush-to-Make-the-Tree-Look-Taller."

In the marketing world, it's long been accepted that when a typical woman chooses a product, 80 percent of the reason is emotional and only 20 percent is rational. Women will generally respond to an entreaty for a conditioner, a new brand of makeup, or even a laundry detergent from an emotional perspective, as in *My mother always used this brand* or *The family down the street drives this car*, before buttressing her emotional decision with a rational argument. This is why most advertising aimed at women tends to play to emotions, like nostalgia or fear or envy. For men, the conventional wisdom in marketing circles has always been that this ratio is reversed, that 20 percent of a man's decision is emotional and 80 percent rational. But I don't believe that for a second! Men and women are both emotional beings, the difference being that men need to disguise their emotional drivers under features and specs. Men's decision making is 80/20, too—I simply call their internal process "emorational," meaning that the practical features of a product permit men to disguise their own emotional natures. And manufacturers are well aware of this, too. Ever notice that marketers of products aimed at men tend to stress specs and numbers, like a 20-gigabyte hard drive or a 14.1-megapixel camera (yes, that *does* make a difference) or an Optimax 225 Sport XS engine, and so on? That's because these numbers provide a rational, quantifiable justification for choosing that product over another (usually cheaper) model. According to *Time* magazine, "Product specifications disproportionately sway our decisions as shoppers, even when our own experiences tell us they don't matter,"[15] and this is generally true more for men than for women.

Yet, the male consumer is changing and so are all the time-tested strategies for marketing to them. These days, if you look in the cosmetics aisle at the products aimed at males, you'll notice their macho names like "Ripped Fuel," "Edge," "Facial Fuel," and "Axe," which evoke associations of sporty, "manly" things like extreme sports, motorcycles, even war. This is because marketers know full well that these tough-guy names allow them to still feel tough and athletic even when buying a product that's in fact all about "beauty," a traditional no-no for most straight males. Advertisers tread carefully around this issue. Even Mënaji, a spectacularly successful online male cosmetics company that offers a full line of natural products including a face mask, a concealer, and an under-eye treatment, gives its products aggressive names like "Camo" and "Eraser." Axe has even rolled out an all-black bottle constructed to look like a grenade, complete with indentations for a young man's fingertips. The underlying emotional promise these brands are making is to smooth out the rough edges and make him look good while still being rugged and masculine at the same time.

This upsurge in male vanity is why men are increasingly falling prey to a cunning trick that retailers used to reserve for women. Ever been shopping for a pair of khakis or jeans, and when you finally find a pair that fits, you are delighted to discover that your size hasn't changed since you were back in graduate school? I have some bad news for you. You've likely fallen victim to "vanity sizing," a devious ploy by which stores make clothes bigger so we *think* we can fit into a smaller size.[16] Many retailers have been doing this with women's clothes for years, but the tactic is now starting to creep into the men's sections of stores as well. When *Esquire* magazine sent reporter Abram Sauer into various stores with a tape measure, he found that pairs of men's pants with so-called 36-inch waists actually ranged in size from 37 inches (at H&M) to 38.5 inches (at Calvin Klein) to 39 inches (at the Gap, Haggar, and Dockers) to a generous 41 inches at Old Navy.[17] It used to be that the typical man couldn't care less what the size of his waistband was, but today experts know full well that *both* genders will be more likely to buy a product that makes them feel trim and svelte.

There's no question that marketers are making a pretty penny by exploiting the fact that it's becoming more and more socially acceptable for men to take an active role in maintaining their appearance. In 1995, 53 percent of men shopped for themselves. By 2009 that figure had risen to 75 percent. As Wendy Liebmann, the founder and CEO of WSL Strategic Retail, a marketing consulting firm, observes, the era of a man needing a woman's opinion before he buys something may be on the way out. "Part of what we're witnessing is a cultural shift," Liebmann says. "Men are marrying later in life and they're living on their own longer." [18] Which means that when men finally decide to walk down the aisle, they already know which brands they like, sometimes even bringing the brands they love into the marriage and influencing what their wives buy. Unlike the males of yesteryear, who went straight from under their mothers' wings to under their wives', today's bachelors *have to* know how to do more when it comes to shopping, like how to get fitted for a suit, how to pick out sheets with the best thread count, and so on.

This goes a long way toward explaining why one smart store, the San Antonio–based supermarket H-E-B, has created a "Men's Zone," a safe haven set apart from the rest of the store, where beauty-conscious men can shop for personal-care items to their hearts' content while still feeling macho and masculine. Adorned with sci-fi blue floor lighting and flat-screen TVs, this stand-alone man cave offers 534 items that promise to do everything from soothe tired skin to tighten baggy eyelids to keep a guy smelling like fresh lemons all day, while five touch screens provide "grooming tips and product advice." [19] And just in case it all starts to feel a little too girly, soccer, car racing, basketball, and other sports play continuously on the flat screens.[20]

Similarly, Procter & Gamble is now ensuring that men's and women's cosmetics will be shelved in different aisles in stores, so that the independent male shopper won't feel uncomfortable or emasculated picking out a facial cream or under-eye smoother as the woman beside him chooses a shade of lipstick. How do these companies know that shelving the men's products separately will increase sales? Thanks to the shadowy investigations they conduct in the dead of the night.

Very few people know this, but most major consumer-goods companies, including Unilever, Kraft, PepsiCo, and Coca-Cola, among others, have set up "fake supermarkets," typically in abandoned warehouses in industrial parts of town. They stock the shelves with their own products as well as their competitors', then late at night, under the cover of darkness, they invite people to come and, well, *shop*. While they're browsing the aisles, cameras and in some extreme cases brain-scanning equipment are measuring what happens in real time as they select and reject various brands and items. Not unlike in the film *Minority Report*, these "supermarkets" generally have a control room lined with TV screens on which reps can actually measure the changes in consumers' brain waves as they encounter different positioning of products. Based on this data, the company develops what in the business is called a "planogram," a model showing where each product should be placed on the shelves to generate the highest sales, then buys shelf space in supermarkets and drugstores accordingly.

As it turns out, the reason that shelving men's "beauty" products separately is such a booster of sales is that even though gender roles may be changing, many men still don't want fellow customers watching them lingering over the grooming shelves. But if they feel like they can browse freely without the scrutiny of other people's stares, they're more likely to go for the higher-end items or pick up an extra item.

So *can* brands traditionally aimed at women (with extremely feminine, ladylike names like "Dove") make a successful crossover to guys? Well, when you consider that Marlboro began as a filtered cigarette marketed to women back in the 1920s, that Nair rolled out a chest and back hair exfoliant for men in 2002, and that Ugg was advertised as a men's brand long before it became known as a must-have female boot, the odds are looking pretty good. And for an example of how even traditionally male brands are catering to men's "feminine sides," recently Dutch electronics giant Philips decided that men wanted "a more robust, heavy-duty tool to tackle hampers of laundry. Something with a larger grip and a more masculine look." So it created the GC4490, which offers "more power, more steam, more performance."

What exactly is this manly item? It's an iron.

Sure, sex in advertising may be one of the oldest tricks in the book, but from what I've seen in my work, one thing couldn't be more clear: whether it's by probing our deepest and darkest sexual fantasies, by engineering nostalgia for the sexual heyday of our youth, or by covertly selling the promise to make us more sexually attractive, today's marketers and advertisers have all kinds of new ways of tapping into our most basic and primal human desire—and making a whole lot of money in the process.

CHAPTER 5

Under Pressure

THE POWER OF PEERS

In 1931, a dedicated bird-watcher named Edward Selous started pondering a curious phenomenon he'd been observing for years. How, Selous wondered, could so many species of birds—rooks, gulls, lapwings, geese, starlings, you name it—rise from a field in complete synchrony, as though doing a choreographed dance? Everyone knew birds aren't that bright and have no way of communicating with one another, so how could they possibly coordinate their actions in such a seamless manner? It must be mind reading, he concluded. At the time, no one gave Selous's ESP theory credence. After all, he had no proof, and the scientific community then, just as now, preferred facts over speculation. Still, back in the 1930s no one could come up with a better explanation.

As it later turned out, Selous wasn't completely crazy. The birds' behavior *was* the result of a mind meld of sorts. The birds weren't reading one another's minds, of course, but they were, in a sense, acting as if they shared one collective brain. This phenomenon isn't unique to birds. The animal kingdom is rife with examples of it. Even termites—yes, those nasty little creatures that were put on earth to gnaw down structures and cause the foundations of houses to buckle—are capable of a collective consciousness. To put it not so kindly, a single termite is spectacularly dumb; its brain doesn't contain enough neurons even to conceive of what it's doing. Yet a *million* termites have enough collective brainpower to build giant, complex structures, some as high as thirty feet tall: the termite mound. The question is how.

It wasn't until the late 1950s that science came up with an explanation. When biologist Pierre-Paul Grasse observed many groups of termites during the early phase of building, he found that each little fellow appeared to be carrying out three simple steps.

First, the termite would chew a mouthful of earth and mold it into a pellet with its saliva.

Second, the termite would wander around directionlessly, and as soon as it stumbled upon an elevated area, it would dump the pellet, just as a golden retriever might drop a spit-covered tennis ball.

Third, the termite would repeat steps one and two over and over.

It's hard to comprehend how these dim-witted insects can eventually construct a giant, well-designed structure through this achingly slow, seemingly random and uncoordinated process. But they can. The more earth pellets the termites drop into place, the higher the ground becomes. And the higher the ground becomes, the greater the chance that all the other aimlessly meandering termites will bash into it, allowing it to grow even more. When these few mounds, or pillars, reach a certain height, Grasse explains, "a new behavior kicks in and the termites start to build arches between them. The whole elaborate termite mound with its chambers and tunnels and sophisticated air circulation channels arises from the work of thousands of termites with no central coordination at all, just a few simple rules."[1] The name Grasse gave to this bizarre phenomenon was "cooperation without communication."

In short, no big-cheese termite queen issued any orders. There was no strategic planning, no formal organizing intelligence telling the termites what to do. They simply created a world by operating as if they were tiny, singular cells in one enormous termite brain.[2]

The process can be explained by a theory known as "complex adaptive systems," which says that many systems in nature (like birds taking simultaneous flight or termites painstakingly constructing a colossal mound) are inherently "emergent" and "nondeterministic," which means, in plain English, that the whole is mightier than the sum of its parts and that you can't predict the collective results simply by looking at the individual actions (like a single termite holding a saliva-drenched bit of sand or one bird about to take flight). According to this theory, although the process might be invisible to the human eye, termites are actually able to intuit "when and where to add to the structure by maintaining a high degree of connectivity to others in the colony." [3] In other words, only by observing and mimicking the behavior of its neighbors can a termite figure out what it should be doing.

We as consumers, I've observed time and again, act in much the same way. Just like those birds and those termites, we, too, are wired with a collective consciousness in that we size up what those around us are doing and modify our own actions and behaviors accordingly. In a 2008 experiment conducted by researchers at Leeds University, groups of people were instructed to walk aimlessly around a large hall, without conversing with one another. But first the researchers gave just a few of the people detailed instructions on where, precisely, they should walk. When they observed the resulting behavior, they found that no matter how large or small the group, everyone in it blindly followed that handful of people who appeared to have some idea where they were going. As the scientists put it, "(The) research suggests that humans flock like sheep and birds, subconsciously following a minority of individuals," [4] and that it takes a mere 5 percent of "informed individuals" to influence the direction of a crowd of up to two hundred people. The other 95 percent of us trail along without even being aware of it. [5]

According to Professor Jens Krause, who engineered the study, "What's interesting about this research is that our participants ended up making a consensus decision, despite the fact that they weren't allowed to talk or gesture to one another." Just like those termites, "in most cases the participants didn't realize they were being led by others." [6]

Want more evidence that it takes only a few people in a group to steer the direction of others around them? In a study conducted in Cologne, Germany, a crowd of two hundred people clustered in the center of a large circle that was numbered like a clock. Researchers then handed out slips of paper to ten "informed individuals" that read, "Go to nine o'clock, but do not leave the group." The others were given no specific instructions, just notes that read, "Stay with the group." For a while, the group seemed to mix and mingle fairly randomly. But soon enough, the "informed individuals" had led all the others to the designated nine o'clock target.[7]

In 2007, the *Washington Post* rolled out an intriguing and now-famous experiment. The newspaper hired one of the best musicians in the world to play a $3.5 million Stradivarius violin on a subway platform during morning rush hour in America's capital city. Most if not all commuters walked right by and ignored him. *Just another downtrodden street musician after my loose change*, they undoubtedly thought. The violinist's final take for the entire morning: $32.17—just a fraction of what a single ticket to one of his performances would cost. On the face of it, it might seem these commuters were just philistines who wouldn't know musical talent if it hit them over the head. But I believe this was an example of our collective consciousness, our herd mentality, at work. Think about it. One harried commuter ignores the performer (maybe she was in a particular hurry that morning or is tone-deaf), and so the commuter behind her, assuming there must not be anything to see here, rushes past him as well. So does the person behind her, and the ten people behind him, and so on and so forth until the entire mass of morning commuters is brushing past a world-class performer whom, under other circumstances, they might have happily paid hundreds of dollars to see perform at the Kennedy Center or Carnegie Hall.[8]

Standing out, or being different from everyone else, causes most of us great discomfort. Sometimes even literally. I'll never forget a Unilever focus group I once observed, where consumers were discussing shampoos. As soon as the moderator brought up the topic of itching, everyone in the room began scratching their scalps. Did they all suddenly develop a head of lice? Of course not. They were simply, and utterly unconsciously, mimicking the behaviors of others in the room.

Over the years, I've noticed another interesting phenomenon. When you show people a stack of photos from a party or an album of pictures just uploaded onto Facebook, the first thing they do is pause and look at the picture of themselves. Not so surprising—we're a vain species. But what's the second thing they do? Pause and look at the pictures of *people surrounding them*. Why? Because once they've taken note of how they appear, they need to analyze how they appear compared to others: Do they look as though they belong? Are they making the right impression? Are others looking on at them approvingly? This is telling. It shows that we as human beings never assess ourselves, our behaviors, or our decisions in a vacuum; we assess them *in relation to everyone else.*

The point is, we're a social species, wired to display this kind of herd behavior. Even fourteen-month-old babies show evidence of it. In a series of studies, researchers trained fourteen-month-olds to play with five distinctive toys. These same children later demonstrated their newly won toy-playing skills to other fourteen-month-old children at a day care, children who'd never seen these particular toys before. Two days later, one of the researchers brought the same toys to each of these second children's homes. Without hesitation, the children began play-ing with the toys *in the exact same way* they'd witnessed at the day-care center. The conclusion? Fourteen-month-old babies automatically imi-tate behaviors carried out by peers and bring what they've learned home with them, even forty-eight hours later.[9]

There is ample research to show that we instinctively look to the behavior of others to inform the decisions we make—everything from which way we should walk, to what music we should listen to, to which kind of car we should drive. It seems, in short, that we instinctively be-lieve that others know more about what we want than we ourselves do.

Psychologists have a name for this phenomenon. It's called peer pressure.

When we hear those two words, we tend to sigh inwardly, as deeply and darkly as we did when we were adolescents. What a loaded and even faintly patronizing expression, conjuring up memories of teenage insecurity, acne, and trying to fit into a small universe where a phan-tom classmate hisses "C'mon, just one of these won't hurt you" into your ear. While that kind of old-fashioned peer pressure certainly ex-ists, that's not exactly the kind I'm talking about here. I'm talking about a more implicit kind that taps into our primitive human desire to be accepted—those evolutionary instincts not to be left out or exiled from the human tribe. As you're about to read, this implicit peer pressure is a far more insidious kind, and companies and marketers are taking advantage of its persuasive powers in ways you couldn't even imagine.

Monkey See, Monkey Spend

Author and social psychologist Robert Cialdini once demonstrated the persuasive power of our peers in a fascinating experiment. Several hundred volunteers took their seats in a room, purportedly to fill out a survey. But that was only a distraction from the real purpose of Cialdini's experiment, which had to do with how our behavior is swayed by those around us. A large glass jar of cookies stood prominently on a nearby desk, filled to the brim with deliciousness.

"Would you like a cookie?" one of the researchers asked the survey takers. Approximately one fifth of the volunteers took him up on his offer. (How very self-disciplined of them.) In the second stage of the experiment, the research team surreptitiously removed most of the cookies from the jar, so that it looked as though others had already taken one. Still, only about one fifth of respondents reached for a cookie.

In the final stage of the experiment, however, a researcher sat behind a desk beside a large glass cookie jar. But this time, before the researcher could ask volunteers if they wanted a cookie or not, a stranger ambled into the room, removed the glass lid, took a cookie in front of everyone in the room, and walked out again. This time, when the survey takers were asked if anyone wanted a cookie, nearly every single person took one.

This experiment revealed something that advertisers and marketers have long been instinctively aware of: humans want what other humans want. And the more visible other people's demand is, the more we want what they are having. In the cookie jar experiment, people didn't want more cookies when they thought that others *might* have taken a cookie. But when they actually *saw* another person take a cookie, their brains said, *Gimme!*

Now imagine it's two weeks before Christmas and you have yet to buy a gift for your young child. Not surprisingly, as was the case with previous Christmases, there appears to be one "it" present that you've read and heard about and that every parent on the playground has already bought (or plans to buy) for their little darling. Those of us with durable memories can cast our minds back to recent Christmas toy fads ranging from Furbys to Beanie Babies to Razor scooters to

Tamagotchis to Tickle Me Elmo, the "it gift" of 1996, which inspired such mania that desperate mothers around America were "duking it out in store aisles."[10] In each case, the furor and pursuit of these must have toys reached the scale of a full-fledged social epidemic, meaning a social trend that spreads quickly and widely, like some kind of consumer virus.

In 2009 the hottest must-have Christmas toy on every child's wish list was the Zhu Zhu pet hamster. Though the actual price was $10, so extraordinary (and, frankly, bizarre) was the national demand that the toy was being sold on Amazon for three times that, and before long people were bidding up to five times its value on eBay. Clearly, fads like this are extremely contagious, and as we've read, when it comes to what we buy for our children, guilt can also play a part. Still, the question remains: what determines which fads catch on and which die, or which brands and products become social epidemics and which don't? Why the Zhu Zhu pet hamster and not some other toy or gizmo? After all, the toy doesn't do anything special. It doesn't sing or dance or grant wishes. It makes a variety of odd sounds, like chirping, beeping, and mooing, but that's about it. Yet by the end of 2009, Cepia LLC, the St. Louis company that created and distributed the hamsters, had sold tens of millions of dollars' worth of the furry things. Turns out this wasn't just a happy accident.

How Cepia made its bizarre product the "it" Christmas toy is a fascinating example of the art and craft of viral marketing—in other words, peer pressure. First, the company staged "hamster giveaways" at hospitals, zoos, and Major League Baseball games. Next, it sponsored roughly three hundred invitation-only "hamster parties" where "influential mommy bloggers" were the fortunate recipients of the toys (as well as Habitrails and a recipe for "hamster crunch," whatever that is). It also hosted a live, nine-thousand-tweet "interconnected Twitter" party (complete with party prizes) on the popular Mom Talk Radio channel, where host Maria Bailey oversaw an interactive discussion in which "fans across the Zhu-niverse share[d] what [made] Zhu Zhu pets so special to them."[11] The result was that soon mothers around the country were hearing and reading about the toy everywhere they went, creating a phenomenon so contagious and a heat so intense that Zhu Zhu hamsters sold out all across the United States.

Then Cepia did something ingenious—and extremely common-place. It started manufacturing fewer Zhu Zhu pets. That's right, *fewer.* Why? Because deliberately limiting inventory makes us think that a product is even more in demand; if "everyone" wants one, in our minds, it becomes more valuable.[12] Creating a sense of scarcity stimulates our pack mentality, our fear of missing out.[13] It's human nature to covet what others have.

This fear of missing out on something being gobbled up by our peers is what drives rabid crowds of shoppers to line up at 4:00 a.m. to get their hands on the newly launched iPad 2 or a pair of Uggs in a hard-to-come-by color,[14] and it's why a few years back a bargain hunter was trampled to death outside a Long Island Walmart on Black Friday. If you've ever bid for an item on eBay, you've probably unwittingly fallen prey to this same trap. With a supply of only one (there can be only one penguin tea set in the world), the panic that some other person might walk away with the matching set of orange-beaked mugs is what can drive people to raise their bid exponentially—and pay far more than what the product is worth.[15]

Once social contagion sets in, it can take on a life of its own. Take another rather bizarre example, a fad called "icing" that caught on a few years ago among college students and males in their midtwenties. No, I'm not talking about the sugary stuff on top of birthday cakes. I'm talking about a phenomenon that the *New York Times* dubbed "the world's biggest viral drinking game." Never played? Lucky you. Here's how it works. First, you give a friend a can of Smirnoff Ice malt beverage. Said friend then has to balance the can on his knee and drink the whole thing at once. The only way to avoid becoming a victim of this uncertain fate is to carry a bottle yourself, in which case you have to drink both bottles—before, of course, going out and "icing" someone else. Sounds absolutely awful, yet somehow this game quickly infected college campuses around the country, spawned several Web sites, and, according to the *New York Times*, "explode[d] from obscurity . . . into a bizarre pastime for college kids, Wall Streeters and minor celebrities."[16]

Smirnoff has emphatically denied that it bears any responsibility for "icing" (and I believe it's telling the truth), but regardless, it's been quite lucrative for the company. As the *Times* reports, the phenomenon has not only raised awareness of the brand but also extended it to young men who formerly saw Ice as "girly" and feminine. And sales of Ice products almost immediately took off in some Southern college towns, where the game took early root. The point is, whether it emerges organically or is deliberately orchestrated by marketers, peer pressure delivers a windfall for brands and companies.

This is exactly why companies of all stripes have become so skilled at planting the seeds of social epidemics and then sitting back to watch them grow (as Smirnoff was accused of doing in this case). As we'll read more about in the last chapter, the most persuasive marketing messages aren't magazine ads or TV commercials or billboards; they're the ones that come from—or at least seem to come from—our peers. In fact, one of the most effective—and sneakiest—viral marketing strategies is for a company to create a blog or YouTube video that is so extreme, funny, outrageous, provocative, or frightening (or a combination of the above) that it raises the question, Is this a joke, or is it real? Among the most successful and talked-about viral marketing campaigns of all time were ones created by John West Salmon (in which a man and a bear grapple over a fish), Trojan condoms (which in 2003 launched the Trojan Games, a sequence of Olympics-like championships based on sexual performance), Levi's (in which men athletically sprang and backflipped themselves into their blue jeans), and surfing apparel manufacturer Quiksilver (which released a memorably phony Internet video showing a group of kids hurling dynamite into a river, then surfing the giant wave it created).

Still, few companies were as downright crafty—or as downright double-talking—in their use of viral videos as Viacom, the media conglomerate. In a 2010 suit against Google (which owns YouTube), Viacom, which has long railed against TV and movie piracy, claimed that YouTube had knowingly allowed its users to post clips they'd illegally downloaded (i.e., stolen) from Viacom's copyrighted movies and TV shows in order to boost traffic and sales. Google countersued, alleging that Viacom had surreptitiously uploaded many of the clips itself—and also manufactured phony YouTube comments—in an attempt to create phony "grassroots" viral marketing campaigns for its TV shows and movies. In fact, Google had evidence that Viacom mandated that its clips "should definitely not be associated with the studio—should appear as if a fan created and posted it."[17] How did the studio manage this? According to unsealed courtroom documents, by hiring at least eighteen third-party marketing agents, who used untraceable YouTube accounts with no connection to Viacom, and by deliberately altering the clips to make them look pirated or stolen. Then marketing agents uploaded the videos from untraceable computers and locations, such as the local Kinko's.[18]

Though YouTube (and Google) won the case when a federal judge ruled the site was protected under U.S. copyright law,[19] one thing is certain: these video clips wouldn't have become the viral sensation they did if YouTube viewers had known they were uploaded by marketers rather than by their own peers.

We've Gotta Have It

Many of us spend our days—at least parts of them—quietly cursing our fellow human beings. The guy in the Hummer who cuts us off at the intersection. The old woman in the supermarket line counting out pennies one by one. The teenagers in blue hoodies perched in front of the convenience store, blocking our path to our cars. They may be annoying, but when all is said and done, we actually rely on these people, and others like them, to help dictate our purchasing choices—with more than a little help from companies and marketers, of course.

When it comes to the things we buy, what other people think matters. A lot. Even when these people are complete strangers. A recent survey by Opinion Research shows that "61 percent of respondents said they had checked online reviews, blogs and other online customer feedback before buying a new product or service,"[20] and a similar February 2008 study commissioned by PowerReviews showed that "nearly half of U.S. consumers who shopped online four or more times per year and spent at least $500 said they needed four to seven customer reviews before making a purchase decision."[21] So persuasive are the opinions of others that though most of us are well aware that *at least* 25 percent of these reviews are fakes written by friends, company staffers, marketers, and so forth, we *purposely* overlook this. As the *Times* of London points out, we are born to believe, in part because a collective belief helps us to bond with others. In short, we *want* to trust in these messages, even when we may also be deeply skeptical.

To see just how powerfully complete strangers' preferences and purchases can sway our decisions, consider the phenomenon of best-seller lists. Imagine that you're entering a big chain bookstore, where you're confronted by square footage that rivals a football field. Given the sheer number of choices, the risk of shelling out $27.99 for a novel or a memoir that you will later deem unreadable is considerable. But wait, what's on that stand-alone shelf directly to your right? This week's *"New York Times* Bestsellers,"* both fiction and nonfiction, perhaps two dozen books in all. Subconsciously you think, *If so many people are buying this book, then it must be good.* Followed shortly by *If so many people are reading this book, won't I be left out if I don't read it, too?* Now not only are you spared the ordeal of wading through the four floors of books and the anxiety of confronting all that choice, but you have a solid endorsement from your book-buying peers.

This is no happy accident for the publishing industry. In fact, despite what publishers might like you to believe, the main reason best-seller lists exist in the first place isn't just to track sales but also to make us think these titles have been "preapproved"—in other words, to imply that if we don't read what everyone else is reading, we'll be uncultured, irrelevant, and excluded from the national conversation.

Best-seller lists work so well in persuading us that they've migrated well beyond book publishing to other products and industries—from Sephora's list of best-selling cosmetics to *Entertainment Weekly*'s Ten Most Popular TV shows to *Variety*'s list of the ten highest-grossing movies of the week to the Apple iTunes music store's list of best-selling or recommended (which, as we'll see in a minute, eventually become one and the same) singles, albums, movies, and music videos. Let's talk for a moment about the latter. Not unlike a Barnes & Noble superstore, the iTunes start page is a cluttered, chaotic place teeming with choices. Luckily for the overwhelmed shopper, however, these endless offerings are organized into tidy recommended categories like "What

We're Watching," "What's Hot," "What We're Listening To," "New and Noteworthy," and, of course, "Top Songs" and "Top Albums."

Two things of interest are going on here. First, I am convinced Apple did this not to make life easier for the casual browser but rather to imply that its team of music experts have spent the past month parsing through thousands of albums and that the dozen or so highlighted on the start page represent their carefully considered picks—the cream of this month's crop. Nothing could be further from the truth. Chances are good that in fact a good deal of money changed hands; in a twenty-first-century version of the old, reviled practice of "payola," record companies pay Apple hefty sums to get these songs and albums featured on the home page (just as publishers, incidentally, pay bookstores to feature their new books on those tables you see when you enter the bookstore). Regardless, the lists on these start pages lead us to believe that an expert, or a team of experts, has waded through the seemingly infinite number of choices and made a discriminating decision on our behalf.

The second thing that's going on here is the classic blockbuster effect. Essentially, a two-tier system is being created, one that puts a small number of brands (in this case, brands being musical artists) on the path to success, while setting up the majority of others for failure. Think about it. Due to the sheer exposure, and the fact the customers believe these are the songs that have been preapproved as the "best," don't many (if not all) of the albums and artists featured on the start page *end up making* the top-songs list? They do—I've seen it happen time and again. And once a song or album makes the best-selling list, that's yet another stamp of approval, and our impressionable minds kick into high gear again: *What do other people know that I don't know? I'm missing out!*

These kinds of stamps of approval can even influence our choice of alcoholic beverage. When the Beverage Testing Institute dubbed Grey Goose the "best-tasting vodka in the world," Sidney Frank, the marketing genius behind the brand, not only promptly created giant ads boasting this new best-tasting-in-the-world status, he "indoctrinated" both hundreds of distributors and somewhere in the neighborhood of twenty thousand bartenders with that very information so that anytime a customer came into a bar or liquor store and asked what the best-tasting vodka was, they would be told it was Grey Goose.[22] The result? By 2004 the company had sold 1.5 million cases and Sidney Frank had sold the company to Bacardi for a cool $2 billion.

Whether it's the world's best-tasting vodka, the best-selling novel of the week, or the highest-grossing movie of the year, you better believe that companies are very deliberately using best-seller lists to persuade us to buy what "everyone else likes." Amazon, the online bookseller (and increasingly, the online seller of just about *everything*), takes this an ingenious step further by actually e-mailing customers to let them know that their fellow purchasers of a certain item have also purchased some new item—and thus that they might like that item, too. This is a case not only of baldly manufacturing peer pressure but also of data mining, a topic we'll be looking at in a later chapter.

An intriguing study published in the journal *Science* shows just how well this can work. The researchers invited twenty-seven teenagers to visit a Web site where they could sample and download songs for free. Some of the teens were told what songs previous visitors had downloaded, whereas others weren't. Indeed, those told what songs their peers had chosen tended to download those very songs. But part two of the study was even more telling. This time, the teens were divided into eight groups and told only what had been downloaded by people from their own group. The researchers found that not only did the teens tend to choose the songs that had been previously downloaded by members of their groups, but the songs that became "hits" varied across all the groups. The implications were clear: whether or not a song became a "hit" was determined *solely by whether it was perceived as already being popular.*[23] This is what I mean about the two-tier system: whatever gains an early advantage in popularity will win. This may not seem so bad at first, but look at it this way: if we're duped into buying something just because it's popular (even if it isn't), think about all the great books or songs or CDs we might be missing simply because they weren't on that "top ten" list.

But this still doesn't explain precisely *why* our buying decisions are so unduly influenced by a brand's supposed popularity. So the authors of the study decided to use an fMRI to see what was *really* going on in these impressionable teenagers' brains when they succumbed to peer pressure. They had twelve- to seventeen-year-olds rate fifteen-second clips of songs downloaded from MySpace. Then they revealed to some the songs' overall popularity. The results showed that when the participants' own ratings of the music matched up with what they had been told about the song (e.g., if they liked a popular song), there tended to be activity in the caudate nucleus, an area of the brain connected to rewards. When there was a mismatch, however (e.g., the teen liked the song but discovered it was unpopular), areas associated with anxiety lit up. The researchers concluded that "this mismatch anxiety motivates people to switch their choices in the direction of the consensus, suggesting that this is a major force behind conformity observed in music tastes in teenagers."[24]

Early popularity is so closely tied to a brand or product's ultimate success that even Hollywood is leveraging the predictive power of the teeming hordes. According to *New Scientist*, one of the most widespread new techniques for predicting the box-office performance of a film is by using something called "artificial markets." On one, dubbed "the Hollywood Stock Exchange," movie fans can buy and sell virtual shares in celebrities and in forthcoming or recently released films. This virtual market, which operates with a virtual currency called Hollywood Dollars, uses these predictions to create a stock rating reflecting the aggregate view of each film's popularity or likely popularity (obviously, people only buy virtual shares in things they expect to be hits). "This is currently the gold standard in the industry for predicting likely box office receipts," says Bernardo Huberman at HP Laboratories in Palo Alto,"[25] and amazingly, the method has been so accurate that it's now even being used to predict the outcomes of political campaigns.

Of course, we aren't always consciously aware that it's perceived popularity that's driving our preferences. Recently, I asked a focus group of ten female Louis Vuitton fans, "Why do you love the brand so much?" Each one spoke of the quality of the zipper, the leather, and finally, the brand's timelessness. I was skeptical. So we took these same ten women and scanned their brains using fMRI. In each case, when the women were shown pictures of Louis Vuitton products, the Brodmann area 10, the region of the brain that's activated when respondents are observing something they perceive as "cool," lit up. The women had rationalized their purchases by telling themselves that they liked the brand for its good quality, but their brains knew that they really chose it for its "coolness."

The fact that even our brains can't seem to bear for us to be left out seems to suggest that whether it's the "hit" song, the "it" gift, or the "in" designer handbag, in the end what we buy really has little to do with what we want and more to do with what we think we *should* want.[26] Even marketers themselves fall for this. For instance, every advertising agency "planner" (a term used in most European ad agencies for the person who conducts consumer research) of my acquaintance owns a fancy Moleskine leather notebook. They don't give these out in orientation; it's simply become an unspoken rule that every ad agency planner has to own and use one. If you don't, it implies you're on the outside, not a member of the "in crowd."

These marketers make their living dreaming up ways to prey on consumers' fear of being left out, but subconsciously they (or may I say *we*) are just as vulnerable to peer pressure as the rest of us.

I've Just Seen a Face

In an earlier chapter, I wrote about how, in our society, cell phones and smart phones have fed a fear of being alone or of being perceived as alone; how, paradoxically, our ability to be constantly connected with others has ignited the fear we have of being unpopular and even unloved.

The Internet, and in particular social-networking sites, have also revealed the extent to which many of us fear that our opinion, and very existence, might not matter. Just as the ability to be connected all the time gives rise to the fear that we are actually alone, the ability to comment, pontificate, and broadcast ourselves all the time gives rise to the fear that no one actually cares what we have to say. I believe it's this insecurity, this feeling of being left out, that's contributed to one of the most contagious social phenomena of our times: Facebook.

First, a few facts and figures about Facebook. As of 2011, Facebook has close to seven hundred million active users, which translates into 22 percent of everyone on the Internet, and it's still growing by 5 percent a month.[27] According to *Time*, "If the website were granted terra firma, it would be the world's third largest country by population, two-thirds bigger than the U.S."[28] Fifty percent of those users log on to Facebook at least once a day, while more than thirty-five million users update their statuses daily, creating a total of over sixty million daily status updates.[29]

But the question is, how did Facebook become the global phenomenon it is today? How did it rise above all other social-networking sites out there (and believe me, there are plenty) to become the one online universe we simply "had" to be a part of? Quite simply because it's where everyone is. It's where invitations are sent, party pictures posted, messages exchanged. Increasingly, it's also where we conduct our social lives. Who wouldn't feel left out of a world where more than twenty-five billion pieces of information are shared a month and where photos are added at a speed of nearly one billion unique images a week?[30] To *not* be on Facebook would guarantee complete social isolation; it would be like moving to a hut in the Shetland Islands.

Most people are more or less aware of this. But what is less known is the extent to which companies are leveraging the persuasive power of connections on Facebook to cleverly advertise and market their products. Take, for example, the feature on Facebook known as the "like" button, formerly known as the "become a fan" button. Originally, people used this to "like" their friends' status updates; it was a way to indicate our approval of the fact that, say, Jenny had just eaten a ham-and-cheese sandwich or Billy had had a great time in Aruba. But increasingly, the site has been encouraging users to "like" their favorite bands, books, movies, brands, and products—so successfully that the site processes a staggering one hundred million clicks of the "like" button daily.[31] Do you happen to enjoy the TV show *Friday Night Lights*? If you go to that show's Facebook page, it will tell you how many friends of yours also "like" the show. Wait, Erica likes *Friday Night Lights*, too? You think Erica is pretty cool and have now received what marketers call "social proof" that it's okay to like the show, giving you a mandate to recommend the show to *your* best friends, so before you know it, you click the "like" button—which has conveniently popped right up on the bottom of the page—too. This will then show up in the newsfeed for all your friends to see, and they in turn may well reach for the "like" button, and so on and so forth until any Facebook user who comes across a mention of the show will spy a little message popping up saying, "Bob and Fred and Martin and 712,563 Facebook users like *Friday Night Lights*." This is peer-pressure advertising at its best, and it works. According to Sheryl Sandberg, Facebook's chief operating officer, marketers have known this for a really long time. "I'm much more likely to do [or buy] something that's recommended by a friend," she's been quoted as saying.[32]

Facebook isn't the only social-media site out there that's making guerrilla marketers and advertisers out of us, either. Take Foursquare, the popular location-based social-networking game we talked about earlier. Thanks to portable GPS apps, it knows where you are at any given time, so all you have to do is tap the Foursquare app on your iPhone or BlackBerry and it will automatically show you a list of nearby restaurants, bars, stores, and shops. But this is more than just a real-time, location-tracking version of Zagat. The point of the game is to "check in" to as many of these establishments as you can, whereupon Foursquare will automatically broadcast your whereabouts to other Foursquare users, and you can also elect to have your Twitter or Facebook feeds immediately updated when you check in to a restaurant, bar, café, or store (which most users do). You earn points for each place you check in, and the user who visits an establishment most is dubbed its "mayor." Not only is this game surprisingly addictive (as we discussed in chapter 3), and not only does it get you to regularly spend money at establishments you might not have otherwise frequented, but because it broadcasts your location to all your fellow Foursquare players, Facebook friends, and Twitter followers, it provides a boatload of free advertising for every establishment you set foot in. As Twitter founder Evan Williams has said, "Many of the great businesses of the next decade will be about making information about our [consumer] behaviors more visible."[33]

Marketers and Mean Girls

It's well known that our culture glorifies the teenage years—just look at how many contemporary movies and TV shows revolve around high school. But rosy retrospection aside, who over the age of thirty would want to relive that torment of uncertainty, self-consciousness . . . and peer pressure? While it's clear by now that peer pressure exists well beyond the high school cafeteria, it's also true that there is no demographic more susceptible to peer pressure than teens and tweens (and it's worth noting here that adolescents today spend five times more money than their parents did at the same age). Why? Largely because teenagers don't know who they truly are yet, so they sport the brands they do as a backup form of ID. In 2010 a longitudinal study by the National Institute of Mental Health found that our brains don't become fully mature until age twenty-five (and sometimes not until later), indicating that in our teen years, our cognitive abilities, and thus our sense of self, are still miles from their final development.

Studies have shown that when tweens ask for a pair of Hollister jeans or the latest hot Wii game for Christmas, they're asking for more than the latest, hippest product; what they're really asking for is a dose of self-esteem. Deborah Roedder John at the University of Minnesota recruited 250 kids ages eight through eighteen and asked them to select among one hundred words and images and create a collage answering the question "What makes me happy?" When she looked at the results, she found that the children with higher self-esteem chose words that represented nonmaterial activities and achievements, like getting good grades or skateboarding with friends, whereas the children with lower levels of self-esteem chose possessions, like new clothes or an iPod.[34]

Thanks to the deliberate marketing strategies by purveyors of everything from cigarettes (look at those smiling, laughing, white-toothed smokers surrounded by friends and having a grand old time!) to razors (if you shave with the Venus razor, the ads suggest, you, too, can end up with a hot, hunky boyfriend) these days, many children are socialized to believe they can buy themselves into popularity and acceptance. Approximately 60 percent of the 2,035 teenagers we polled in our national SIS study for this book believed that wearing or owning the right brand of clothes, gadgets, or cars could help them "buy" happiness. Moreover, compared to adults, teens were more likely to buy famous brands, more likely to believe that having the right clothes, gadgets, and cars could help them become more popular, and more likely to display expensive items such as makeup and perfume conspicuously in their bedrooms and bathrooms. While teens believed that their favorite brands made them feel cool, confident, friendly, self-expressive, creative, and passionate—they couldn't have cared less about whether a brand actually *did!*—the adults said their favorite brands made them feel more reliable, practical, effective, and—yes—nostalgic. According to a study in the *Journal of Consumer Research*, "Starting at 11 or 12, children begin to understand so much about the complex meanings of products and brands, and that is the exact time when their self-esteem drops. They're thinking, 'I don't think I'm so popular. I don't think kids like me. How do I solve that? Well, I know that popular kids wear Gap clothes and Nike shoes. So if I wear those, then I'll be popular.'" [35] In short, the less confidence or self-esteem they had, the more they seemed to be dependent on brands. (One might even conclude from this that the larger the logo we wear, the less self-esteem we have.) In a way, it makes sense; it's easier, after all, to fit in with your peer group by buying the same brand of sneakers than it is to transform your personality. According to Amanda Grum, a psychologist who specializes in play and parenting, peer pressure "is most effective in children aged five to 12, as they are starting to develop their own identity. . . . Belonging is a powerful urge for young children, especially before their sense of self is fully developed. By aligning themselves with an external force, they are able to use the attributes of that object or group to help define themselves." [36]

According to a poll of 112,000 teenagers in thirty countries, just under half of all teenagers factor in the brand when making purchase decisions, with Nike, Lacoste, Adidas, Sony, and Apple being the most popular among the boys, and Zara, H&M, and Roxy among the girls. What's more, just under half of all the teens said if there was no visible branding, they wouldn't buy an item of clothing at all. [37]

In a focus group I recently conducted (in conjunction with the Murray Hill Center) with female teens and tweens, I found that the more popular a brand, the more aware these young women are of its high cost. Hollister and Abercrombie weren't just "cool girl" brands by virtue of how they looked; they were "cool girl" brands because they *cost more* than other brands. Clearly, companies know that teens (and often adults) are willing to pay more for brands they deem cool or popular—which is why Apple can get away with charging $229 for the iPhone 4 and Abercrombie can charge forty dollars for a tank top.

The widespread belief that expensive, high-end brands will bring popularity, acceptance, or status goes a long way toward explaining the universe of knockoff clothing sold on the streets of many cities. Ironically, while we may often buy those fake Coaches, Versaces, Pradas, and Ray-Bans to feel better about ourselves, recent research shows they may in fact have the opposite effect. Three psychologists—Francesca Gino of the University of North Carolina at Chapel Hill, Michael Norton of Harvard Business School, and Dan Ariely of Duke University—gave a large sampling of women what appeared to be Chloé sunglasses, then told half the women they were fake and the other half they were real. Then they had the women carry out complex math puzzles, grade themselves on the honor system, and take money for each correct answer. Well, it turns out the women wearing the "fake" Chloé glasses (in reality, of course, they were all fake) cheated a whole lot more; a whopping "70 percent inflated their performance . . . and in effect stole cash from the coffer." [38] The authors concluded that "wearing counterfeit glasses not only fails to bolster our ego and self-image the way we hope, it actually undermines our internal sense of authenticity. 'Faking it' makes us feel like phonies and cheaters on the inside." [39] I guess it's true what adman David Ogilvy once said: "A fake Rolex will fool everyone but you."

Lacoste is another high-end brand that has been extremely successful in using peer pressure to draw teenagers and college-aged kids to its products. Three decades ago, that little crocodile was one of the hottest logos in Europe and the United States. *Everyone* wanted to wear it. Then Bangkok-manufactured "fakes" began swamping the market, and the brand's reputation went down the drain (Lacoste came close to filing for bankruptcy). So to resurrect its image, it gave out free shirts to cool-looking people at colleges and universities (as well as famous tennis players) and paid for product placements on MTV ... and suddenly the brand was back in action. Today—go figure—Lacoste is as popular as it was thirty years ago.

As many people know, few brands have shrewdly amassed a more cultlike, almost religious following than Apple (and in fact, in an experiment I conducted for my last book, when I studied the brains of Apple fanatics using an fMRI, I found that their brain activity was similar to that of those devoted to Christianity), and peer pressure has been central to many of its strategies. One such strategy is early recruitment, or in other words, very deliberately marketing to kids aged thirteen to seventeen. This campaign has been so effective that today a staggering 46 percent of Americans in that age range own an iPod, the product teens talk to one another about most is the iPod, and one survey found that 82 percent of high school students who own a portable music player own an iPod.[40]

Once these kids get to college, Apple even starts "recruiting" officially, going so far as to hire kids to become "Apple campus reps" and turning entire sections of college bookstores into mini Apple emporiums. "This is a great opportunity to represent Apple and to have some fun," says the online recruiting ad. The job description includes hosting workshops, throwing events, and building relationships with students, faculty, and parents, and to top it off, "You'll collaborate with the Apple team to run marketing programs on campus, from sales promotions to increasing awareness of Apple products. . . . It takes a leader, someone who can inspire peers and work with campus organizations."[41] This is a clever touch: who doesn't want to think of him- or herself as a leader, a trendsetter, a person who inspires peers? (I might add here that if you are a frequent moviegoer, you would probably assume everyone on earth uses an Apple—a triumph of product placement and peer pressure all in one. In 2009 nearly one in two popular Hollywood movies—roughly 46 percent—featured Apple or its products. Though it's generally agreed that no money changed hands, Apple couldn't have bought better advertising or brand exposure.)

Kids and teens want what the popular kids have, plain and simple. A colleague once told me an intriguing story about a computer game that was released in California not too long ago. Instead of advertising the product in a traditional way, the game's savvy developer simply identified the hundred most popular kids in a high school in Southern California, gave them free versions of the game, then sat back to watch it catch on like wildfire.

There's an actual biological reason for why kids are so drawn to the classmates they deem more popular. Years ago, the BBC carried out a fascinating study. It showed kids a stack of photos of other kids who were either laughing or smiling and asked them to pick out the kids they would most like to be around. Every single person picked the laughing kids. On the face of it this seems obvious. Who wouldn't want to be around someone who's laughing and appears to be having a good time? But there's another reason behind it; laughing actually makes us feel good on a physiological level. When we laugh, we're flooding our brains, organs, and tissues with oxygen, which is one of the "primary catalysts for biological energy in the human body." [42] So the popular kids at school didn't just get that way because of their personalities; they got that way because it physically *feels good* to be around them.

That said, as powerful as peer pressure is in persuading teens to buy, when a brand becomes *too* popular, too widespread, it can backfire. From studies I've conducted over the years, it's become clear that young people will always deny being "a part of " any new trend. What's more, I've found that once an older generation catches on to a new brand or trend, it becomes unhip, and fast. It's what I call the "generation lap" problem, because it's what happens when the younger kids jump ship in an attempt to create the "generation lap"—meaning a psychological distance between them and older generations.

The generation lap, though, is in itself a form of peer pressure; a reverse peer pressure, if you will. Take what happened with the Levi's brand. In the eighties, Levi's were *the* jeans to have. Anyone who was anyone wore Levi's. But by 2001 the brand had taken a major hit. Its revenue was slashed in half and market share had dropped to 12.1 percent, from 18.7 percent in 1986.[43] Levi's was suddenly the brand that no one cool would be caught dead in. Why?

It's a rite of passage for every child to pass through a rebellious phase. (That said, a study has shown that men and women both recognize that they are similar to their parents, or accept the strength of their parents' influence, by the time they turn thirty-five.) Many companies, knowing this, often market their brands and products to seem "bad" or "subversive." Which is what Levi's did . . . only a little too well.

Levi's was the brand of rebellion for the baby boomer generation. That rebel without a cause, James Dean, wore them. In the sixties they were practically the uniform of hippies and protesters. In the seventies they were among the first brands to introduce bell-bottoms. But once the boomers grew up and started having kids of their own, the generation lap set in. No rebellious youth wants to be seen wearing the same jeans as his *dad*. How can you distance yourself from your parents' generation if your parents are into the same trend? So the kids started wearing other jeans, ones different enough to distinguish them from their parents. (Now you know what skinny jeans are all about—this style is adult-proof. Let's face it, the trendiest adult on earth knows he can't fit his fortysomething legs into those pipe-cleaner holes.)

This is exactly why I recommend that companies create more and more "brand *dis*approved" concepts—ideas or products or gadgets deliberately built to court parental disapproval. A concept so outrageous, so provocative, so different, so . . . *anything!* . . . that adults will react against it. This is harder to do than you might imagine, yet my research has shown that once such a concept has been identified, there's almost a 90 percent chance that it will turn out to be a success among the younger set.

Peer pressure may sometimes work in backward ways, but the psychology behind it—the desire for acceptance—remains the same. I've seen again and again that there's a certain type of consumer who will run *away* from what's popular, even among the people in their own generation. If their peers start to like "indie bands," they'll turn up their noses. If their friends are decked out in Abercrombie & Fitch, they'll head for the local Goodwill or Salvation Army. If they go to a school that champions the football team, they'll spend their Saturdays playing the xylophone, or maybe just sit in their rooms scowling and smoking. They presume that anything that's popular, that's universally adored, or that involves long lines snaking around a block is probably substandard, populist swill. To them, it's cool to be *un*cool.

But this isn't really as counterintuitive as it seems. Because these people tend to flock together with people who feel exactly the same way. So when one of them bashes the band Arcade Fire for being "sellouts" or declares that Converse sneakers are for "posers," it's likely because he's observed those around him doing the same. In the end, nonconformity is a form of conformity as well.

Peering Overseas

In all my years in the marketing world, I've consistently found one fact to be true: nowhere in the world are people more easily brandwashed than in Asia. In Asian countries, it's perfectly normal for a man to own half a dozen expensive Swiss watches or for a woman to carefully put aside a month's salary for a pair of Prada shoes. In Asia, more so than even in the United States, a person is what he or she wears. But the really interesting thing about this is how socially contagious brand preference is over there. Most Asian women who carry a Louis Vuitton bag don't do so because they're enamored of the brand. As one expert explained, "The ability or need to fit in is a strong driver. Asians are a collectivist society, and group identity is important. So in Japan, if one office lady carries a Louis Vuitton bag, then it means that to fit in, the rest would do the same." [44]

Louis Vuitton has very cleverly capitalized on the herd mentality of Asian culture by playing on a dream that is common to 78 percent of Japanese women: getting married in Paris. How? By playing up its "Frenchness" in its marketing, advertising, and stores. First off, in Japan, even more than elsewhere, the store design is made to look French-inspired—with its glamorous, old-fashioned Parisian street scenes and paintings of iconic French landmarks like the Eiffel Tower or the Arc de Triomphe. Store managers in Japan are often French-born (with accents that typically manage to outdo even Maurice Chevalier's), and the brand's suitcases, or "trunks," are embossed with French name tags and placed conspicuously in the foyers of the company's flagship stores (the stores even serve French-made Moët & Chandon champagne to their best customers). The photos in the Louis Vuitton catalogs are also set against Parisian backdrops, and even in Japan the models are *never, ever*

Japanese. They're either ambiguously ethnic or stylishly "French look-ing." And no matter what country you're surfing the Web in, when you go to the Louis Vuitton Web site, you'll immediately be asked if you want to read the site in French—even though globally, French consumers are responsible for only a minuscule percentage of Vuitton sales (fact is, the French elite largely eschew the brand). And finally, even though Louis Vuitton in fact manufactures a number of its products in India, it continues to manufacture the luggage it sends to the Japanese market in France, just to keep up that "French" image.

Based on what I've seen in my travels, it's also fair to say that in places where money is relatively new—like China and Russia—you'll find the greatest obsession with brands. I believe that this, too, comes back to insecurity and the desire to fit in. For a long time, both China and the Soviet Union felt like the underdogs of the global economy—many of their residents have felt as though the rest of the world doesn't yet accept or respect them. So they tend to overcompensate for this national lack of self-esteem by buying brands—the louder, bolder, and more in-your-face expensive the better.

I won't ever forget a story a Russian man once told at a conference. He was recalling the first time he received special permission to travel from his home state to America. At the Dublin airport, where he was changing planes, he dashed into a small kiosk and, using the only money he had on him, bought a can of Coke. But the snap top broke off, and he couldn't open the can. When he tried punching a hole in the top and the whole thing exploded, he didn't care. He didn't care about actually drinking the beverage. The point was, he'd bought an original can of Coca-Cola, and for him, that Coke symbolized nothing less than America.

Scol! Nastrovia!

To leave you with one final story of how marketers engineer viral trends, let's take a trip to Russia, where last year Greg Tucker and Chris Lukehurst of the UK's Marketing Clinic and I were summoned to develop a market-leading brand of (what else?) vodka. I remember the first time I set eyes on the vodka section of a Russian supermarket. There weren't tens or even hundreds but thousands of varieties of vodka (and this wasn't a monstrous superstore, either). Later I learned that Russia boasts roughly *three thousand* different vodka brands and *five thousand* different vodka flavors. Greg's and my challenge was to create brand number 3,001 and somehow turn it into the market leader.

I had another mission, too—to transform the Russian population's drinking habits. I'm sure you're familiar with the place's reputation. It's mostly true. And the amount of drinking that goes on there has caused major societal damage, which the Russian government has been struggling to combat for many years. Now you might wonder (and rightly so) why a vodka company would want to figure out a way to get Russian citizens to drink *less*. Good question. The company's reasons were twofold. The first was that cognacs are making significant inroads in Russia and becoming serious competitors to the long-standing Russian vodka industry. The second is a twist on the generation-lap problem—the rampant drinking among the older generation of Russians is turning off the younger generation, who look at their soused parents and think, *Dude, I don't want to end up like that.*

So I was tasked to travel around the country and find out why Russians drink as much as they did, and whether there was anything I could do about it. And paradoxically, at the same time could I help create a successful new vodka brand? To me these missions seemed incompatible, if not impossible. That is, until one night when I discovered something about *why* Russians drink as much as they do.

Not completely unlike the viral drinking game "icing" we talked about earlier in the chapter, it all comes down to a socially contagious ritual, only this one is a century old. The *scol* ritual begins with pouring vodka into a large—typically fifty-milliliter—glass. Then, all at once, everyone downs the stuff and cries out *"Nastrovia!"* No sipping here, either—you have to drink it down straight. This is one of Russia's oldest and most widespread customs, and it's a major part of every occasion or celebration, from birthdays to dinner parties to funerals. (Not doing it, in fact, is considered bad luck.) But once I began talking to hundreds of Russians in cities and villages across the country, I discovered something surprising. Most Russians *hate* the taste of vodka *and* hate the accompanying ritual (they even have to scarf down food afterward to get rid of the burning taste in their throats). In other words, they don't do it because they enjoy it—they do it because it's simply *what everyone else does*—it generates a sense of belonging and camaraderie. Plus, there were no alternative rituals.

Which is when I thought, *Huh*.

By introducing a *new* drinking ritual, one that people actually enjoyed, maybe I could not only gain awareness for a new brand but also show the Russians a new (and healthier) way to drink vodka.

Now, the thing about the *scol* ritual is that it requires that everyone drink at exactly the same speed: fast (which was actually bad for the vodka company, because a person who drinks too much too fast will also be on the floor that much more quickly, thus *reducing* overall vodka intake). This countrywide ritual was like a fraternity during hazing week; it was creating peer pressure to binge drink. By altering the ritual, my hope was that we could change at least the speed of drinking.

This turned out to be just what many Russians had been waiting for but no one had ever dared to say aloud. In the rough-and-tumble Russian culture, sipping a drink slowly is generally perceived as weak, overdelicate, and effete. No red-blooded Russian man would ever dare take the risk. The key, therefore, would be to introduce a whole new *masculine* way of drinking vodka, this time slowly and out of a small glass, that would still be perceived as "Russian." So I borrowed from a country that many Russians respect and admire—Finland.

By setting up hundreds of testing groups and analyzing consumers' taste palates across Russia, we crafted a vodka product that lacked the harsh burn everyone loathed—and by combining this new taste with a newfound ritual of drinking out of a smaller glass (and I'm afraid I'm contractually bound to secrecy, so I can't divulge anything more), a new vodka brand hit the market. Time will tell whether the brand will take off, and whether we actually managed to create a healthier kind of peer pressure.

6

Oh, Sweet Memories

THE NEW (BUT ALSO OLD) FACE OF NOSTALGIA MARKETING

An American woman I know who spent her childhood years in Paris is obsessed with the taste of Mars bars. Not American Mars bars. Just French Mars bars. She will raise her right hand and swear that the U.S. version cannot compare with the taste of the Mars bars she snacked on growing up. She can't explain why. When pressed, she'll say only that the chocolate tastes sweeter and the caramel tastes creamier. When friends visit France, she begs them to bring her back supplies.

I have to admit, I feel as fondly about my memories of the holidays I spent growing up in Denmark, though I haven't lived there for years. The snow coming down outside, the smells drifting out of the kitchen, the family members gathered around the tree. The simplicity of a time that, looking back, seems so far superior to the strident commercial machinery that defines the holidays today. Though I've had fantastic holidays in recent years, in my mind none compare to the ones I had when I was a child.

While we're on the topic of the past, wasn't the music you grew up listening to and the TV shows you liked to watch way back when all frankly *better* than the newfangled bands and songs and shows that are on TV and the radio today? Or have you noticed that 99 percent of the time we derive the most pleasure from our first experience of something? That the original version of a song or movie is the best; that the house we grew up in is better and more attractive than any future home; that a story is more enjoyable *and* more believable the first time we hear it than the second or third time (in fact, I once conducted a study to investigate that last one and indeed found that 72 percent of people believed that the first source of a story was more authentic than subsequent retellings).

Sometimes the first experiences were objectively better, though not as a rule. But objectively better or not, they always *seem better in hindsight.* That's because as humans (and consumers) we've been fooled into thinking the past was perfect, and by our own brains, too. The culprit? A simple and very powerful psychological persuader known as nostalgia—one that marketers know all too well.

Case in point: the 2009 Super Bowl, an event that's almost become better known for its high-priced commercials than for the game itself (some of us can't remember who played, others don't care, but almost all of us can remember which commercial we liked best). During this particular Super Bowl, 151.6 million people,[1] the largest TV audience ever, sat back and watched ads starring Don Rickles (for the flower company Teleflora), Abe Vigoda and Betty White (for Snickers chocolate bars), Stevie Wonder (for Volkswagen), and an antique sock monkey (for a new model of Kia).

What's more, the soundtrack accompanying the commercials that spanned the roughly three-hour show featured songs by seventies funk stylists Kool & the Gang (for the Honda Accord Crossover); the classic rock band Cheap Trick (for Audi); the British symphonic rockers Electric Light Orchestra, whose global fame peaked in the midseventies (for Select 55 beer); and seventies singer-songwriter Bill Withers (for Electronic Arts' Dante's Inferno video game). During the halftime show, the eighties sensation Bruce Springsteen and the E Street Band came out and performed "Tenth Avenue Freeze-Out," "Born to Run," "Working on a Dream," and "Glory Days."

What decade were we in, anyway? What was going on here?

Nostalgic for Nostalgia

The word "nostalgia" comes from the Greek compounds *nostos*—meaning "to come home"—and *algos*, or pain. It was coined in 1688 by a Swiss physician, Johannes Hofer, in reference to a bizarre malady affecting Swiss nationals stationed overseas (homesickness, basically) that Dr. Hofer believed could ultimately lead to widespread desertions and even death. In our modern parlance, however, it's generally used to refer to, as *Webster's* puts it, "a wistful or excessive sentimental yearning or return to some past period."

In a 2006 study carried out at the University of Southampton in the UK, 79 percent of the 172 students polled claimed they experience nostalgic thoughts at least once a week, while 16 percent reported having such fond moments daily. Turns out there's a reason we as humans are prone to these thoughts; nostalgia is good for us. According to *Scientific American*, "Rather than being a waste of time or an unhealthful indulgence, basking in memories elevates mood, increases self-esteem and strengthens relationships. In short, nostalgia is a source of psychological well-being."[2] What's more, when the same researchers asked those subjects to assess their social competence in three areas (their capacity to build relationships, their ability to be candid with others about their feelings, and whether or not they could offer their friends emotional support), they found that "the participants most likely to engage in nostalgic thinking did better in all three measures of social skills than those in the control group,"[3] concluding that "nostalgic thinking . . . breeds happier moods."[4]

Another reason we have a predilection for nostalgia is that our brains are wired to recall our past experiences as having been far better and more pleasurable than we experienced them to be in the moment, a phenomenon that goes by the names "rosy remembering" or "rosy retrospection." As Bryan Urbick, the CEO of the UK's Consumer Knowledge Centre, theorizes, rosy retrospection may be an adaptive mechanism designed to erase and protect us from painful memories. Evidence suggests it may even have evolved to help ensure the continuation of the human race; after all, if women accurately remembered the pain of giving birth, chances are that few of them would voluntarily go through the experience again.

Though surprisingly little research has been done on *why* this nearly universal psychological phenomenon exists, countless studies have shown that we indeed have a strong tendency to assess past incidents or events more favorably after the fact than we did while those same events were taking place. (Interestingly, our brains are also prone to a phenomenon known as rosy *prospection*, whereby our anticipation of certain events is more positive than our actual experience of the event.) In one such study, psychologist Terence Mitchell and a team of colleagues had students who were about to embark on one of three vacations (a two-week tour of Europe, Thanksgiving weekend with their families, or a three-week bicycle tour across California) rate their anticipation of the trip, their level of enjoyment during the trip, and their memory of the trip after it took place. In all three cases, both the students' anticipation and memories were more favorable than their feelings during the trip itself. As one study brief points out, "As memory takes over . . . the unpleasantness fades and the good parts remain, perhaps . . . even get amplified beyond reality." [5]

Other studies show that we're so determined to remember the past favorably that on occasion we "remember" pleasant incidents that never took place. In one, individuals remembered seeing Bugs Bunny during a visit to Walt Disney World, an impossibility since Bugs Bunny is a Warner Bros. creation, not a Disney character. The experiment concluded that "even knowing a memory is not real does not make it any less meaningful or enjoyable" and that "the memory of an event is more important than the actual experience." [6]

The point is, we tend to live in the past (and to some extent the future), and our brains like it that way. This is part of the reason why, in my experience, no one believes that on the inside they're truly their chronological age. In fact, I have a theory that most people have a psychological age that remains fairly stable and consistent throughout their adult life, no matter how many candles burn on their birthday cake. I once asked a top banking CEO who was around fifty what his "inner age" was. "Nineteen," he said at once. Ask the same question of a roomful of people, and I guarantee not one person will answer their actual age. It's almost as if we're two people: the one inside us and the (older) one others see. After all, who hasn't felt incredulous at hitting each milestone birthday, whether it's twenty, forty, or sixty? Naturally, no one likes the thought of getting old, but I believe this phenomenon is rooted in something more than just a fear of aging. I believe it has to do with our rosy remembering of what our life was like when we actually were that "inner age."

At this point, you might be thinking, *Okay, this rings true, but what does it have to do with how companies trick us into buying things?* Well, a lot, actually. Companies and marketers know full well that our "perceived" age is a huge factor in our shopping decisions and buying habits. Why does a fifty-year-old woman buy hair dye or wrinkle cream? Why does a forty-year-old man buy Ray-Bans or a Ferrari convertible (otherwise known as a midlife-crisis-mobile)? Not just to look or seem younger (though that's part of it) but to bridge the gap between how old they are . . . and how old they *feel* inside. It's the very same human tendency that drives grown men and women to buy all those things they loved (or *remember* loving) when they were younger, like tight jeans, fast cars, Converse All-Star sneakers, Pink Floyd CDs, and so on. All the kinds of stuff that will make us feel younger again or, rather, make us feel the age we actually believe we are on the inside.

Clever companies know that the older we get, the more intense our longings for the past become. They also know that our preferences for music, movies, trends, and products we enjoyed in our carefree childhoods, adolescences, and early twenties remain with us our whole lives. In a 1998 *New Yorker* article, neuroscientist and writer Robert Sapolsky pondered his disintegrating interest in new things: food, experiences, and especially music. Why, Sapolsky wondered, did he keep playing *Bob Marley's Greatest Hits* over and over while his twentysomething lab colleagues were bopping around listening to every hot new (or old but trendy) thing from Sigur Rós to Sonic Youth to the Black Eyed Peas?

In an attempt to understand why he was musically stuck in the seventies, Sapolsky set out to study "the windows in which we form our cultural tastes, and [in which we] are amenable to new experiences." Was there, he wondered, an age at which these "windows of openness slammed shut?"[7] Indeed, Sapolsky concluded, there was. He and his research assistants called radio stations that specialize in the music of various periods and asked the same two questions of each station manager:

When was most of the music that you play first introduced? And what is the average age of your listeners? Based on their responses, Sapolsky found that most of us end up playing and loving the music we're exposed to when we're around twenty years old (or younger) for the rest of our lives, and that if a person is over the age of thirty-five when a new pop music style makes its mark, there's a greater than 95 percent chance he or she will never listen to it. After conducting similar inquiries about food and fashion, he concluded that our "window of openness" for new experiences, like getting our tongue pierced, slams shut at age twenty-three and our openness to trying out new foods (say, sweetbreads or calves' livers) pretty much closes for good at thirty-nine.[8]

In my career, I've found time and again that there is often a specific moment or time in our lives when we form such powerful memories involving a brand that we decide (subconsciously) to consume the product for life. When I began working for Pepsi and Coca-Cola, I remember speaking with a fifty-five-year-old woman who was a lifelong fan of Coke. Why? When she was six years old, her parents allowed her to walk alone to a local candy store where the owner served "real Cokes" by mixing together soda and syrup and pouring the concoction into an iced glass bottle. It was cold, frothy, and delicious, the highlight of her day. She would then traipse back to her neighborhood, where she would play on the street with the other kids until it got dark. It was what I call an "oasis" memory, when everything seems all right with the world—safe, contented, fun, protected, shimmering.

Today, this woman's life is difficult. She works two demanding jobs and juggles several children, one severely handicapped. But when I stood before her and watched her take a sip of her Coke, I swear the look in her eyes changed. The taste had taken her back to that moment, that neighborhood, that oasis.

Such is the power of nostalgia.

Golden Oldies

Nostalgia marketing is a perennial—and, I should add, wildly successful—strategy by which advertisers resurrect the sights, sounds, and feel of a previous decade to sell us a brand or product of today. Sometimes it's by reviving a commercial or a style of packaging or even an icon or spokesperson (like in those Super Bowl commercials) that those of us over thirty or forty are guaranteed to recall fondly from our own childhoods. Other times it's done more subtly, by implicitly evoking the feel or texture of a simpler time. And sometimes it's done by reviving an old brand itself.

Recent research from the University of Arkansas shows that the older a brand is, the more favorably it will be perceived, regardless of how well it works. One reason is that when we see a nostalgic product from the past, whether it's a brand of breakfast cereal or a make of sneakers, we are reexperiencing the world as we first encountered it when we were young—that time when everything (thanks to our brains' rosy remembering) was safer, simpler, better.

Few people know this, but one of the main goals of any brand or ad campaign is to own a "moment." What do I mean by owning a moment? Well, if you're in your late forties or early fifties, no doubt you remember Kodak Instamatic cameras. Peaking in popularity between 1963 and 1970, Kodak Instamatic cameras were inexpensive, point-and-shoot apparatuses that created a phrase that became so ubiquitous as to secure a place in our cultural mythology: the "Kodak moment." A Kodak moment, as many know, is an instant in time that captures a one-of-a-kind, emotional experience—that second before your son blows out the candles on his first birthday cake, the instant your daughter reaches out her hand to accept her high school diploma, and so forth. Though Kodak no longer manufactures Instamatics, the expression refuses to die. And for marketers, the "Kodak moment" is pure gold.

Owning an instant in time is a product's equivalent of a landgrab, meaning that it keeps other brands out and in their place. *No trespassing; this moment is mine!* Nesquik, whose slogan is "They Only Grow Up Once," has grabbed the moment you pack a milk box in your child's lunch on his first day of kindergarten and realize he is morphing from toddler to boy before your eyes. The Jenny Craig weight-control program has co-opted the "seatbelt moment," the instant when a woman secures her belt across her lap only to find it no longer reaches the clasp.

What these slogans ingeniously do, of course, is subtly link their products not just to those fleeting moments but to our *emotions* surrounding those moments. So that when little Billy's middle-school graduation makes us feel wistful (where did the time go?), we reach for Nesquik, and when we feel insecure and embarrassed because our jeans feel tighter than usual, many of us automatically think, *Time to call Jenny Craig.* It's all subconscious, of course, but that's part of the reason it's so powerful.

The *really* ambitious marketers and companies even try to lay claim to not just a moment but an entire era. Amazingly, McDonald's has successfully managed to lay claim to the last thirty years, with slogans like "It's a good time for the great taste of McDonald's" or "It's MacTime," because together we've shared "30 years of good times and great taste." [9] The result? Three entire decades' worth of emotions and associations linked in our minds to their burgers and fries.

It's worth noting that allusions to time persuade us to buy in other ways as well. Did you know that just *mentioning* time in an advertising campaign makes us more likely to buy a product? It's because as soon as we're reminded of how fleeting time is, we think, *I'd better have and enjoy this before it's too late.* And did you also know that when we're "primed" to think about time, the chances we'll feel a personal connection to a product increases exponentially? [10] For example, if a suitcase manufacturer or coffee company announces, "It's time for a new set of rolling wheels," or "It's espresso time," we're more likely to respond positively to these ads than not. Why? Because time, quite simply, is one thing we all wish we had more of yet rarely give ourselves permission to savor.

Our tendency to romanticize bygone eras helps explain why nostalgia marketing is especially potent during uncertain economic times. When the stock market is down, personal debt is up, climate change is in the news, and job security is a thing of the past, anxious consumers seek nothing more than the retail equivalent of comfort food: the sounds, the smells, the appearance, and hence the memories and familiar fonts of the best-loved brands from our childhoods. In other words, an era before we were plagued with these grown-up worries.

In the face of insecurity or uncertainty about the future, we want nothing more than to revert to a stable time. And what time could seem more stable, simple, and quaint than the past (even though it was in reality crazy and turbulent, and we're just not remembering it accurately)? Plus, oddly enough, recalling the past not only provides us a source of comfort and security; it even makes us feel more hopeful and optimistic about the future, more equipped to deal with the challenges that lie ahead.

This is why during hard times we eat more "retro" foods, like macaroni and cheese and mashed potatoes, and flock toward classic, ever-iconic brands that have been around forever, like Hershey's, Maytag, Heinz, Hellman's, or Hunter Boot (a brand of shoe that's been around for 150 years and is carried in high-end retailers like Bergdorf Goodman and Bloomingdale's).[11]

This is also why nostalgia marketing boomed during the turbulent years of World War II and has resurged at certain points throughout just about every decade since. It tends to conform to a particular pattern, too. Generally, marketers and advertisers home in on cultural trends that are most dissimilar (and therefore most romanticized) to the ones of the current age. For example, during the economic and political turbulence of the 1970s came a nostalgic fad for products that recalled the staid, conservative 1950s. During the buttoned-down Reagan-era 1980s, marketers paid tribute to the freewheeling 1960s, and in the tumultuous first decade of the twenty-first century, which saw 9/11, two wars in the Middle East, and the worst economic downturn since the Great Depression, marketers were harkening back to the trends and styles of the flush and relatively peaceful eighties.

Does anyone recall the 1986 commercial featuring Marvin Gaye crooning his 1967 tune "I Heard It Through the Grapevine" to a bunch of raisins? What about Wendy's dusting off its 1984 "Where's the beef?" TV commercial in 2010 or Coca-Cola reviving its famous 1971 "I'd like to teach the world to sing" ad for its thirty-fifth anniversary (the company even went so far as to hire a detective agency to hunt down the men and women who'd first sung the song decades earlier)?

Here one can't help but note the popularity of "oldies" television channels like TV Land, Nick at Nite, and American Movie Classics. And what about the recent cultural phenomenon, the AMC series *Mad Men*, which so impeccably captures the aura, essence, and glamour of Madison Avenue in the early 1960s? And it's not just the show (which, by the way, has been deliberately advertised to play into this sepia-toned nostalgic sentiment) we're obsessed with. We're also preoccupied with (and willing to spend money to enjoy) its trends and fashions in our own lives—all kinds of nostalgic items from tunic dresses and skinny ties to martinis and old-fashioneds.

Today countless companies and brands, from Coke to McDonald's to General Mills to Target to Unilever, are turning huge profits by deliberately playing into our human fancy (and fantasy) that the past was better—simpler, quainter, more authentic, more secure—than our lives are now (there's even a mall in Shanghai devoted exclusively to nostalgic products known as Zhonghua Laozihao Shangcheng, which translates to "Time-Honored Chinese Brand Shopping Mall").[12] However, the risk of this approach for marketers and advertises is that if they play up the past *too* much, we might begin to see the product or brand as dusty, outdated, or out of style. Which is why a lot of brands and companies, like the ones you're about to read about, have developed some incredibly inventive—not to mention psychologically sophisticated—strategies for toeing this delicate line.

Feasting on the Past

As I enter the Time Warner Center in New York's Columbus Circle, a Midtown "mall" largely populated by high-end retailers, and descend the escalator to Whole Foods, which we visited in chapter 3, it doesn't escape my attention that the music playing faintly overhead is a dance hit that weaves in a sample of Abba's 1979 "Gimme, Gimme, Gimme (a Man After Midnight)," providing quite a shot of nostalgia and familiarity for shoppers over thirty-five.

Talk about having it both ways. Here at Whole Foods, we see the latest agricultural and dietary fads of the twenty-first century—from grass-fed beef to gluten-free cookies to pesticide-free produce to cask-ale microbrews—united with the carefree tunes from an era before any of these things even existed. (Oh, and it's no coincidence that this particular song is playing, either. In a later chapter we'll be exploring the world of data mining, at which time you'll discover that there is no such thing as a melody playing "randomly" overhead while you shop.)

The connections between the gleaming, auditorium-sized, state-of-the-art Whole Foods and nostalgia marketing may not seem apparent at first. After all, isn't Whole Foods about as modern as you can get? The past was a much quainter, far less complicated place than labyrinthine Whole Foods, right? For most of us, "the good old days" were a time before chain stores, anxieties about industrialized food, or even the term "organic" ever existed, an era when produce was fresh and no-frills and there weren't ten different brands of everything from garbanzo beans to graham crackers.

Perhaps we "remember" a time when grocery shopping meant stopping with our parents at a roadside fruit and vegetable stand, where we sniffed and unpeeled ears of corn harvested just that morning, filled a basket with apples picked from a nearby orchard, or grabbed a bunch of flowers whose prices were hand-scribbled on a small slate board. Or was that in a movie we once saw? Doesn't matter. I once screened photographs with consumers in five different countries, asking them to rank each photo in order of which most evoked a sense of freshness. The unanimous winner was a photograph of a twentysomething farm boy, wearing a cowboy hat and holding a wooden box laden with fresh vegetables. When I asked the respondents how many of them had seen this image in real life—not the farm boy in question but *any* farmer—only one person out of four hundred raised his or her hand.

The point is, whether or not we've actually set foot on an old-time farm stand in our lives, emotionally we associate things like old wooden boxes, flowers, and hand-scrawled signs with authenticity, history, and a better, simpler time (as well as with freshness, as we saw in chapter 2); in other words, everything that the modern-looking Whole Foods is not. Or is it? It might not be obvious at first, but the ingenious marketers who designed Whole Foods did so very carefully, to trigger these very associations of a simpler era.

For example, about a dozen feet into the store sit a dozen stacked cardboard boxes with anywhere from eight to ten fresh cantaloupes packed inside each one. These boxes could have been unpacked easily, of course, by any one of Whole Foods' unionized employees, but they're left that way on purpose. Why? For that rustic, *aw-shucks* touch. In other words, it's a symbolic to reinforce the idea of old-time simplicity—as if our mythical farmer ran out of cantaloupe crates and had to make do with used cartons.

But wait, something about these boxes looks off. Let's move in and take a closer look. Funny, upon close inspection, this stack of crates looks like one giant cardboard box. It can't be, can it? It *is*. In fact, it's one humongous cardboard box with fissures cut carefully down the side that faces consumers (most likely by some industrial machinery at a factory in China) to make it *appear* as though this one giant cardboard box is made up of multiple stacked boxes. It's ingenious in its ability to evoke the image of *Grapes of Wrath*–era laborers piling box after box of fresh fruit into the store. But like a lot of what goes on at Whole Foods, this image in false.

In the industry, these cardboard boxes are known as "dummies." And for good reason! We've been punked by nostalgia again.

Whole Foods' ongoing salute to the roadside stand of bygone days continues with a display of apples perched atop a wooden crate. The crate is deliberately distressed looking and grainy gray, suggesting that the apples on display were shipped to this store in a dirty flatbed, as they might have been in the 1940s. *The Apples of Wrath!* This crate is another symbolic, as are the two bottles of organic apple juice perched behind the apples, like Ma and Pa Apple overseeing a litter of baby Granny Smiths. Only a person with six-foot-long arms could ever hope to actually reach these bottles. But that's not the point. Organic apple juice steers our brains to the old-fashioned notion of homemade cider—yet another marketing trick designed to recall a time when life was simpler and better and more delicious.

Yet there's an interesting paradox at play here. The past is perfect, and so is its produce, right? Well, not exactly. Because what I've found in all my years of studying consumers and their responses to branding is that one essential component of the nostalgia factor is authenticity, and nothing authentic is truly perfect, is it?

A bruise on the apple. A chip in the china. A scratch in the veneer on an old armoire. Just enough imperfection to create that authentic, slightly "used" feel can go a long way in evoking memories of that battered old toy we dug out from the attic or the scuffed bracelet we inherited from our grandmother. Have you noticed the market for "prewashed" T-shirts? Rationally, we tell ourselves that we buy them because they don't shrink in the washer or dryer, but emotionally, it has more to do with their "authentic," tattered look. Goodwill and the Salvation Army are among the most popular destinations nowadays among teenage girls, for whom it's become cool to doubt the "authenticity" of such manipulated clothing emporiums as Abercrombie & Fitch, Hollister, and American Apparel.

I recently visited a Trader Joe's where they were having a sale on the luxury chocolate Ghirardelli. But the usual fancy wrappers and glitz boxes were nowhere in sight. Instead, they were selling "bulk" Ghirardelli chocolate chunks packed in large brown paper bags branded with old-fashioned handwriting. Inside were bits of chocolate cut into uneven pieces—as though a chocolate maker at a mom-and-pop candy shop had chopped them by hand. There was no doubt that this looked as authentic as could be—until I happened to buy two bags and coincidentally discovered that the pieces were identical. The broken chunks were not hand cut at all; they were molded by a machine to look like randomly broken pieces.

Most consumers are drawn to small imperfections, and companies know it. It's an aesthetic the Japanese term *wabi-sabi*, which can be translated as the art of finding beauty in nature, whether it's a brown spot on a banana or a knot in the bark of a tree. To illustrate, I have a friend whose father was the Australian ambassador to Japan. One day, she told me, her father was seated in his garden in the middle of Tokyo, sipping tea. Fifty feet away from him, a gardener was going around picking up fallen leaves. It took him two full hours to complete the job. Then, when there was not a single leaf remaining on the ground, the gardener disappeared for twenty minutes, came back, and started carefully and tenderly placing leaves randomly onto the lawn. One here, two over there, and so on. Why? Because the leafless lawn looked unnatural. It looked *too* perfect.

Perfection makes us as consumers leery. As everyone knows, nothing is truly perfect, ever, and so when it appears to be, we subconsciously seek out the flaw, the inauthenticity. We glimpse a perfectly shaped hamburger in the supermarket, and it suddenly reminds us that we're eating mass-produced beef from an industrial slaughterhouse. We see a wall at Old Navy lined with impeccably stitched and identically dyed pairs of jeans, and we can all but picture them rolling off the assembly line in a Chinese sweatshop. We're sick and tired of picture-perfect babies and flawless models. Why do we love YouTube videos so much? Because they're imperfect, amateurish, and the people in them remind us of us. Recently there's been a trend of using "real" people in mainstream movies and TV shows, and it's one I predict will get bigger and bigger. According to a 2010 article in the *New York Times,* "Television executives at Fox Broadcasting, for example, say they have begun recruiting more natural-looking actors from Australia and Britain because the amply endowed, freakishly young-looking crowd that shows up for auditions in Los Angeles suffers from too much sameness." [13]

But what is "authentic," anyway? *Webster's* defines it as "worthy of acceptance and belief," but when it comes to the shady corners of the marketing and advertising world, that can mean a lot of different things. Is canned laughter authentic? Is the Paris Hotel in Las Vegas authentic? Is the sweater from H&M or the skirt from Zara that looks just like the one we saw on the runways during Fashion Week (but at quadruple the price) authentic? I would answer technically yes, as in all cases each one is true to what it intends to be. But at the same time, one could also argue these are mere imitations, clever ploys to trick our brains into thinking we're getting "the real thing."

These kinds of strategies are old hat for marketers and advertisers, but I've recently begun to notice an interesting shift. These days many marketers are introducing tiny, subtle imperfections into their products in an attempt to create the *impression* of authenticity, or what I call "inauthentic authenticity." This is why, in places like Whole Foods, we're seeing more and more Brussels sprouts and tomatoes still tethered to their stalks, many with dirt still clinging to the roots and leaves still hanging from the stalks. We're seeing more handwritten signs that mimic the messy scrawl of a roadside fruit and vegetable stand; more dusty wooden crates; more rustic cardboard boxes; more packages that look as though they were wrapped casually, messily, by loving human hands (when in fact a machine packaged these containers, in some cases with the sticker deliberately attached crookedly, in an overseas factory). And all in the service of pushing our nostalgia buttons, evoking a rosy remembrance of a simpler time that may or may not have ever existed.

But the tricks Whole Foods plays aren't the only ones companies have in their nostalgia playbooks. So let's focus now on another variant of nostalgia marketing: the old-fashioned kind.

Haven't I Seen You Somewhere Before? ·

One of the classic (literally)—and most effective—ways companies create the nostalgia factor is by dusting off and rereleasing commercials, slogans, or ad campaigns from the past. Few have pulled this off better than Heinz did in 2009, when it revived its famous 1970s tagline, "Beanz meanz Heinz."[14] Heinz's new (or rather, old) advertisement features loving mothers feeding their kids plates heaped with Heinz Beans to the backdrop of catchy slogans, like "Sometimes when I'm feeling sad my mum will read the signs. She knows the thing to cheer me up and she knows that beanz meanz Heinz." This ad was so memorable, it was voted the most popular slogan by the Advertising Hall of Fame nearly three decades after its original launch.

The British company Hovis has adapted an identical approach. In one advertisement, consumers see a retake of Ridley Scott's original 1973 ad showing a "boy on a bike" riding through dodgy eras in British history, from the Blitz to the miners' strikes. The implicit message: no matter what we've been through, Hovis has always been there for us.[15] It worked in 1973 and worked again in 2009—so well that it boosted sales 11 percent.[16]

Even banks and tire makers have gotten into the slogan-repurposing act. Citigroup has recently brought back its original 1978 tagline, "The Citi never sleeps," in an attempt to seem safer and more trustworthy by harkening back to a time before just about everybody hated and distrusted banks. And Michelin is bringing back its celebrated icon, the Michelin Man, created way back in 1898 (though in its latest incarnation, bowing to contemporary health concerns, he's slimmed down).[17] Allstate insurance's new TV ads feature a spokesperson strolling through a montage of Great Depression–era photographs while intoning, "Nineteen thirty-one was not exactly a great year to start a business, but that's when Allstate opened its doors. And through the twelve recessions since, they've noticed that after the fears subside, a funny thing happens. People start enjoying the small things in life. It's back to basics, and the basics are good. Protect them. Put them in good hands." [18]

I began working for Pepsi around the time the company launched its retro-inspired "real sugar" versions of two of its most beloved drinks, which it decided to nostalgically dub "Mountain Dew Throwback" and "Pepsi Throwback." Using all-natural sweeteners popular during the 1960s and '70s, the "throwback" campaign even included a Facebook app designed to make a Facebook user's photo "retro" or pose him or her behind a retro-looking template. Well, the viral buzz was absolutely staggering, garnering "over 2 million website mentions, 24,000 blog posts, hundreds of YouTube videos combined with a whirlwind of Facebook and Twitter activity." [19]

On the luxury side, Louis Vuitton recently rolled out nostalgic ads featuring Sean Connery and Catherine Deneuve, symbols of the lacquered glamour of Old Hollywood. Another Vuitton ad recalls a bygone era by featuring astronauts Buzz Aldrin, Sally Ride, and Jim Lovell, each representing a past generation of space explorers. They're perched in a secondhand Western pickup truck, gazing up at the night sky, but they might as well be glancing back, awestruck, at history itself.

When you think about it, this strategy is really quite brilliant. By rereleasing ads and commercials from our youth (or in the case of Michelin, our grandparents' youth), companies are not only triggering our nostalgia for that time; they're creating an association in our brains between our rosy memories of the era and their product. It doesn't matter if we never once ate Heinz beans or banked at Citibank in our lives. Those old ads still trigger memories of all the other things we lovingly remember from that time (while at the same time costing the company next to nothing).

In Boynton Beach, Florida, a town populated mostly by retirees, a new free publication entitled *Nostalgic America* attempts to hook senior citizens by pairing local ads with iconic images from yesteryear. For example, a photograph of the Beatles' 1964 *Ed Sullivan Show* appearance accompanies an ad for a long-term-care facility, and a photo of Gene Kelly crooning "Singin' in the Rain" is pictured alongside a business selling "final-expense insurance." [20] What about the 1951 ad for the debut of the

TV classic *I Love Lucy* situated next to a reverse-mortgage pitch? Still, few crafty advertising campaigns aimed at seniors can compare with the Social Security Administration tapping musician Chubby Checker to promote its program in ads that feature a black-and-white video of Checker doing the twist with dancers dressed in 1960s attire. As Mr. Checker comes into color, he says, "A new twist in the law makes it easier than ever to save on your Medicare prescription drug plans."[21]

It might not surprise you to learn that your everyday supermarket, not just those high-end megastores like Whole Foods, is lousy with examples of nostalgia marketing. Let's look at cereals. Note that the iconic Tony the Tiger—who has been around since 1952—on the box of Frosted Flakes is appealing to the child buried inside the adult who dreamed of growing up to be strong and powerful. Similarly, the Australian brand Neutragrain, most commonly consumed by males between the ages of forty and fifty, is aggressively marketed to the little boy who wants to someday grow up to become an Iron Man hunk (the brand is the official sponsor of the 2011 Iron Man series, and if you go to the Web site, you'll be assaulted by photos of youthful, ripped athletes). I would also argue that cereal in and of itself is a nostalgia product. Go to any college or university cafeteria and you'll find a surprising number of homesick students shoveling the stuff into their mouths. Why? Sure, they might like the taste, but it's also a lifeline to their parents, to comfort, and to the familiarity of childhood. Cheerios, Trix, and Cocoa Puffs have all undergone a 180-degree retro repackaging and are sold nowadays in vintage boxes. And if you really want to step into a time machine, watch one of those "new" black-and-white Rice Krispies commercials in which Mom, Dad, Grandma, and their precious band of little ones mix up some Rice Krispies treat memories.

The retro food marketing trend doesn't stop with cereal. In 2009 Nabisco brought out vintage renditions of Ritz crackers and Oreo cookies, while Hawaiian Punch has brought back its classic tagline, "How about a nice Hawaiian Punch?" and Jiffy Pop popcorn tells consumers, "Some things are even better than you remember." And a few years ago, Anheuser-Busch rolled out a reproduction of its first-ever Budweiser can from 1936, complete with a three-step illustration showing consumers how to drink the thing (back in those days, beer in a can was unheard of). Speaking of dated beverages, could that possibly be Tab on the soda shelf? Tab, the favorite soft drink of countless female dieters from the 1970s, is still around? You bet, and its original lettering in an oversize, jutting font has even been retained. It's straight out of *That Girl* or *The Partridge Family*.

Past the soda aisle, we make our way toward a vast selection of chocolates. Whitman's Samplers? Funny, the box looks like a patchwork quilt, just like the one Grandma used to have. Werther's caramels? Anyone remember the TV ads where Robert Rockwell played the kindly grandfather lovingly offering a caramel to his sweet, innocent-looking grandson? Talk about nostalgia.

And in 2007, the frozen food brand Swanson, rebranding itself as "Swanson classics," relaunched a line of "original TV dinners," which included such 1950s staples as chicken pot pie, Salisbury steak with corn and mashed potatoes, and meatloaf—all served in that iconic, segmented Styrofoam tray of our youth, of course.

Marketers know that we as consumers are hungry for any relic of our past, and not just when it comes to food. When we buy a Monopoly or Parcheesi set or a Rubik's cube, for example, we aren't just buying a toy or a game; we're purchasing a trip back to our childhood. This is why Target has reintroduced what the chain calls "selected retro toys," including sock monkeys and gumball machines. We're even more likely to buy a game that a brand rolled out last week but that *looks* like a relic of our youth. Take the popular Hasbro game Taboo. It was introduced in the late nineties but includes an old-school hourglass instead of a timer (which always makes me think of *The Wizard of Oz*, another childhood classic) and has a very simple, retro look.

Nostalgia is also one reason why Best Buy, the giant electronics retailer, has recently devoted shelf space in one hundred stores around the United States to LP records (yes, you read that right, LPs, those bizarre black spinning things that make a crackling sound when the needle reaches the end). Despite the fact that most CD stores have closed to make way for the MP3 generation, vinyl is making a serious comeback. Go on eBay and you'll find people auctioning off thousands of old records—sometimes for hundreds of dollars or more. Facebook groups and fan sites for lovers of vinyl abound, and Best Buy has deemed its vinyl experiment an unqualified success.

Some brands and products are even going so far as to make up a past they don't have. How old do you think Baileys, the Irish whiskey-and-cream-based liqueur, is? A hundred? A hundred and fifty? After all, it terms itself "The Original" and comes in an "authentic-looking" bottle designed to denote the good old days. But in reality, Baileys Irish Cream will turn a mere thirty-seven this year. And those brands unwilling to invent a history can buy one; in an auction held last year in New York, defunct names like Lucky Whip, Handi-Wrap plastic wrap, and Snow Crop orange juice—and even such old-time media names as *Collier's* magazine and *Saturday Review*—came up for sale.[22] The winners not only bought a trusted, time-tested brand name; they purchased the memories of an entire generation.

Even *places* designed to recall the texture of a bygone era can be extraordinarily seductive. Think about your favorite restaurant or watering hole. Does it have the thick oak bar and wood paneling of a twenties saloon? The chrome booths, fluorescent lighting, and tabletop jukebox of a fifties diner? The dark mahogany and leather of an old eighteenth-century steakhouse? Does it actually date back to the era it's meant to re-create? Probably not. More likely some smart marketer knew that making it look and feel "old-fashioned" would help lure in crowds—and dollars. As a recent *New York Times* article reported, this has become a trend in New York's hip West Village neighborhood, where "a pride of reincarnated restaurants . . . each taking a different area of history for inspiration," have turned the neighborhood into a "theme park of the past." As the article goes on to note, "designers say it is important to give a room a detailed storyline that harks back to a more intimate way of life."[23]

The Future of the Past

"Happiness is not something you experience; it's something you remember,"[24] Oscar Levant was once quoted as saying. All these brands and companies I've talked about know that for most of us, the past is *always* better than the present; quite simply, it is how our brains are hard-wired. When you think about it, it's one of the nicer tricks our brains play on us, as it protects us from painful memories and instills in us an optimism that things will be good again. But the danger, of course, is that it also makes us unwitting suckers for anything—from bruised apples to sock monkeys to classic motorcycles—that reminds us of being young. And scarier still, sometimes all it takes is a subtle, subconscious cue like a few bars of a song or some old-fashioned lettering or a picture of a dead movie star to unleash that sly seductress, nostalgia, in us.

As America's roughly seventy-eight million baby boomers reach their sixties, there is no doubt in my mind that nostalgia will most likely play an even more integral role in marketing than it does today. At a time when technology is advancing at an ever-increasing pace, legendary brands and institutions from Woolworth's to Tower Records are toppling left and right, and nothing feels durable or lasting, we as consumers are clinging even more protectively to those brands that not only have endured from our childhoods but reawaken us and allow us to relive the memories from that simpler, more stable time.

Speaking of which, remember the woman I spoke about earlier in this chapter, who swears that the Mars bars from France taste better than the same Mars bars manufactured in the United States?

I believe her. Bear with me for a moment and you'll see why.

For the past few decades, I would say, nine out of ten new French parents have given their babies Evian water. For French parents, it's become a minor superstition of sorts: unless they give little François or Odile a bottle or cup of Evian, the child won't turn out to be a successful adult. Many young French families keep two separate bottles of water at home: Evian for their babies and another brand of bottled water for themselves. In the introduction to this book, I spoke about the influence parents have over their children's choice of brands and how, whether it's the ketchup or mustard in the fridge or the scent of shaving cream or perfume our parents used, we carry throughout our adult lives a fondness for those products we grew up with.

As it turns out, it's not just our personal past that can affect our brand preferences for years to come. We also have an abnormal attachment to past tastes and flavors of our history and culture. A few years back,

Danone, one of the world's largest food and beverage companies and the manufacturer of Evian water, decided that since it was so successful in France, why not try to penetrate China, which, with its more than one billion potential Evian drinkers, was a potentially lucrative market?

Normally, Danone taps its Evian water in the French Alps before shipping it to retailers and customers across the globe. But given that water is quite heavy, the costs of shipping all the way to China proved to be so financially challenging that Danone made a fateful executive decision. The company executives summoned French water-quality experts to inspect hundreds of local Chinese wells in an attempt to find one that met the quality of the French Evian water. Millions of dollars in expenses later, they uncovered the perfect well (or so they thought) and began pumping and manufacturing the Chinese variant of Evian water.

It was a flop, an across-the-board disaster. When you think about it, it's not hard to see why French consumers would turn their noses up at the stuff. After all, for many Westerners, China connotes pollution and industrial waste, not exactly qualities we'd want in our drinking water, especially if we were used to getting it from the verdant, picturesque, natural wonder in our backyard. But as it turned out, Chinese consumers wouldn't touch it either. What was going on?

As everyone knows, the taste of water is frustratingly difficult to put into words. Water tastes like everything; it tastes like nothing. It tastes like air; it tastes like glass; it tastes like a cold night. So an Evian research group tasked with figuring out why the Chinese hated the water so much decided not to bother asking them what they thought of the taste of the water; instead they asked them questions about their childhoods. Among them were "Where did you play when you were young?" "What was the first drink you recall drinking as a child?" and "Which drink did your parents forbid you to drink—but you drank anyway?"

The results explained everything.

Just two decades earlier, metropolitan cities like Beijing, Shanghai, and Guangzhou had been farmland, complete with crops, cows, and farming traditions. Roughly 60 percent of the Chinese labor force worked in agriculture; by 1990 this number had fallen to 30 percent. In the mid-1990s, it dropped further once the Chinese Industrial Revolution reorganized certain cities into economic redevelopment zones and the government bulldozed farmland in preparation for building factories.

Remember that most of the time we as consumers are seeking to activate and re-create taste memories from long ago, though we're not always conscious of it. This was what was going on with Evian water in China. Chinese consumers weren't used to the bustling, urban China of today. Most of them had grown up in agrarian surroundings that were more like the French Alps than modern-day Shenzhen—and had grown accustomed, like the French, to the faintest, subtlest taste of green vegetation in their drinking water, even the bottled stuff. Farmland can turn into factories, but memories are forever green, so when Evian rolled out the new China-sourced water, Chinese consumers felt deprived of the taste of their childhoods.

Which is where Evian's experts had gone wrong. They thought they were marketing to the China of today, not the China of yester-year. Based on the answers to the survey questions, Evian had no choice but to hunt down wells in China that, after filtration, still boasted a faint, grassy, moldy note. This wise shift in strategy not only altered how Danone and Evian decided to operate their future international businesses but today has made Danone the third-largest player in the Chinese water market.

Which is a long way of saying that I'll bet my American friend is right about those French Mars bars. To her, at least, they *do* taste better than the American ones.

Oh—this same friend recently joined Facebook. She's refriended several of her old classmates from her old French *lycée* (talk about reliving old times), and they all agree with her about the Mars bars. The probable cause: French cows, French milk, French grass growing on French soil. And maybe—okay, just maybe—nostalgia.

CHAPTER 7

Marketers' Royal Flush

THE HIDDEN POWERS OF CELEBRITY AND FAME

A ccording to nationwide polls, a faraway royal family's popularity ratings were tanking. The public was questioning, as they tended to do every few years, whether the royal family was really worth it. All that tax money spent maintaining palaces, paying guards, keeping up regal appearances, and for what? What exactly do the royals *do* to earn their keep? The royal family was facing a PR crisis, and their advisers were desperate. Which is when my telephone rang.

Would I be available to help strengthen the royal family's image? To advise it on how it might restore its high national ratings? In other words, could I help reinvent and reinvigorate the royal family's brand?

After a few conversations, I found myself in the employ of one of the more recognized families in the entire world.

There's something about royalty that ignites most people's imaginations and aspirations. After all, who wouldn't want to be a member of royalty and live a life of swank balls, elegant clothing, sumptuous food, shimmering diamonds, and attentive waitstaff? Royalty plays a part in every fairy tale and fantasy most children (and plenty of adults, too) ever read or see in the movies. As Marta Tantos Aranda, a design manager at LEGO's concept lab in Barcelona, Spain, notes, according to the company's studies, young girls are hardwired to grow up wanting to be princesses. "They even want to sleep with their princess costumes," she told me. Even the richest and most powerful people on earth, from billionaire CEOs to Hollywood megastars, turn into flustered, tongue-tied children when they come in contact with royalty, and even the richest, most successful CEOs in the world, including Bill Gates, pony up enormous sums to dine with the UK's royal family. It's because in our culture, royalty is the highest class there is: it's the ultimate celebrity, the pinnacle of fame, status, and envy.

What most people don't know, however, is that this image doesn't come easy. That behind the scenes, a royal family is actually a high-end brand like any other, one that is carefully, deliberately, and consistently cultivated and maintained. So much so that royal families across Europe actually meet on a regular basis to compare notes and exchange experiences and craft long-term strategies. As someone in the know once said to me, "The difference between a royal family and a brand is that a brand is focused on the next six months, while a royal family typically has a marketing plan for the next seventy-five years." Among other things, keeping up a royal image involves maintaining the delicate balance between fantasy and reality, distance and familiarity. It's important for the royals to stay relevant, but when they become *too* real, or overly familiar, they lose their magic.

In 2003, for example, when a reporter for the UK's *Daily Mirror*, working undercover as a palace footman at Buckingham Palace, snapped a photo of a Tupperware container adorning the royal breakfast table, the public was horrified.[1] They didn't want members of royalty using Tupperware! They wanted them to be eating from gilded bowls, using spoons of antique silver! But at the same time, if royals behave too loftily or high-handedly, they risk that the public, who generally foots their bill, may perceive them as haughty, remote, and out of touch.

In the industry, we call this the "pixie-dust phenomenon," and it springs from the idea that every time celebrities (and what they stand for) interact with the public, they either gain or lose some of their magic—their "pixie dust." When they become too familiar or reachable, the pixie dust dissipates. I've spent my fair share of time around celebrities, and it's true that the more time you spend with them, the more "normal" they become. Their mystery, magic, and authority vanish—a "brand withdrawal" occurs. Maintaining just the right amount of pixie dust is a fine balance that celebrity "brands" have to juggle every day—which is why when celebrities meet with their "real fans," managers and publicists typically limit these encounters to a half-hour maximum. And not many people know this, but the reason many royals wear those long gloves isn't just for elegance; it's to create an intentional psychological distance from members of the public.

From a historical standpoint, royal families really are the world's first-ever celebrities. Since practically the beginning of civilization, they've been the public face of their countries. They symbolize a nation's values and traditions. By commemorating anniversaries, birthdays, deaths, and even the passage of a new year, they unite a country's citizenry. They're living, breathing tourist bureaus, and as a result they bring in enormous amounts of capital, business, and industry. In short, they're brands, and lucrative ones, too. In the case of the British royal family, "the link between the British Crown and Corporate Brand management is not as obtuse as might first appear," says one study, which points out that many of the royal family's members refer to the monarchy as "The Firm" . . . and goes on to quote a prominent British historian as saying, "In the age of democracy, the crown has to be like any other brand. It has to win the respect of the people."[2]

The present-day English House of Windsor can even be said to have invented the concept of "merchandising" royalty. In order to control the Queen's image and ensure she appeared exactly as we recognize her from stamps, coins, currency, and posters, the British royal family rolled out an "image-control system." Then, as now, whenever the public interacts with the Queen at dinners or receptions, the royal photographer is the only person permitted to take her photograph. Well, naturally, everyone and her mother wants to have their photo taken with the Queen, so the royal photographer will sell these photos to you, for a hefty price (online, you can also buy your picture of yourself standing beside the Queen).

But back to *my* royal family and its brand, which two years ago was in trouble and needed a shot of pixie dust. I started off with a campaign that appealed to that country's (sorry, I can't say which one) sense of national responsibility, reminding the public that every great monarchy needs to trust and *believe* in its royal family. Study after study shows that if a citizenry believes in something, the national death rate goes down and people generally are happier, live longer, and use fewer social services—all information I took pains to make very public. I also felt we had to remind the country's citizens that the royal family was the pinnacle of citizenship, responsibility, and public service; royal dinners and champagne brunches would no longer do the trick. Accordingly, we arranged for members of the family to carry out a new set of duties for assorted handpicked, high-profile charities.

Next I hired an archivist to plumb the history books to uncover forgotten rituals we could resurrect. My research over the years has shown that consumers forge greater emotional attachments (and are therefore more loyal to) brands that have rituals surrounding them—and that creating a sense of mystery around a brand or product is another highly effective branding strategy. Lucky for me, royal families have many centuries-old rituals, stories, mythologies, symbols, and ceremonies unknown to the general public. Many of these rituals are, in fact, designed to protect the royal family from embarrassing moments—and in general to "control" the public (like the unspoken rule that commoners should never address members of the royal family unless the royal addresses them first and that commoners *must* use the right titles, both of which serve as reminders that commoners are subordinate to the glittering, highborn royals standing before them). The royal family I work for actually offers training sessions for its younger members in which, among other things, they're taught the proper way to shake hands with "commoners."

In my time working for the royal family, I've learned about many secret rituals and traditions that I'm not permitted to divulge, but I can tell you this much: every single royal family in the world knows that the best—and quickest—way to boost its popularity ratings is to host a royal wedding. (Think of the publicity storm surrounding Prince William's wedding to Kate Middleton and you'll know what I mean.) A close second? The arrival of a royal baby. Make that lots and lots of royal babies. You want a royal home run? Have twins! This was a feat the Danish royal family managed to carry off in 2011 for the first time in modern history—boosting its countrywide popularity ratings by several percentage points. Remember, the more little princes and princesses that pop forth, the greater likelihood of future weddings and future births and thus continued popularity (now you know what I mean when I say that royal families have a marketing plan that extends for decades).

At this point you might be thinking, *Okay, well, this is interesting, but what does it have to do with us?* After all, the United States doesn't even have a royal family. Well, while that's true technically, we do have our own variation on royalty. There are Brad Pitt, Angelina Jolie, Julia Roberts, Reese Witherspoon, George Clooney, Tom Cruise, Katie Holmes, Will Smith, Justin Timberlake, Kim Kardashian, Ryan Seacrest, Barack and Michelle Obama, and so many more the head reels. In our culture, celebrities *are* the kings and queens. And you'd better believe that our marketers and advertisers are just as shrewd at using their fame to brandwash us as the royal family's advisers are at selling their royal brand to their constituencies.

Cinderella Really Did Eat Our Daughters

At this point you might be wondering, *Can a famous face really have that much of an impact on how we spend our money?* Surely we're not that naive, are we?

The answer is yes, we are. What's more, the lure of celebrity begins earlier in life than you'd think. By the time most young boys reach the ripe old age of three or four, they've already begun to worship super-heroes like Batman, Superman, Spider-Man, X-Men, or whoever the marketers at Marvel or Pixar have decided the popular new hero du jour should be. By the time they're seven or eight, many have transferred this giddy adoration onto flesh-and-blood heroes—usually athletes like David Beckham, Dale Earnhardt, Derek Jeter, and Peyton Manning. Companies, of course, know this, which is why there are so many celeb-rity spokespeople for products marketed to young boys. "When LEGO signed an endorsement deal with Ferrari when [racecar driver] Michael Schumacher was still driving, the license became huge in Germany," re-calls Mads Nipper, executive vice president of market and products for LEGO. "And LEGO was able to ride that wave." In short, LEGO may have been a strong brand, but celebrity was even stronger.

Why superheroes and sports stars? Remember in chapter 2, when I talked about how fear-based marketing plays on our insecurities about becoming some feared future self? Well, marketing strategies centered on celebrity do the exact opposite: they appeal to fantasies about our *idealized* future selves. Thanks to the psychological studies they conduct and the consultants they hire (I know because I'm one of them), marketers are keenly aware that the vast majority of young boys dream of growing up to become strong and powerful. And, in turn, they will be drawn to heroes with special powers—supernatural, athletic, or otherwise. Case in point: I know one American man whose mother gave him a jet-black Batman suit, plus accessories, when he was five years old. He's well into middle age now, but he still remembers how powerful he felt, with his chintzy little bat boomerang cinched to his waist. He wasn't just dressed as Batman, he recalled forty-five years later—he *was* Batman.

As for girls? In general, young girls are seduced less by powerful figures. Their ideal future selves are graceful, feminine, and stunningly beautiful—hence the princess fantasy that is so pervasive in our culture. In her recent book, *Cinderella Ate My Daughter*, journalist Peggy Orenstein looks at why the princess has become synonymous with the feminine ideal. Among other things, she cites the "princess industrial complex" and all the ways in which companies and marketers are peddling the princess fantasy to our young daughters (and making boatloads of money in the process). As Orenstein points out, with more than twenty-six thousand Disney princess items on the market, " 'princess' is not only the fastest-growing brand the company has ever created; it's the largest franchise on the planet for girls ages two to six." [3]

Marta Tantos Aranda explains that little girls start out wanting to be princesses, but later on "their role model isn't just Hannah Montana or a young gymnast they've seen on TV, but very often an older, typically gorgeous teenage girl with long blond hair." So if the Disney princess is the idealized image of girlhood, the brand that best represents teens' and tweens' idealized (if completely unrealistic) image of womanhood is none other than Barbie (who will turn fifty-three this year). To be sure, this blond bombshell has had her critics, but whether you approve of her and her unnatural proportions or not, you can't deny her celebrity—or her profitability; Mattel estimates that two Barbie dolls are sold somewhere in the world every second of every day, with total sales around $1.5 billion annually[4] (which represents one fifth of Mattel's yearly revenue). When you think about it, it really isn't altogether shocking that Barbie has endured as one of the most famous cultural icons—and one of the most famous brands—of the past half century. After all, she was designed and marketed to represent exactly what every girl, no matter what decade she's born in, wants to be: beautiful, glamorous, popular, and adored.

This is also the appeal of a much newer pop-culture idol, Miley Cyrus. In case you don't have a preteen daughter at home, this famous young lady is the star of *Hannah Montana*, a wildly popular TV show about a teenager named Miley Stewart who's an ordinary schoolgirl by day but by night, disguised in a blond wig, is a hugely successful pop star known as Hannah Montana. Just as sports stars do for boys, Hannah Montana appeals to tween and teen girls' fantasies about their ideal selves; Cyrus is unselfconscious, fun, wild, and bold—everything an insecure teenage girl would like her future self to be (plus, name me one kid who hasn't lip-synched with a fake microphone before a bedroom mirror).

If these are the heroes we have as children, what happens when we grow up? Clearly our obsession with fame and celebrity doesn't end in childhood. Well, in the same way that most young boys want to grow up to be superheroes and most young girls want to be princesses (though granted, there are exceptions), the ideal "future self" for most adults, male or female, is more or less universal: rich, attractive, and famous.

I've been asked more than once to "brand" a celebrity, the most recent being a well-known television star. In general I use the same playbook I use with royalty, with a few crucial differences. Unlike royal families, celebrities lack bloodlines, history, timeworn rituals, or pageantry (other than strolling the red carpet at one of the year's countless awards ceremonies). And unlike royal families, traditional celebrities have attained fame through talent (though this is becoming less and less the case, and if you don't believe me, watch a season or two of *Dancing with the Stars*), whether that talent is acting, singing, dancing, or athleticism (although sheer good looks don't hurt either). Yes, our celebrities are like disposable royals in that they are wealthy, powerful, and surrounded by a squadron of agents, managers, publicists, and bodyguards.

But the most important thing they have in common is our envy. We want to *be* them. Barring that, we want to be *like* them. So I suppose it's no surprise that advertisers and marketers pay celebrities of all stripes—from actors to athletes to reality TV stars—enormous sums of money to sell us everything from clothing to cars to breakfast cereal to sports drinks.

Most people are aware that celebrity marketing exists (after all, it's hard to miss). But what many are unaware of is how well it's working. According to an online survey sent to eleven thousand adults and teens across the country, the large majority of us believe that the celebrities who appear in advertising or endorsements do not—repeat, *do not*—affect our purchasing decisions. In fact, more than 80 percent of respondents claimed they would buy the products they like, regardless of whether or not there was a celebrity endorsement.

Well, guess what? I believe them. At least I believe they don't *think* they're being seduced or persuaded by celebrity advertising. But that's exactly the point. As the chief industry analyst of NPD Insights, Marshal Cohen, points out, "Sometimes it is an unseen influence that triggers the consumer's attention or encourages a product purchase. A celebrity-associated product can be a very powerful, subliminal purchase influence. In some cases, it may even be the reason a consumer recognizes a brand or product, just based on the mere fact a celebrity is associated with it." [5]

Studies have also shown that when celebrities appear in advertisements or endorse products, not only do we perceive the brand message as more authentic, but it also enhances our recognition and recall of the product in question. So when we see that product (whether it's Sarah Jessica Parker's perfume, the Triscuits with Rachael Ray on the box, or the Nike sneaker endorsed by Rafael Nadal), we reach instinctively and often quite unconsciously for that product over the non-celebrity-branded variety.

There's even evidence to suggest that the persuasive power of celebrity is biologically based. One Dutch study found that seeing a celebrity endorse a product—in this case a pair of shoes—actually alters a woman's brain activity. In this fascinating study, researchers scanned twenty-four women's brains as they viewed forty color photos of both famous and nonfamous women, all wearing the same footwear. Results showed that when the women looked at the celebrity photos, there was heightened activity in a part of the brain associated with the feeling of affection (the medial orbitofrontal cortex), activity that was absent when the women looked at the photos of the noncelebrities.[6] Another recent UK study, which found that even average, ho-hum-looking celebrity models in ads produce a more intense emotional response in us than breathtakingly gorgeous noncelebrity endorsers, concluded that not only is fame even more powerful than beauty in persuading us to buy something, but there may actually be *a dedicated area of the human brain* that's become hardwired to respond positively to celebrity-endorsed products.[7]

Given that humans appear to have a practically innate attraction to fame (it also helps that talk of celebrities, like the weather or sports, establishes common conversational ground among relative strangers and helps us feel a sense of belonging), I suppose it's no surprise that over the past decade the number of "famous" people in the press has tripled. You read that right: *tripled.* Thanks to reality TV and the Internet, both of which have provided all kinds of new (if somewhat ridiculous) avenues for celebrity, the boundaries of what it means to be "famous" have expanded beyond our wildest imaginations. Celebrities aren't just athletes and movie stars anymore; today they include YouTube sensations (like Chris Crocker, the Britney Spears "superfan"), MySpace phenomena (think Tila Tequila), celebrity bloggers (like Perez Hilton), and, of course, reality television personalities (too many to name), many of whom have inexplicably managed to parlay their fifteen minutes of fame into an hour, at least. Accordingly, the percentage of ads worldwide using celebrities has doubled (to roughly 17 percent) in the past decade.[8] And let's not forget celebrities who are famous just for *serving* celebrities: all the doctors, dentists, plastic surgeons, real estate agents, chefs, bloggers, fashion designers, cosmeticians, hairdressers, party planners, choreographers, and florists to the stars. As Hamish Pringle writes in *Celebrity Sells*, the proportion of UK ads featuring a celebrity is now one in five, an increase of nearly 100 percent in a single decade. In the United States, this figure stands at one in four.[9]

It's not just actors, rock stars, and basketball players, like it used to be in the old days of celebrity marketing. Today's product sponsors and spokespeople include talk show hosts (Kelly Ripa for Electrolux), TV chefs (Gordon Ramsay for Gordon's Gin), former boxers (George

Foreman hawking his best-selling grill), politicians (Bob Dole for Viagra), business moguls (Twitter cofounder Biz Stone for Stoli vodka), celebrity spawn (Billy Joel and Christie Brinkley's daughter Alexa Ray Joel for Prell), and home wreckers (golfer Tiger Woods's alleged mistresses for the auction site Bidhere.com).

As you're about to read, companies and marketers not only recognize that the boundaries of fame are expanding, they are coming up with all kinds of sneaky and underhanded new ways of exploiting our obsession with this new breed of celebrity to the fullest. *That's* what makes celebrities such a powerful hidden persuader.

I Want to Be Like Mike

Just so we're all on the same page, let's define a celebrity as a symbol or an icon who possesses and represents a variety of desirable attributes to which many of us aspire. It could be beauty, charm, sex appeal, glamour, coolness, suaveness, outrageousness, musicianship, or athleticism—you name it. When I talk about celebrity-driven marketing or advertising, I'm not talking about celebrities simply lending their names to a brand or slapping their faces on an ad or package. Of course, these tactics do work, but it goes deeper than that. I'm talking about a more subtle psychological maneuver whereby we as consumers are duped into believing that a celebrity has almost alchemically transposed his or her attributes onto a food, a drink, an automobile, a perfume, a face cream, a luggage brand, a credit card, and so forth, in a process so seamless that we're subconsciously persuaded that by purchasing said product we are essentially purchasing a piece of the celebrity.

To many of us, celebrities are living the dream. Each time we pick up a gossip magazine or watch an awards show, we're instantly seduced by the red carpets, $10,000 dresses, attractive spouses, perfect complexions, Fifth Avenue penthouses, and beachfront Malibu estates. During insecure economic times, celebrities' lives appear especially idyllic, seemingly untouched by the everyday troubles and responsibilities that mark most of our days (interestingly, Peggy Orenstein writes that the princess craze escalated during the recent recession). *I'll bet Julia Roberts doesn't have to take out a second mortgage,* we think sourly. *Why can't my life be that easy?* Well, buy Julia's brand of lipstick, or perhaps a handbag, advertisers imply, and it can be.

If this sounds overly simplistic or as though perhaps I'm not giving consumers enough credit, think again. An interesting study carried out by researchers at Duke University's Fuqua School of Business and Canada's University of Waterloo found that even fleeting exposure to an established brand—like Apple or Coke—can actually cause us to *take on the behaviors* championed or represented by those brands.[10] For example, just being exposed to an Apple logo, a brand widely associated with creativity, made people think more imaginatively. So, since celebrities are fabulous, can't exposure to their brands cause some of that same fabulousness to rub off on us, too?

There's no question that slathering on a movie star–endorsed face cream, perfume, or eye shadow makes us feel that much closer to our favorite celebrity and everything about that celebrity we envy. We carry him or her with us all day. And in turn, we adopt his or her values and attributes, too—his or her swagger, attitude, talent, individuality, coolness, or allure. In short, in effect we *become* that celebrity—in the deeper recesses of our brains, at least.

Wear the same Dolce & Gabbana makeup Scarlett Johansson wears, and you can become as sultry and beautiful as Scarlett is. Buy a house that bears Fergie's provenance, however tenuous (e.g., she lived two blocks over, once), and you can look out onto views Fergie's eyes once scanned. Spritz on Jennifer Lopez's or Halle Berry's perfume, and you can smell as irresistible as they do, and so on. This may sound a little extreme, maybe even hard to believe. But in fact it's a common psychological phenomenon known as transference, a term that refers to our tendency to subconsciously transplant our feelings about some person or thing onto another.

Ever try the South Beach Diet? Named for a glamorous, art deco Miami neighborhood and created by Dr. Arthur Agatston, a Miami cardiologist, it's an eating plan designed to help you lose weight by eliminating cravings for sugar and refined starches. Anyway, you probably would never have heard of the book, which was published in 2003 by Rodale Press, if something incredible hadn't happened.

When former president Bill Clinton, renowned for his love of fast food, announced in late 2004 he was waiting to undergo heart bypass surgery, he made reference in interviews to losing weight on the South Beach Diet.[11] And not only that, he told the press, but Hillary Clinton was on it, too. Suddenly, sales of the book went through the roof, and today, the South Beach Diet is not only one of the best-known diets in the United States (perhaps second only to Atkins), the book has sold more than five million copies.[12]

This seemingly mundane episode highlights exactly why celebrity is such a powerful persuader. By buying *The South Beach Diet*, consumers were able to share the eating habits of one of the most famous and powerful political couples in American history. As an added bonus, they could even shed excess pounds of their own along the way. Whatever your politics, whatever your values, I'm betting that the Clintons embody *some* attribute to which you aspire. Power. Brains. Charisma. Charm. Determination. Plus, studies have found food to be a powerful emotional connector. So if we sample, say, the recipe for chicken puttanesca that Bill Clinton favors, it literally makes us feel closer to the former president, just as when we wear Michael Jordan's sneakers and feel the same bounce to our step, we imagine we can play just like him. Or when we wear Kate Moss's Calvin Klein underwear and feel how it must feel against her hips, we imagine ourselves as sultry and seductive as she is. Or when eating Campbell's Chunky soup, we can feel as mighty as Philadelphia Eagles quarterback Donovan McNabb—and picture the fans cheering for us as we stride onto an (imaginary) field.

Rationally, we know this is foolish and delusional. But emotionally? That's another matter.

A Star Is Born

To better understand just how companies prey on this fundamental aspect of our psychology, let's look at Vitaminwater, a brand (now owned by Coke) that would be nothing without celebrities. A few years back, the marketers of Vitaminwater came up with a very clever plan. Why not give celebrities shares in the company in return for endorsing the brand? This shrewd arrangement accomplished two things. First, it got Vitaminwater an all-star team of celebrity endorsers (including rapper 50 Cent, who's made a fortune from the shares he owns in the company) fairly cheaply. Second, and perhaps more important, now that these celebrities had some stake in the company, it gave them the motivation to position themselves on camera, whenever possible, sipping the sugary drink. Most recently, Ellen DeGeneres conducted a live commercial for noncaloric Vitaminwater Zero, right in the middle of her popular TV talk show. After taking a few sips, Ellen, or rather, a very athletic stand-in, did backflips across the stage to show how much energy the stuff gave her. Quite an endorsement indeed.

Marketers are very aware that when celebrities are photographed or caught on video with a product, sales go through the roof, particularly when the photo is a "candid"—a shot of said celebrity using or enjoying the product while simply going about his or her "normal" routine. Take, for example, what happened in 2007, when former Spice Girl and soccer wife Victoria Beckham was caught on camera buying the then-unknown cookbook *Skinny Bitch* in an LA boutique. Though it had been a best seller in the UK, you could barely give it away in the United States. That is, until Beckham came along: as soon as that photo hit the entertainment mags, online sales shot up by 37,000, inaugurating the book's eighty-four weeks on the *New York Times* best-seller list.[13]

But of course, these photos aren't nearly as "candid" as they seem. Knowing full well what a gold mine such a photo can be, marketers and advertisers have been even more persistent—and clever—in their attempts to "catch" celebrities on camera using their product or brand. Vitaminwater did this quite successfully during Fashion Week 2009, when the company placed free bottles on the seats closest to the runway—the seats typically occupied only by A-list celebrities—ensuring that legions of A-list attendees, from Sarah Jessica Parker to Tyra Banks to Heidi Klum, would be seen drinking, or at least holding, a bottle of the drink for a couple of seconds before taking their seats.

Apparently, celebrities don't even have to be human to be effective persuaders. In South America, one of the sponsors of a TV reality show called *La Granja VIP* is a dog food brand known as Masterdog. In order to shine through the clutter of thirty-second ads (as you may remember from my last book, the more a brand is integrated into the content of a TV show, the more likely consumers are to remember it), Masterdog insisted the show it was sponsoring add another recurring contestant—a golden retriever known as (what else?) Master. The canine contestant was so popular and talked about, Master became a celebrity virtually overnight. Of course, dog food sales skyrocketed.[14]

Interestingly, the power of celebrity even has a trickle-down effect to celebrities' children. Several years ago, Fox News reported that Angelina Jolie and Brad Pitt's children are "the world's most imitated little nippers. . . . From baby carriers to hairstyles to T-shirts to international adoption," the article stated, "people are literally copying the ways of Jolie's adopted . . . Cambodian son Maddox and his wide-eyed . . . Ethiopian sister Zahara."[15] Case in point: When Maddox was photographed wearing a T-shirt reading, "Human Cannon Ball," shirt maker Inky-DinkTees' sales shot up.[16] Apparently, according to a company spokesperson, the company's online store has a "How did you hear about us?" section, and most of the people who bothered to write in wrote, "Saw it on Maddox." We seem to quite literally want *everything* Jolie and Pitt have; as Cheryl Carter-Shotts, director of Americans for African Adoption, told *People* magazine, her organization "began to be flooded with calls and e-mails from people wanting information" after *People* magazine ran a story about Jolie's adoption of her Ethiopian daughter.[17] From the BabyBjörn Original (the brand of stroller favored by the rich and famous) to Marc Jacobs diaper bags to even designer diapers (yes, the designer Cynthia Rowley has joined forces with Pampers to create eleven different styles and patterns, available at Target),[18] if we associate something with a celebrity, we just have to have it for our child.

And what about this? Celebrities even influence the names we choose to give our children. In 2009, according to the Social Security Administration, the names growing fastest in popularity were Malia (the name of President Obama's older daughter) for girls and Cullen (the surname of the heartthrob vampire protagonist in Stephenie Meyer's *Twilight* series of megabest-selling books and blockbuster movies) for boys. Sharing the number one spot were names of two other *Twilight* characters, Jacob and Bella (okay, to be fair, Jacob and Isabella have been popular names for more than a decade, but it's no coincidence they rose to the top the year *Twilight* mania reached its peak).[19] Also on the rise in 2009 were such famous names as Khloe (as in Kardashian), Scarlett (as in Johansson), Violet (the name Ben Affleck and Jennifer Garner gave to their daughter), and Valentina (as in Salma Hayek's daughter) for girls; and for boys, Jett (the name of John Travolta's late son), Romeo (David Beckham and Posh Spice's newborn baby), and Maddox (see above). Among the names disappearing from the top-hundred list—as the careers of their namesakes either imploded or faded away—were Lindsay (as in Lohan) and Tori (as in Spelling).

Making us feel like celebrities or royalty (or some unholy combination of the two) has long been a marketing strategy of choice within the travel, hospitality, banking, and gaming industries. These companies know full well that none of us likes to think of ourselves as mere ordinary citizens. That's why, for over thirty years, American Express has trotted out its celebrity "members," including Robert De Niro, Jerry Seinfeld, Quincy Jones, and, most recently, Tina Fey to lure customers into its exclusive "club" (which, of course, isn't exclusive at all—anyone willing to pay the exorbitant annual fee can join). Creating this illusion of exclusivity has been so effective that companies of all stripes are trying to seduce us with everything from "preferred member" upgrades and priority statuses to sapphire cards, silver cards, gold cards, platinum cards, and titanium cards to presidential limousines, Emerald Club memberships, and executive elite suites—the vast majority of which, I might add, are advertised by some famous face or another. Remember the funny American Express commercial from a few years back in which Tina Fey gets shut out of the executive airport lounge and almost misses a chance to sit down with none other than Martin Scorsese . . . that is, until a cheerful airline employee informs her that, not to worry, her AmEx Green Card allows her entry! The message of ads like this is *Buy our product or use our service, and you can enjoy the same status, perks, and even fame as your favorite celebrity.*

"Thanks to marketers and reality TV shows that have shown access to excess, VIP status has become more attainable," confided a Las Vegas nightclub impresario I spoke to. "It has nothing to do with social status. It's purely monetary, a form of peacocking—a momentary experience of elitism." He sighed. "You have to wonder, is it really worth it to pay six hundred dollars for a bottle of thirty-dollar Grey Goose vodka, just to feel like a celebrity for one night?"

I admit it, even a marketing guy like me isn't immune to these tricks. For more than a dozen years, I've been traveling the world with Lufthansa Airlines. Because of my chaotic traveling schedule and innumerable frequent-flyer miles, I've long been one of the airline's top-rated members. Recently I checked in at the Zurich, Switzerland, airport and proceeded to the first-class lounge, where the hostess politely informed me that because of internal changes too boring to go into, I was now two thousand miles short of becoming "a member of the club." I'd been demoted to the "Senator" level, and I wasn't happy about it. Hey, I didn't want to be a senator! Like George Clooney's character in *Up in the Air*, I wanted to achieve the most elite flying status there is! Even though I *knew* the whole club thing was a marketing tactic carefully devised to seal my loyalty to Lufthansa, I still felt the sting of rejection and inadequacy. *How pathetic can you get, Senator Lindstrom?* I wondered.

I Feel Pretty

A poster bearing life-sized images of actresses du jour Dakota Fanning and Kristen Stewart greets me as I walk into Sephora, the global cosmetics chain. It's a promotional ad for their new film, *The Runaways*, which chronicles the mid-1970s evolution of rocker Joan Jett and her grungy all-girl band. According to the ad copy, "These Make Up Essentials were used on the set of 'The Runaways,' to re-create the film's smoky-eyed 1970s look." It would seem that the collection's three products are key to achieving dark, smudgy lids—the epitome of rocker-girl chic.[20]

In short, what this ad is saying is that young women can not only get the look of Dakota Fanning and Kristen Stewart, but they can also channel Joan Jett herself. It's a one-two punch: the cosmetics secrets of an iconic rock star, plus those of hip young celebrities playing iconic rock stars!

I don't know, they all look like burned-out baby raccoons to me.

Those aren't the only famous faces you'll find in the Sephora aisles. There might be roughly 250,000 products in the store, but my eyes can't help but be riveted to the back wall where I can make out the oversized letters spelling out, "The Doctors."

Since the boundaries of celebrity are bulging at the edges, why shouldn't Sephora promote a celebrity doctor or two? Let's take a look. First up is celebrity dermatologist and best-selling author Dr. Nicholas Perricone, MD, who "recommends"—i.e., advertises—not only an assortment of high-priced skin-care products and kits (his RX3 anti-aging regimen retails at $603) but also a line of "nutriceutical" dietary supplements—Dr. Perricone's special blend of ninety-nine nutrients that allegedly enhance our health, optimize our energy, and help us manage our weight. Garbed in a white medical smock, Dr. Perricone, who has appeared on *Oprah, Today,* and *20/20,* has been featured in virtually every major newspaper and can be seen regularly on QVC (naturally, he also has a popular blog, an impressive Twitter following, and even his own iPhone app) and looks uncannily like David Hasselhoff's wiser, sterner brother (the one who refused to go into the water because it was bad for his skin). Some of Dr. Perricone's wrinkle serums and moisturizers are even packaged in old-fashioned brown bottles like you might see in an old apothecary, to emphasize the "medical" feel. Celebrity tinged with nostalgia, anyone?

The famous physician's "Camera Ready" box is an ensemble that trumpets "Dr. Perricone's celebrity secrets for creating luminous, youthful, gorgeous skin." Among other things, the box includes "Neuropeptide Facial Contour, a true Hollywood must-have," which, at $325 an ounce, also serves as a "red-carpet-prep secret weapon."[21] Next to the shrine to Dr. Perricone sits the skin-enhancing beauty line promoted by another celebrity doctor, Dr. Dennis Gross. Gross is consistently featured in fashion and beauty magazines including *Vogue, Elle,* and *Harper's Bazaar*—at least according to his Web site, where, in another nod to the power of exclusivity—or at least the illusion of it—we are invited to join the "Beauty VIP Club."[22] In short, it's star doctors telling us how we can look like a star. What could be more persuasive than that?

The infiltration of the medical profession within the beauty industry would seem to be the ultimate seal of approval, the equivalent of getting the go-ahead from an actual general practitioner. Which is why, more and more, consumers are seeing the reassuring stamps "Doctor-Recommended" and "Dermatologist-Approved" atop their medicine bottles and skin-care products. There's even an entire brand known as Physicians Formula, but when you go to its Web site, there's not a doctor in sight.[23]

Yet who *are* these famous doctors and dermatologists who go around giving their seal of approval to various medicines? What are their credentials, exactly? Good question. A quick glance at the bottle's small print says nothing (except in Germany, where many brands get around this problem by announcing, "Approved by Doctors' Wives"). The truth is that all pharmaceutical companies employ well-compensated physicians as advisers; and many doctors even sit on cosmetics company boards. In other words, the doctors and dermatologists who "approve" these products are usually positioned to reap some of the company's profits. Still, companies are more than happy to keep these doctors on their payroll. Why? Because as we'll see later in this chapter, recommendations from "experts" are worth their weight in gold.

Back at Sephora, the lure of celebrity picks up again two aisles later, with a line of skin-care products created by Philosophy, a brand whose Web site proclaims it is "adored by celebrities, dermatologists and most importantly, their customers."[24] Many of Philosophy's clever product names are borrowed from Hollywood, like Dark Shadows (after a popular vampire-themed soap opera from the 1960s and '70s) and Miracle Worker (after the Oscar-winning movie). And nearby, the LORAC brand (which bills itself as the "Red Carpet authority") Hollywood Insider Collection offers an "All-access pass to Celebrity Make-up Artist Carol Shaw's Red Carpet beauty tips and tricks." The ad copy continues: "Carol hand-picked her favorite LORAC must-haves for this essential makeup collection that contains Perfectly Lit in Spotlight, Couture Shine Liquid Lipstick in Vintage, Baked Matte Satin Blush in Hollywood, Special Effects Mascara, and the exclusive Bronzed Bombshell Eye Shadow Trio. Get behind the scenes beauty with LORAC's Hollywood Insider Collection!" These ads whisper (or shout), *These are the products that all your favorite celebrities are using. Why aren't you?*

I Am a Celebrity and the Brand Is Me

Believe it or not, we're still not finished at Sephora. And what better place to see celebrity marketing in action than the perfume aisle, where among the brands for sale are perfumes named after Halle Berry, Mariah Carey, Elizabeth Taylor, Shania Twain, Britney Spears, Faith Hill, Gwen Stefani, Sarah Jessica Parker, and Beyoncé Knowles (who, incidentally, also appears in ads for Pepsi, Verizon, Samsung, L'Oréal, Vizio, Nintendo, American Express, House of Deréon, Samantha Thavasa handbags, and Crystal Geyser water).

On the male side, there are colognes attached to the famous names Justin Timberlake, David Beckham, Usher, Tim McGraw, Andre Agassi, and even Donald Trump. "We are confident that men of all ages want to experience some part of Mr. Trump's passion and taste for luxury," said Aramis president Fabrice Weber.[25] Actually, it appears they don't. In one of the few cases where putting a celebrity name on a product *didn't* work, a few years after it hit the shelves, according to one gimlet-eyed blogger, Donald Trump for Men could be found on clearance at T.J. Maxx for $8, down from $48.[26] The latest scent? Eau de Bruce Willis, which the manufacturer describes as the "manliest scent in the world," an aroma that allegedly captures the actor's "strength, self-assurance and single-mindedness."[27]

Of course, celebrity branding is nothing new in the multibillion-dollar fragrance industry. Decades ago, perfume companies and advertisers realized that a famous name could goad consumers into forming an intimate connection with a brand. And at the same time, celebrities realized they could potentially earn many millions of dollars licensing their names and images to a fragrance. Quick—can you name the most successful celebrity perfume of all time? Answer: it's Elizabeth Taylor's White Diamonds, with more than $1 billion in sales to date (typically, with this sort of arrangement, a celebrity takes anywhere from between 5 percent and 10 percent of a fragrance's total sales).[28]

Celebrities have long been aware of their value not just to fragrance and beauty companies but also to fashion designers. Giorgio Armani, the Italian designer (now a celebrity in his own right), got his start by setting up a Los Angeles studio and recruiting celebrities to wear his outfits, thus helping to create today's obsession with the outfits celebrities wear to the Oscars, Golden Globes, and countless other awards shows.

In recent years, however, celebs have taken this even one step further, as fading stars have realized that owning and launching their own product line can not only be lucrative but can help breathe new life into their careers. For Jennifer Lopez, who's licensed her name to a handful of scents, this tactic has paid off staggeringly well. In 2006, according to *Forbes*'s list of the twenty richest women in entertainment, sales of her fragrances not only accounted for $77 million of her net worth of $100 million,[29] but they gave JLo the added visibility and publicity boost that undoubtedly helped her end a dry period and snag a series of producer gigs as well as roles in the films *Monster-in-Law* and, more recently, *The Back-up Plan*.

A fragrance executive who had been involved in the launch of a global celebrity's line of perfume once told me an interesting story. The famous singer/actor in question had never worn cologne in his life (*sssshh!*) and hadn't a clue what he was doing, so fragrance company representatives visited the star at his home in search of inspiration. They went from room to room, jotting down notes about his sense of style and design (which weren't much to speak of, according to my friend) in an attempt to figure out both the values he projected and what he symbolized to his worldwide fan base. From there, the fragrance reps went back and created an assortment of scents. The star selected one, and the rest was all profit. The bottle and "the juice" cost next to nothing to produce, but thanks to the celebrity brand name, people were happy to shell out $60, $80, $100, or more for a few mere ounces of it.

Of course, celebrity brands are inordinately successful in other product categories, too. If you were to ask a group of fifteen-year-old kids today who Paul Newman is, most of them would answer, "a salad dressing" or "lemonade." That's because in 1982, after Paul Newman retired from his long film career, he rolled out a small Connecticut-based packaged foods business with his friend, the writer A. E. Hotchner. Having started the company on a whim, Newman had anticipated sales of roughly $1,200 annually; instead, over the past twenty-six years, Newman's Own has made close to $300 million (which it has distributed to various charities).

Then there are those countless celebrities who don't just create and sell a brand but *are* the brand. David Bowie was the first big pop icon to use classic marketing tactics to brand (and rebrand) himself. Just as successful brands like Pepsi, Old Spice, and Nike are constantly revamping their packages, redesigning their logos, and reinventing their public images, in 1973, at the height of his fame, Bowie shed his multiple identities as a glam rocker, a disaffected friend of Warhol, and Ziggy Stardust. Good-bye Ziggy, hello, well, you name it. On the cover of *Diamond Dogs*, Bowie appeared as half male, half canine. For his next album, he'd transformed himself again into an elegant, if unsettling, Aryan persona known as the "Thin White Duke." During his late-1980s world tour, when Bowie announced to his fans it would be the last time he would be playing "old material," "it was a huge public relations success, prompting sales of his newly re-mastered albums to skyrocket."[30] And as any lucrative brand would be clever to do, several years later, in 1997, Bowie issued "Bowie Bonds," asset-backed securities of both current and future revenues. The deal (and the attendant PR) netted the singer a cool $55 million up front.[31]

Madonna, of course, is another master at the art of personal rebranding. Most people are aware that she's gone through quite a few "looks" over the years, but what most people don't know is how strategically and shrewdly she works to project a new "brand image" of herself with each of her new musical releases. Whether it's the good girl gone to seed, a virgin dressed all in white, a spirit attired in Kabbalah beads, a pale, Michigan-born version of Marilyn Monroe, a cone-breasted robot, or a yoga-obsessed UK expatriate, the way she transforms how others see her is nothing short of marketing genius. As Jeffrey Katzenberg, the former chairman of Walt Disney Studios, was once quoted as saying, "She is always evolving: she never stands still. Every two years she comes up with a new look, a new way of presenting herself, a new attitude, a new act, and a new design. And every time it is successful."[32]

Now I'm going to let you in on how she does it. For each new CD, Madonna creates a collage of magazine photos, illustrations, and news stories about the latest and most cutting-edge trends in today's—and tomorrow's—culture. Rumor has it that she and her creative and production team then proceed to create a persona, to which they tailor everything from the CD case to the clothes she wears to the rhythm of the actual music. This is one way Madonna manages to maintain her strong brand while simultaneously remaining culturally relevant, even one step ahead of the game. It is also why her audience never perceives her as getting old (as evidenced by the fact that the number of teenagers in her audience is legion, even though she's old enough to be their mom). It's also how she manages to remain, in some respects, "out of time."

This is *exactly* how many successful brands are created. Trust me, I've used these very same techniques hundreds of times. I'll ask a large consumer group to rip out photos and headlines from magazines to illustrate a "feeling" or a "sense" or a "value" that a client is looking to instill in its brand, then present the collage to a design company. In fact, I've often asked CEOs and CFOs if they could pick a person whose business and marketing acumen they admire and from whom they think they could learn valuable lessons, and nine out of ten say, "Madonna." Why? She's able to reinvent herself and react instantaneously to trends. As a result, her fans are emotionally engaged not just with her music but with the brand *Madonna*.

Speaking of celebrities being out of time, some have cleverly managed to become so timeless as to basically achieve immortality. Remember how, in the early 1980s, Michael Jackson was filming a TV commercial for Pepsi when his hair accidentally caught on fire? Well, evidently, executive producer Ralph Cohen swept up Jackson's seared locks, kept them under wraps for almost thirty years, and, when Jackson died in 2009, sold them to a collector named John Reznikoff, who then contracted with a Chicago-based jeweler called LifeGem, which makes expensive diamonds out of hair samples. The upshot: LifeGem has announced plans to release (i.e., sell) a "limited edition" of diamonds made from Jackson's hair or, as LifeGem founder Dean VandenBiesen phrases it unforgettably, "Our plan is to give people an opportunity to own a diamond made from Michael Jackson's DNA. . . . We anticipate great interest."[33] Is it any surprise at this point that in an auction held last year in Beverly Hills, an X-ray of Albert Einstein's brain was sold for $38,750, while a pair of Marilyn Monroe's empty prescription bottles (I kid you not) went for $18,750?[34]

These days, celebrities—particularly in the music industry—don't exist without a marketing plan. More and more pop music stars are surrounding themselves with marketing experts to help them not just define their image and their values but also decide what to do, where to go, and how to target specific audiences. In short, to manage their brand.

Music manager Larry Rudolph is widely recognized as one of the best at this in the business. He is the guy credited not only with discovering Britney Spears (whom he picked out from the many soon-to-be-famous alumni of *The Mickey Mouse Club* for her plucky, "schoolgirl sexy" look) but with managing her brand from 1999 to 2004 and again in 2007. It was Rudolph who encouraged Spears to enter rehab when she famously hit rock bottom in 2007, at which point he and Spears parted ways. Once she got clean, though, she rehired him. Thus, it was Rudolph who engineered her comeback after many months of, shall we say, "unconventional" behavior—a marketing feat in and of itself. Integral to the success of the Spears comeback campaign was an "uncensored documentary" of her life entitled *Britney: For the Record* that MTV broadcast in 2008. Most viewers were struck by how down-to-earth, beleaguered, humbled, and human the singer came across—and came away with a new sympathy for the pressures that accompanied tabloid superstardom. Naturally MTV failed to note—and why should it?—that the selection of all this "uncensored" documentary footage had been carefully overseen by Britney's manager, Larry Rudolph (I should add here that Rudolph also represents other megabrands such as Justin Timberlake and 98 Degrees).

Being brands in and of themselves is what allows many stars to charge top dollar for the honor of their presence at events ranging from movie screenings to fashion shows to bar or bat mitzvahs. A 2010 ranking by fashion blog Fashionista claims that appearance fees for A-list celebrities including Beyoncé, Rihanna, and Maggie Gyllenhaal *begin* at $100,000. For that same ten minutes, says Fashionista, B-list celebrities, from Hilary Duff to the cast of *Gossip Girl*, receive somewhere in the vicinity of $25,000. However, there is a limit: the D-list—whose members range from Paris Hilton to the cast of MTV's reality TV show *Jersey Shore*, are just plain unwelcome.[35]

I Just Play One on TV

In 2002 the hosts of the *Today* show decided to roll out a monthly book club. The day they announced the selections, those books immediately shot up to the top of the Amazon rankings, and the following week occupied prominent positions on the *New York Times* best-seller list. The only thing that could have catapulted their sales higher was if they'd been recommended by Oprah.

If you've ever visited one of those ginormous Barnes & Noble or Borders superstores or, for that matter, any oversized superstore, be it Target, Best Buy, or Walmart, it's easy to understand why consumers appreciated being steered through the seemingly bottomless pool of choices and pointed in the direction of a worthy book.

It's an intriguing truism that more choice often leaves consumers less satisfied *and* less likely to buy something. You heard that right: when it comes to shopping, less *is* always more (and you've wondered why you generally walk out of Best Buy empty-handed or why a twelve-page restaurant menu makes you want to walk right out and find the nearest McDonald's). Quite simply, we are paralyzed by the fear of making a wrong, and expensive, choice.

To prove this point, in one of my all-time favorite experiments, I gave a dozen people two options: they could choose a chocolate from a box that contained thirty different types of chocolates, or they could pick one from a box that contained only six varieties. Can you guess what happened? A huge majority ended up picking from the box with only six chocolates—another argument that the fewer choices and selections we face, the more likely we are to pick up, and buy, something.

Recently I had a long conversation with the managers of a well-known bookstore chain. As I was leaving, I asked the employees to carry out a similar experiment for me: to remove all but one of the seven or eight display tables situated up front and in the center of the store. On that single table, I had store personnel place only a dozen or so books. (The average table in a bookstore holds at least forty.) A week later, we looked at the store's overall revenue. In the course of only seven days, book sales had gone up 2 percent (which may not sound like a lot but is a *huge* margin for a bookstore) storewide. In short, when they didn't have to deal with all those choices, hundreds more readers walked away with a purchase.

So given how petrified we are of making choices, wouldn't it be great if someone else—and not just anyone, but a *celebrity*—made that choice for us? After all, even the UK royal family issues a century-old "royal warrant," a seal of approval, prestige, and high quality that appears on a range of luxury goods. "People apply for the warrant because it is a mark of excellence," said Pippa Dutton of the Royal Warrants Association. "It's very helpful for trade because people say, well, if the Queen shops there, then it must be good. It's very good for trade abroad." [36] For a company or manufacturer, gaining recognition as a royal supplier means reaching the top of the aspirational hierarchy—while consumers, in turn, believe, *If the royal family uses it, it* must *be of the highest possible quality*. As a result, thousands of product samples show up every month at the royal doorsteps.

Isn't this the exact phenomenon that explains not only why we run out to buy the books recommended on the *Today* show book club but also why there are so many celebrity doctors hawking their beauty products in Sephora? I call it "turning our brains off."

In a 2009 study, Emory University School of Medicine scientists led by Gregory Berns, MD, a professor of neuroeconomics and psychiatry at Emory, found that people will actually stop thinking for themselves when a person they perceive as an expert offers them advice or direction. In the study, experimenters asked volunteers to make a decision about their finances. In one trial, volunteers were asked to make decisions on their own. In another, they received conservative advice guaranteed to minimize their gains from a financial "expert." Then the researchers scanned their brains.

Fascinatingly, the fMRI showed that in the face of "expert" advice (even though it actually wasn't particularly good advice), the parts of the volunteers' brains involved in considering alternatives became almost completely inactive. [37] It seems that receiving "expert" advice shuts down the areas of our brains that are responsible for decision-making processes, especially when the situation involves risk (interestingly, the areas of the brain responsible for skepticism and vigilance also become less active when a person is engaged in prayer). [38] "The brain activation results suggest that the offloading of decision-making was driven by trust in the expert," according to C. Monica Capra, PhD, a coauthor of the study. Added Berns, "This study indicates that the brain relinquishes responsibility when a trusted authority provides expertise. "The problem with this tendency is that it can work to a person's detriment if the trusted source turns out to be incompetent or corrupt."[39]

Because we are so in awe of fame and fortune, the line between expert and celebrity can be surprisingly thin. Remember the old joke, "I'm not a doctor, but I play one on TV?" Turns out there's a lot of truth behind it. Take Bill Cosby, for example. As one study notes, at the height of the popularity of *The Cosby Show*, in which he played a physician (and loving father to a large brood of children) named Dr. Huxtable, Cosby also appeared in a series of extremely successful TV ads for Jell-O gelatin and pudding. Why did these ads work? Because people confused him with the discerning doctor and doting father he played on television—someone you'd expect to endorse only the very healthiest and most wholesome food items. What was going on in their brains as they watched those ads? A summary of the experiment in *Social Cognitive and Affective Neuroscience* "found that a single exposure to a combination of an expert and an object leads to a long-lasting positive effect on memory for attitude toward the object."[40]

Is it any wonder celebrity experts like Dr. Gross, Dr. Perricone, Martha Stewart, or anyone who offers advice or counsel on television (many of whom, paradoxically, are experts only because they are famous and famous only because they are experts) have the rapturous and devoted followings they do? When we hear their "expert" advice, we unwittingly shut down the critical decision-making regions of our brains. As a result, we blindly heed that advice, often to the tune of hundreds or thousands of dollars.

Ready for My Close-up

Andy Warhol's legendary quote about fame—"In the future everyone will be famous for fifteen minutes"—was repeated back to him so many times over the years, it eventually made even his own eyes glaze over. "I'm bored with that line," he announced in the late 1970s. "I never use it anymore."[41]

Today, it's more like fifteen seconds. "The price of fame has hit rock bottom," writer Bruce Horovitz remarked in *USA Today*, when, last year, apparel maker American Eagle announced that for the mere price of a shirt, jeans, or a pair of socks, customers could get their face flashed to the world on the store's twenty-five-story-tall Times Square billboard. But what American Eagle's savvy marketers have actually figured out is how to make a few fleeting seconds of stardom last forever—and get an everlasting supply of free advertising in the process. They knew that in today's digital world, these young, wired consumers would whip out their digital cameras or smart phones, take a photo of their face on the billboard, post it on their Facebook pages, blast it to their Twitter followers, and so on, giving American Eagle countless millions of dollars of free publicity—and more celebrity of its own.[42]

Fact is, it's unbelievably easy nowadays to become a celebrity. So easy that last year I made a bet with a *Today* producer that I could manufacture a celebrity from scratch.

I got to know Krista Brunson, who works behind the scenes (not on camera) at the popular morning show over the course of appearances to promote my last book. I'd been explaining my thesis on celebrity—that if a person surrounds herself with the right accoutrements (and the right people), the public will be seduced into believing that she's famous—and was challenged to prove it. So I decided we would transform Krista into a "celebrity" and see if people bought it.

At 6:00 a.m., Krista showed up in the NBC makeup room looking like her usual fantastic self: young, attractive, and pulled together, though admittedly nervous. Ten minutes later, at the request of a specially hired cosmetician, Krista had removed her usual makeup and a personal stylist got to work on her head-to-toe transformation. Before long, Krista's hair had gotten big, her lips glossy, her cheeks bronzed, and her eyes smoky. Next, we outfitted her in a tight leather dress, textured tights, patent leather boots, an expensive Chanel handbag, oversized sunglasses, and—the pièce de résistance—a yappy, microscopic dog named Zak. But wait, we weren't done. Everyone knows that celebrities seldom travel solo, so we set her up with a phony entourage, including a personal photographer, a security guard (to keep adoring fans at bay, of course), and an NBC cameraman.

Krista Brunson was ready to be the star of her own life—an overnight sensation, a national treasure in the making.

With a camera team trailing us, we made our way out of the *Today* studios in Rockefeller Center and up toward Fifth Avenue. The photographer began snapping away as Krista, per my instructions, began window-shopping at Saks Fifth Avenue. I'd also instructed her to move slowly and languidly, as celebrities are wont to do, and to remain stubbornly in character, no matter what happened. At first, not a single person approached us. Then—and I'd never seen anything like this before—people appeared from out of nowhere and began swarming around like she was Julia Roberts or Keira Knightley. *From out of nowhere!* Many were convinced they'd seen her before and began snapping her photograph, and those who were simply convinced she was important kept sidling up to Krista's entourage to ask who she was.

At one point, a member of Krista's entourage filled her in about her schedule for the rest of the day. In response Krista, keeping in character, loudly announced that she wanted a champagne mimosa for lunch and later that afternoon a deep-tissue massage. As she continued along Fifth Avenue, the crowds multiplied. "Krista, what are you wearing to the Oscars?" one of our fake paparazzi called out. "Are you sleeping with Peyton Manning?" another asked. When people came forward to ask for Krista's autograph, she repeatedly scribbled her real name. No one noticed.

And as we headed back to the studio, one man mentioned to me that he'd seen Krista in concert and even briefly exchanged words with her after a show. He wasn't confusing her with someone else, either; he was thoroughly and completely convinced it had been her.

As I'd predicted, creating a celebrity was just that easy. Expensive accoutrements. Dark glasses. Great clothes. Designer shoes. A purebred dog the size of a rat. Which suggests that if we can simulate celebrity so easily, maybe it's less about who we actually are and more about the brand we project to those around us.

But then again, most companies and their marketers already knew that.

CHAPTER 8

Hope in a Jar

THE PRICE OF HEALTH, HAPPINESS, AND SPIRITUAL ENLIGHTENMENT

W ay, way high up in the hills of the Himalayas, in northern Nepal, beyond the moon, beyond the stars, its stems grazing the heavens, there grows a small, magical berry known as the goji.

Best of luck trying to track down the meaning of this word in any language, though one unconfirmed source once told me "goji" means, simply, "happy." Whether or not that's the real meaning, today the goji berry, or wolfberry, which resembles a shriveled red raisin, has been squashed, pulverized, crushed, and strained into a juice that resembles sewer water and is sold in health-food and organic markets for anywhere from $30 to $50 for a thirty-two-ounce bottle.

Chinese medicine has used *Lycium barbarum* and *L. chinense*—the scientific if slightly less marketable names for the goji berry—for centuries to help protect the liver, improve eyesight, and boost immune function and circulation. Today many makers of these juices—which include PepsiCo (makers of SoBe Lifewater Goji Melon), Coca-Cola (Honest Tea's Honest Ade Superfruit Punch with Yumberry and Goji Berry), Schweppes (Snapple Goji Punch), Anheuser-Busch (180 Red with Goji), Dr Pepper (Goji Fruit Punch Skinny Water), Campbell's (whose V8 V-Fusions include Goji Raspberry as well as Passionfruit

Tangerine), and FreeLife International (which today carries the tagline "The Himalayan Goji Company" and which makes up 90 percent of the global goji business across twenty-six countries, with annual sales estimated to be in the range of $250 million to $500 million[1])—assert that daily consumption of goji juice may help cure almost every human ailment in existence, from depression to anxiety to sexual impotence to lower-back pain to circulatory problems to blood sugar imbalance to autoimmune deficiencies to liver failure to macular degeneration to some forms of cancer (some suppliers distributing goji juice go so far as to claim that a man named Li Qing Yuen ate goji berries every day and lived to be 252 years old).[2] Yet as the back of one bottle admits somewhat sheepishly, "These statements have not been evaluated by the Food and Drug Administration. This product is not intended to diagnose, treat, cure or prevent any disease."

So *does* this pricey little fruit actually have any real proven health benefits, or is it all just one big sham? One published study suggests cautiously that the goji berry "certainly deserves further investigation."[3] Another study found that hairless mice who'd been given goji juice and then zapped with SSUV irradiation showed fewer incidents of sunburns, suggesting that "consumption of this juice could provide additional photoprotection for susceptible humans."[4] In another strange-sounding 2004 study carried out by the College of Public Health at China's Wuhan University, diabetic bunnies were found to have "an increase in HDL, or 'good,' cholesterol and a reduction in their blood glucose level"[5] after consuming goji.

Well, that's fantastic for diabetic rabbits and sunbathing rodents, but what about the rest of us?

Though there may be a great deal of quixotic charm surrounding the folklore, legend, and provenance of the exotic goji berry, there's just not much concrete scientific proof it actually *does* anything—except perhaps cost a lot of money. Yet we keep buying it by the caseload; in 2009, goji products were a $145 million industry, reaching well beyond the juice market to include nine product categories, including tea (Celestial Seasonings' Goji Berry Pomegranate Green Tea), cereal (Me & Goji Custom Artisanal Cereal), and candy (Vosges's dark chocolate goji bar).[6] But if goji berries haven't been proven to have any real medicinal properties, that raises an obvious question: how exactly are we being brandwashed to buy the stuff in such quantities?

Turns out the real magic of the goji berry has less to do with our hearts or our circulatory systems or our blood glucose and more to do with our brains.

As I wrote about in my last book, *Buyology*, our brains are prone to forming mental shortcuts, or bookmarks, known as somatic markers, that link cues from our physical world to specific emotional states or properties. Well, I've seen over and over in my work that shrewd companies are able to actually plant these somatic markers in our minds by creating associations between some positive emotion and their product. It seems that's exactly what's going on when it comes to the goji berry. Now, bear with me for a minute. The goji berry is found in China and Malaysia but is most often linked with the Himalayas, former home to the Dalai Lama. And when we think of that part of the world, what comes to mind? Could it be Buddhism and everything Buddhism symbolizes: purity, simplicity, compassion, wisdom, selflessness, and, ultimately, enlightenment? Marketers of these products know this, which is why they have very cleverly prodded our brains to associate their products with these spiritual properties. How? For one thing, by taking great care to emphasize the berry's Far Eastern provenance in their packaging and advertising.

Look, for example, at a bottle of FreeLife's Dr. Earl Mindell's Authentic Himalayan Goji Juice (available in Amazon's health and beauty section, among other places). Its stylish, expensive-looking bottle pictures snow-dusted Mount Everest ascending majestically into the clouds, seemingly uncontaminated by humanity. In the foreground, like a small miracle, there dangles a cluster of bloodred goji berries, affixed to a gently bent, leafy stalk. The price of four one-liter bottles? $186.11. Or take Goji Gold 100% Pure Organic Juice, created by Dynamic Health Laboratories, which comes wrapped in similar packaging picturing distant, vaguely Himalayan mountains, seemingly reaching into the heavens and therefore unsullied by man. The company Steaz, maker of organic green teas and energy drinks, too, markets its products using images meant to imply a Far Eastern origin. If you go to its Web site, you'll be greeted by yet another Himalayan scene—dark mountains covered with snow; clear, babbling brooks; untraveled pathways; a far-off red pagoda; and even computer-generated hummingbirds swooping in to feed on the nectar of virgin flowers—not to mention the words "Wisdom Can Be Obtained Within."

While these brands would have you believe that the contents of their bottles are grown, hand harvested, and shipped from the pristine mountaintops of Tibet or Nepal, that couldn't be further from the truth; FreeLife products are mass-produced and bottled in a giant factory in Phoenix, Arizona, Dynamic Health Laboratories is based in Georgia, and Steaz's operations are headquartered in Newtown, Pennsylvania.

I've long considered the strongest brands on earth—from Apple to Harley-Davidson—to be intriguingly akin to the world's religions, in that they tend to inspire in us a strong, ritualistic, almost evangelistic faith. In this chapter, though, we'll be talking about a different way faith works as a hidden persuader. We'll be talking about how marketers, advertisers, and purveyors of everything from food and beverages to clothing to cosmetics and more have embarked on an almost religious—and highly profitable—quest of their own: to ignite desire for their brands and products by imbuing them with such intangible yet emotionally powerful "spiritual" qualities such as health, hope, happiness, faith, clarity, good luck, and even the betterment of the human soul.

Dan Ariely, professor of behavioral economics at Duke University and author of the best-selling book *Predictably Irrational*, notes that what we buy is often not only some thing but also an idea embodied by that thing.[7] Whether that embodied idea is health, happiness, enlightenment, or social responsibility, it's this very universal psychological tendency that makes the hidden persuaders we'll read about throughout this chapter so incredibly powerful.

It Was a Berry Good Year

As anyone who has visited a health-food store in the past few years is well aware, goji isn't the only "miracle" berry in town.

Take acai, the fastest-growing product in the herbal subcategory, with 2009 sales just under $300 million dollars (it's the biggest-selling botanical product today).[8] The acai berry is a miniature, grapelike fruit that grows profusely in the rain forest of Brazil and is available today in the form of various tablets, juices, smoothies, yogurts, and instant drink powders (there's even a goji-acai drink I saw once in a health-food store, which is like the marketing version of a double-bill concert featuring the Rolling Stones and U2). Again, the ads and the packages deliberately play up the berry's "exotic" provenance; the box of Good Earth's Rainforest Red Tea (with acai and tropical fruits, of course) pictures a savanna on which a mother lion sits nursing her cub, whereas Rainforest Therapy's Acai Powder (fresh from the Brazilian Amazon) shows simple wooden vats overflowing with the life-giving fruit.

At first glance this seems perfectly harmless; we can't imagine we'd be so gullible as to be duped into thinking a berry has magical properties just because there's a picture of a rain forest on the box. But that's exactly the point. The reason these subtle, seemingly innocuous images are so insidiously persuasive is because they operate deep within our subconscious. What's happening here, though we're barely aware of it, is that when we read the words "rain forest," or "Brazilian Amazon," the somatic markers in our brains perk up and begin connecting various dots. Peacefulness. Serenity. Nature. Purity. And soon our brains begin to ascribe all sorts of spiritual and medicinal qualities to the product—which, of course, is exactly what the marketers want.

If this sounds a bit far-fetched, remember that our brains are *hard-wired* to connect these dots and to make associations that sometimes aren't even there. Countless studies have shown that thanks to this pattern-recognition skill humans are born with, we often "see" connections that don't exist. Remember the *Today* show experiment I described earlier? The one where I fooled crowds of New Yorkers into assuming that Krista, one of the show's off-air producers, was a celebrity? It was because their brains had simply put together various dots: The dark glasses. The hair. The entourage. The paparazzi. The tiny dog. From these assorted cues, many concluded they'd not only seen Krista before but had attended her concerts, loved her music, and so on. In a sense, this is exactly what is going on with acai and all the other products marketers would have us believe possess miraculous, restorative, even spiritual properties. External cues trigger associations so powerful that the thought of questioning or second-guessing them doesn't even occur to us.

However, companies and retailers that sell acai products don't stop there. Not by a long shot. They aren't content just sitting back and hoping that we'll associate good health and spiritual well-being with their products; instead, they come out and make all kinds of highfalutin, preposterously unsubstantiated claims that acai juice increases energy, helps you lose weight, improves digestion and sexual performance, detoxifies the body, relieves insomnia, reduces cholesterol, rejuvenates your complexion, and helps with heart disease and diabetes and more. Yet profoundly little evidence that acai berry juice improves human health actually exists. Like most berries, acai has good nutritional qualities, but "there is not a drop of research" that supports marketing claims that it prevents weight gain and facial wrinkles, says Jonny Bowden, a certified nutrition specialist and author of several health books.[9] "The expensive Acai berry is the triumph of marketing over science, that's the bottom line," Bowden says. "[The berry] isn't useless, but it's not anything that people are claiming it is."[10]

I really have to tip my hat to whoever's out there marketing acai and all these other "superfruits." Sure, there are vitamins and omega-3s in the acai berry—just as there are in all the other (markedly less expensive) fruits, like bananas, grapes, and cranberries. And yes, one study by the University of Florida did suggest that an acai berry extract may indeed retard the growth of leukemia cells—in a petri dish, not in actual humans, that is.[11] According to acai drink manufacturers, if you drink four ounces of acai berry juice daily, it's the equivalent of scarfing down more than two dozen fruits a day—well, that may be true (only because it's highly concentrated), but according to the FDA we actually need only about two cups of fruit a day.

As you may have surmised by now, acai juice isn't cheap. A week's supply will cost you roughly $40, which, if you do the math, comes to nearly $2,000 a year. And acai has even migrated over to the skin-care category; for approximately $40, we can now buy acai hydrating facial cream and antiwrinkle hydration cream infused with acai and mulateiro, rosewood, or copaiba (it would seem that the harder it is to pronounce, the more it costs).

Some online sellers of acai berry go even further over the line in their sneaky efforts to sell us the stuff. Some use a tactic called network marketing, a clever technique that also incorporates a healthy dose of peer pressure. What this means is that one day your friendly neighbor Maureen will knock on the door, claiming that the acai juice she is holding (and by holding, I mean selling) has cured her of all that ailed her—from hangovers to varicose veins. A number have gone so far as to offer consumers a free trial, which seems fairly harmless—that is, until the trial ends and the consumer discovers that the company has covertly signed her up to automatically keep receiving shipments, to the tune of $80 a month; "some [have] had to cancel their credit cards just to break free from the scheme," according to Arlene Weintraub in her book *Selling the Fountain of Youth: How the Anti-Aging Industry Made a Disease Out of Getting Old—and Made Billions.* The practice was so widespread, Weintraub writes, that "the consumers' site Complaints Board (www.complaintsboard.com) collected more than 17,000 posts from furious buyers of Acai."[12] Sneakier still, according to CNN, many online acai vendors, like FWM Laboratories of Fort Lauderdale and Hollywood, Florida, Advanced Wellness Research of Miami Beach, Florida, and others stand accused of using fake diet blogs to steer consumers to sites plugging these free trials.

While we're on the topic of "magical" fruits, what about pomegranate? That one really *does* have actual health benefits, doesn't it?

Well, like the goji, the pomegranate has been used for centuries in traditional medicine across the world to treat everything from mouth ulcers to dry coughs to diarrhea to conjunctivitis to tuberculosis. (I might add that artwork from the earliest days of Islam, Judaism, and Christianity shows pomegranates symbolizing both unity and eternal life.) More recently, pomegranates have been shown to reduce UVB-induced skin damage[13] and "exert favorable effects on lipid profiles" (whatever that means).[14] What you have to keep in mind about these claims, though, is who is funding these studies: companies like POM Wonderful, maker of those wonderfully weird-shaped bottles of pomegranate juice. (Incidentally, in case you were wondering why those bottles are shaped that way, they were deliberately designed not only to resemble one pomegranate on top of another but also to evoke associations of the "ideal" female form—a little fuller on the top and bottom with a cinched waist. Similarly, the heart in place of the *O* in the brand logo is meant to evoke associations of cardiovascular health.) In any case, it turns out that if you fund enough scientific studies—and the owners of POM have not only funded over fifty-five of them, but they've also donated over $34 million in research support to scientists and universities all over the world—you can find *something* redeeming in just about any product under the sun. Sure, pomegranates have a handful of health benefits, but again, so do fruits, vegetables, fish, oatmeal, olive oil, a healthy lifestyle, exercise, and weight control.

Did I forget to mention that pomegranate juice also contains "valuable antioxidants"? If you're not sure exactly what antioxidants are or what they do—other than bellow at us from the shelves of the supermarket and health-food store—you aren't alone. For the record, antioxidants neutralize and stamp out the errant, unstable molecules known as free radicals that damage our body's cells (our bodies produce free radicals naturally, as do pollution, the environment, too much sunlight, and an unhealthy lifestyle). But just so you know, you don't need to pay two dollars an ounce for some weird purple juice to stamp out these free radicals (nor do you have to travel to Nepal or the rain forest); antioxidants occur naturally in fresh fruits and vegetables. According to Dr. David Gems of University College London, "It is not the antioxidant content of your food that is critical, it is that you don't eat too much [food]. . . . Get plenty of exercise. Get a dog and take it for a walk."[15]

But that doesn't stop POM Wonderful from claiming (on its Web site) to be the "antioxidant superpower" and "far and away the top performer in terms of antioxidant potency, defined as the in-vitro ability to scavenge free radical molecules." Nor does it stop the company from marketing a line of teas, bars, pills, and supplements containing the "super antioxidant extract" it calls POMx—the *x*, of course, meant to imply a medical prescription, despite the fact that the products have never been medically or clinically tested. So specious are the brand's health claims, in fact, that in 2010, POM Wonderful received a warning letter from the FDA, stating that "the therapeutic claims on your website establish that the product is a drug because it is intended for use in the cure, mitigation, treatment, or prevention of disease"[16] and that the marketing of POM Wonderful using these claims was in violation of the Federal Food, Drug, and Cosmetic Act.[17] Similarly, in 2009, regulators accused Kellogg's of deceiving consumers with claims that their Frosted Mini-Wheats cereal improved children's cognitive health and attentiveness.

While Kellogg's quickly agreed to a settlement, POM, at time of writing, has repeatedly claimed innocence and, according to the company Web site, was "currently reviewing FDA concerns."[18]

What That Nutrition Label Is Really Saying

It should come as no surprise that selling health (or the illusion of health) is hugely profitable. In fact, it is so profitable that it has spawned an entire exploding industry of products marketed as "functional foods"—one that pulled $37.3 billion in 2009 in the United States alone. Naturally, companies have a lot of tricks up their sleeves for snagging a share of this hugely profitable (and rather bogus) market; witness, for example, the cash cow known as "one-hundred-calorie packs," which cleverly allow manufacturers to create smaller servings typically at twice the price. In industry parlance, this is a well-known strategy called selling "perceived health and wellness," with the major word here being "perceived."

This illusion of "healthy" is perpetuated by the fact that many of us don't know what many of the marketing buzzwords really mean; and of course marketers work hard to keep it that way. A national survey conducted by the Shelton Group found that, when asked whether we'd rather buy a product billed as "natural" or "organic," we choose "natural," "thinking organic is more of an unregulated marketing buzzword that means the product is more expensive," says Suzanne Shelton, who conducted the survey. But she explains, "In reality, the opposite is true: 'Natural' is the unregulated word." And other popular buzzwords—like "organically grown," "pesticide free," "all-natural," and "no artificial ingredients"—actually mean very little.

Given how freely companies throw these terms around, one can hardly blame us for being confused. For example, in a clever bit of bait-and-switch marketing, when Silk Soymilk recently introduced a line of milk made from nonorganic soybeans, it simply switched its organic soy milk to a green box and began selling the new, nonorganic version in the original red packaging, with only one perceptible change: replacing the word "organic" with the word "natural." [19]

Companies have gone to great lengths to convince us that "natural" equals "healthy," but that couldn't be further from the truth. Believe it or not, because the term is unregulated by the FDA, a company can dub just about any product "natural." Potato chips made from actual potatoes instead of potato flakes may technically be natural, but they are still processed, high in fat, high in sodium, and lacking in nutritional value.

Or take English muffins. As someone who has been eating this breakfast staple for years, you can imagine how delighted I was to pull a package off the shelf and learn that they are now made with "unbleached enriched white flour" and contain "hearty grains." *How nutritious*, I thought, feeling more virtuous than ever as I placed one in the toaster. But alas, this actually just means they are made with white flour and contain wheat—a standard ingredient for any bread or starch. As for "multigrain," well, this more-grains-the-merrier approach sure *sounds* convincing, but all it means is that more than one type of grain is involved (which doesn't automatically make it healthier). And what about products that boast they contain "isolated fibers"? Sorry, but this, too, is meaningless. To reap any actual health benefits, you have to consume "intact fibers," such as oats or legumes. As the *Washington Post* points out, "Fiber One Oats & Chocolate bars say they provide 35 percent of daily fiber, but the fiber comes mainly from chicory root extract," [20] which isn't one of the healthy fibers.

With all this linguistic smoke and mirrors, is it any wonder we have no idea what it is we're actually eating?

My favorite sleight of hand is the claim that a food or drink can give you "energy." Well, I have news for you. "Energy" is just another way of saying "calories." Which makes this a very clever way of putting a positive spin on what would otherwise be the kiss of death for a "health" product—can you imagine a company touting the fact that its product is high in calories?

What about those claims "made with real fruit" or "contains real fruit juice," which regularly appear on the packages of fruit snacks, soft drinks, cereals, cookies, and pretty much any food item marketed to children (or, rather, the guilt-laden *parents* of children)? Again, considering that there is no law in place governing how much "real fruit" a food or drink must contain to make this claim, don't be surprised if those strawberry-flavored fruit rolls contain maybe half a drop of fruit juice and are spiked with eight grams of sugar apiece (a perfect example of how food companies target children and their wallet carriers at the same time). And speaking of juice, what about those foods advertised as being fortified with nutrients, like calcium-fortified orange juice? According to the *Washington Post*, "fortifying a junk food does not offset the food's negative qualities. Example: Fruit Loops says it 'now provides fiber.' But the 9 grams of sugar in each ¾-cup serving of the cereal could have far more negative effects than any benefit from the slim amount of added fiber." [21]

Another favorite among marketers is the "low trans fat" claim. Recall that several years ago, the FDA proclaimed that trans fat, the fat created when oils are hydrogenated during food processing, contributed to coronary heart disease, the biggest killer of Americans. Naturally, every food product under the sun was immediately proud to boast "zero trans fat" on its package. Problem is, products with "zero trans fat" (and by the way, thanks to labeling guidelines, these actually include any foods containing 0.5 grams or less per serving) are typically teeming with saturated fat, which can be just as bad for our hearts as trans fat. It's kind of like saying "I'm not carrying a gun!" while neglecting to mention you *are* packing a hand grenade or a switchblade.

Genie in a Bottle

These are just the shenanigans being pulled with FDA-regulated products; when it comes to nonregulated products, like cosmetics (which are not considered drugs and thus can sidestep many of the clinical trials required by the FDA), marketers and advertisers can get away with saying just about anything. Makers of face creams, for example, are happily peddling all kinds of clever and often blatantly unproven claims. The La

Prairie brand, for example (which, by the way, is sold in a jar the shape of a genie bottle to imply magical wish-granting powers), actually promises to reduce stress levels—a claim that one doctor I spoke to assured me is a medical impossibility. "Ninety-eight percent of the 'cosmeceutical' industry is all about marketing," Eric Finzi, a dermatologic surgeon in Maryland, was quoted as saying. "If you buy a $1,000 cream, there's no reason to expect it's better than the $50 cream. It might be worse."[22]

La Prairie's Cellular Serum Platinum Rare claims to "maintain your skin's electrical balance while warding off pollutants." Givenchy's Le Soin Noir contains black sea algae, which, according to the company's ad copy, "reconstructs a catalyst in the skin to counteract the signs of aging." Should you be so bold as to ask exactly how it does this, a Givenchy spokesperson will offer you nothing more than the assurance that the company's clinical tests "speak for themselves." And Lululemon, the maker of popular, overpriced yoga wear, got into hot water in 2007 when the *New York Times* reported that a product called VitaSea, which the company claimed contained a stress-reducing, underwater healing property known as Seacell, in fact contained no seaweed, no marine amino acids, no minerals, and no vitamins whatsoever, as the label claimed.[23] Evidently, Lululemon "agreed to withdraw the claims immediately," at least until it could prove them scientifically. The world is still waiting.[24]

Finally, there's La Prairie's Skin Caviar Crystalline Concentre, which retails for $375 an ounce and contains (I'm not kidding here) "stem cells from the rare Uttweiler Spatlauber Swiss apple, so rare that only three trees remain in existence,"[25] implying some magical regenerative or restorative properties. The problem with this deranged claim is that, as Finzi explains, "Number one, no cell would stay alive in a cream. A cell is a very delicate living thing, and unless it's in the right environment, when you take the apple off the tree, it's starting to die. Number two, a plant's stem cell is not going to do anything for human skin."[26]

Unfortunately, the fact is that most face creams that promise to prevent aging (many of which are loaded with antioxidants for no good reason other than to give marketers an additional tagline) have next to no effect. According to one prominent British researcher quoted in the UK's *Daily Mail*, "Rather than spending money on vitamin-loaded potions and pills, people who want to retain a youthful look should instead concentrate on eating healthy foods in sensible amounts and exercising."[27]

And while we're talking specious marketing claims, what about the multibillion-dollar supplement business, which has migrated well beyond chains like GNC and is now taking over aisles and aisles of most drugstores and health-food stores? Shark cartilage "may be used to help treat arthritis and cancer"; bee pollen is "a storehouse of all naturally occurring multi-vitamins, minerals, proteins, amino acids, hormones, and enzymes"; ginkgo biloba "may support mental sharpness"; and then there's my personal favorite, horny goat weed, which we're only told has a "long history of traditional use by men in China and Japan" (for what, you can draw your own conclusions). I could go on and on. And despite the fact that "these statements have not been evaluated by the FDA" and these products are "not intended to diagnose, treat, cure, or prevent any disease" (as their labels are required by law to read), we continue to buy into them; according to a 2009 survey conducted by Ipsos Public Affairs for the Council for Responsible Nutrition in Washington, DC, some 65 percent of Americans label themselves "supplement users."

According to Dr. W. Steven Pray, Bernhardt Professor at the College of Pharmacy at Southwestern Oklahoma State University, "All this crazy junk became available thanks to the 1994 supplement health act. It's a completely unregulated industry. . . . It just means that you or I could find a weed in our backyard and start marketing it as a dietary supplement. There have been reports of kidney stones and liver damage—no one knows what's in this stuff."

It's true—the 1994 regulations (or lack of them) allow just about anyone to start up a company and roll out a supplement in record time, no medical license or credentials necessary. In general, supplement makers aren't even under any responsibility to register their products with the FDA. As another source puts it, "The Dietary Supplement Health and Education Act of 1994 opened a floodgate of questionable health claims and advertising for herbal and dietary supplements. Although lawmakers didn't intend that the supplement industry be unregulated, this has been the practical result."[28]

Given how easy it is for anyone to get in on this very profitable game, it's no surprise that the so-called nutraceuticals industry—worth

$25 billion in the United States alone—continues to expand. At time of writing, though, several senators, including John McCain, are behind a new Dietary Supplement Safety Act, which would require dietary supplement manufacturers to register with the FDA and fully disclose their ingredients. Fingers crossed that it becomes law.

The High Price of Doing Good

Ever since the 2008 economic downturn, the cult of consumption in our culture has lost a lot of followers. Over the past couple of years, many of us have traded our worship of money and things for an almost fervent devotion to a "new frugality." Forced to adjust to the new economic climate in which we suddenly found ourselves, our lives became smaller and simpler in a hurry. We stayed home, hunkered down. We quit eating out at restaurants. We sold off some of the junk collecting dust in our basements and storage lockers. We clipped coupons, shopped for bargains, made do, and wondered, sensibly, too, how on earth we'd gotten so caught up in this spending spiral in the first place. So if we've stopped praying at the church of the material gods, what's standing in the wings? Answer: something no company can put a price, or even a discount sticker, on: Serenity. Simplicity. Equilibrium. Happiness. Balance. Virtue. In short, spiritual enlightenment, in its many purchasable forms.

It seems that in a world that's increasingly hyperconnected and always "on," today more than ever we're searching for a simplicity in life that few of us have ever known. This "back to basics" sentiment has become so pervasive, in fact, that it has spawned a number of popular trends, from urban farming (think chicken coop on a fire escape) to "freeganism" (consuming only discarded food and goods) to "clean eating" (a strict regimen of natural eating popularized in part by best-selling author Michael Pollan).

Marketers and companies have jumped right on these trends. Which is why today so many products are marketed in a way that emphasizes Mother Earth. Their packages are plastered with words like "wellness" and "natural" and "environmentally friendly" (buzzwords that have particular meaning and significance for women, who influence roughly 80 percent of all consumer purchases).[29]

The irony of all this is that "green" and "ethical" and "organic" products often cost more. Hey, virtue, charity, health, benevolence, and social responsibility are expensive! According to a poll conducted by GfK Roper Public Affairs & Media and the Yale School of Forestry and Environmental Studies, nearly half of all people, women in particular, say they are willing to pay more for "environmentally responsible" products,[30] and according to that same survey, the majority of women polled believe not only that "consumers have a personal responsibility to take care of the earth" but also that "being green is good for your health and well-being."[31]

Companies know this and are exploiting it in all kinds of ways. Take how Procter & Gamble's best-selling Tide laundry detergent has begun using social responsibility as a marketing tool with its hugely successful "Loads of Hope" campaign. Evidently, in the wake of Hurricane Katrina, P&G decided it would form a "Tide Loads of Hope" team to travel to Louisiana and other afflicted areas to supply clean (washed with Tide, of course) clothes to displaced residents. According to the online magazine *Slate*, "the team . . . arrives in a rolling Laundromat, a gigantic orange truck (the color of the original Tide box) carrying thirty-two washers and dryers." Then, "for two or three weeks, the team, wearing bright-orange Tide T-shirts, will wash, dry, and fold the sheets, towels, and clothes of families and aid workers for free. It's got to be a huge relief for displaced people. It's also likely to produce a very pleasant association the next time anyone who's been helped sees a bottle of Tide on the grocery shelf," the article notes.[32]

But is shelling out the extra money for these "responsible" products actually doing any social good? Or are they just making us *feel* more virtuous, in the same way that drinking acai juice makes us *feel* more healthy? Signs point to the latter, given that research shows that when we make these kinds of purchases we tend to give ourselves permission to make less responsible decisions in other areas of our lives—say, failing to recycle our Coke can after scarfing down an organic hamburger, or pressing the gas on our eco-friendly Priuses with an alligator-skin boot—thus undoing our efforts to "do good." One study found that the owners of hybrid cars drive more miles, are more ticket and accident prone, and even bash into pedestrians more.[33]

More ironic still is that today, buying "responsible" products, like hybrid cars, is actually an act of conspicuous consumption—a way of purchasing the respect and admiration of our peers (an old episode of *South Park* didn't refer to it as the "Pious" for nothing). And in fact, Toyota engineered this quite deliberately. Not only were its designers the first to make an environmentally friendly car stylish, even *sexy*, with its sleek design, powerful engine, and cool-looking solar-powered moonroof, its marketers made the Prius nothing short of a status symbol by taking swift advantage of our devotion to celebrity. How? The company turned to Mike Sullivan, the owner of Toyota of Hollywood, and arranged for him to transport twenty-six Priuses to the 2003 Oscars, and "before long," *BusinessWeek* notes, "such stars as Cameron Diaz and Leonardo DiCaprio were being photographed ('Look, we're so green!') with their Priuses, and 'It became the cool thing to do,' says Sullivan."[34] Toyota also loaned cars to an LA public relations agency, thus ensuring snapshots of such stars as Harrison Ford and Calista Flockhart in Priuses, and also provided Priuses for use on such TV shows and movies as *CSI Miami*, *Weeds*, *Evan Almighty*, and *Superbad*, where the cars ended up being featured prominently (always driven by the lead characters, no less).[35] With celebrities like Meryl Streep, Brad Pitt, Kirsten Dunst, Will Ferrell, Miley Cyrus, Tim Robbins, Larry David (who owns three Priuses, including the one his character drives on his HBO series, *Curb Your Enthusiasm*),[36] and others singing the praises of Toyota's environmental marvel, and both the Sierra Club and the National Wildlife Federation endorsing the Prius[37] (remember the power of experts?), it's no wonder that as of this writing, the hip brand is Toyota's third-best-selling model, just behind the far more affordable Camry and the Corolla.[38] In fact, several consumer studies today rank Toyota as one of the most environmentally friendly brands in the world. But hold on a moment—isn't Toyota a *car* company?

The appeal of the Prius is a perfect example of what psychologists call "competitive altruism," a widely accepted theory which asserts that people do socially responsible things (like buy hybrids and other environmentally friendly products) not so much to do good but rather to show off their benevolence and enhance their social reputations. One study supporting this theory found that even the most (ostensibly) environmentally conscious consumers tend to actually *avoid* buying green products when no one else is around to witness their selfless, mindful behavior. When people buy lightbulbs over the Internet, for example, they tend to choose the nongreen, politically incorrect (and less expensive) option. But if they're buying in the store, where other people can see them, they will typically go with the longer-lasting LED bulb in the recycled package. As the researchers explain, "Status motives led people to make a rather economically irrational decision, at least from a superficial perspective. When people are thinking about status, they in fact want to spend more—to demonstrate not only that they are environmentally conscious, but also that they can *afford* to be environmentally conscious."[39]

Is it any coincidence, then, that in July 2007, according to data from CNW Marketing Research, when asked why they bought a Prius, most people gave the one answer that every marketer loves to hear? The main reason for buying a Prius, said 57 percent of owners, was because "it makes a statement about me."[40]

The Church of Persuasion

I guess it should come as no surprise, given the turbulence of these times and the return to basics that it has inspired in many of us, that spiritual marketing—the term for trying to pass off products as having soothing, magical, or summoning qualities—has become a popular strategy for all kinds of unlikely brands and products, ranging from candy to sports drinks to even cars and computers.

Today, those seeking "a taste of nirvana" can munch Hampton Chutney or suck on "Classy Yoga Candy" or "Karma Candy." And if this leaves you thirsty, Anheuser-Busch recently rolled out a series of ads featuring parched Tibetan lamas gazing longingly at a blimp labeled "Budweiser." Still, when it comes to spiritual marketing, few edible products can compete with the invention of one Gao Xianzhang, a Chinese farmer who has actually come up with a way to grow Buddha-shaped pears. Sure, they cost about $7.50 apiece, but that hasn't stopped this ingenious farmer from selling close to ten thousand of them.

A commercial for the 2010 Hyundai Sonata features a "suggested daily routine for achieving inner peace" (essentially just a handful of yoga poses including one cleverly christened "the Sonata"),[41] while in one spot for Gatorade, basketball legend Michael Jordan hikes up a rocky mountain (Himalayan, no doubt) in search of a spiritual guru whose sage wisdom turns out to be the brand's slogan, "Life's a sport. . . . Drink it up." And the computer maker IBM and Web search engine Lycos have both built advertising campaigns around Sherpas and Tibetan holy men.[42]

Sometimes holy people even participate in this brandwashing. For example, a rustic Cistercian abbey in the Midwest has a for-profit arm called LaserMonks.com. When not praying or fasting, these monks—yes, actual monks—will refill your used printer cartridges. The monks claim that they have served more than fifty thousand customers to date and that they process anywhere from two hundred to three hundred daily orders. Their 2005 sales? $2.5 million.[43] (Oh, and the Web site also indulges Internet prayer requests.)[44] And one Los Angeles company, known as Intentional Chocolate, goes so far as to employ a recording device that captures the electromagnetic brain waves of real-life meditating Tibetan monks before "exposing" the recording to the chocolates in the assembly lines for five days per batch. According to company founder Jim Walsh, "Whoever consumes this chocolate will manifest optimal health and functioning at physical, emotional and mental levels and in particular will enjoy an increased sense of energy, vigor and well-being for the benefit of all beings."[45]

If New Age spirituality has really become the new consumer religion, is it any wonder that there is a moisturizer called Hydra Zen or that a campaign for the beauty company ghd, which refers to itself as "a new religion for hair," explains how users can live their lives according to the "gospel of ghd"? Or that the logo for Brazil's Sagatiba, a popular sugarcane-based liquor, is Rio de Janeiro's Christ the Redeemer? Similarly, Guerlain, the upscale Parisian perfumer, distributes a fragrance known as Samsara, which is named after the Buddhist cycle of birth and rebirth and whose ad copy reads, "Samsara is the symbol of harmony, of osmosis between a woman and her perfume" (the perfume stopper even resembles the eye of Buddha).

The reason all this works so well? Well, remember that our brains are predisposed to believe in something—anything. You might say that as humans we *need* to believe. Which is why companies are constantly coming up with new and ingenious ways to capitalize not just on New Agey spirituality but also on traditional, old-world faith and religion. To give one rather surprising example, I've noticed that in recent years the increasing number of modern-leaning Muslims in our society have presented companies with an unexpected yet very lucrative opportunity. A little background: If you're a devout Muslim, your religion dictates that you can only eat foods designated "halal," which is an Arabic term defined as "lawful" or "permitted" (among other things, this excludes pork and its by-products, animals not properly slaughtered, carnivorous animals, and alcohol). Now, historically, buying halal food meant going to a Muslim grocer or butcher, who cut the meat in accordance with Islamic principles.[46] Such a person might not be hard to find in downtown Baghdad, but here in the States, there aren't exactly Muslim butchers on every corner. Which is why food companies have begun to offer thousands of new products boasting the halal label. This business, according to the *Halal Journal*, is worth roughly $632 billion per year—a staggering 16 percent of the global food industry.[47]

Today companies are slapping the halal label on everything from food to makeup to even furniture (in this case, it could be the oil, paint, or soap used to stain the wood that claims halal certification). Canadian drug companies even sell halal vitamins, which claim to be "free of the gelatins and other animal derivatives that some Islamic scholars say make mainstream products *haram*, or unlawful," and there are multiple halal cosmetics lines, including a brand called OnePure, which has supposedly been certified in Malaysia by the same Islamic body responsible for certifying meats. "People are always looking for the next purity thing," confirms Mah Hussain-Gambles, who built the halal makeup firm Saaf Pure Skincare.[48] Whether or not all these religious claims are legitimate, they certainly are persuasive. A Muslim taxi driver in New York once told me that to make up for his lack of devoutness, he'd begun buying more and more halal-branded products; they made him feel better about his spiritual lapses. Which is exactly the point. These shrewd brands aren't really selling food and perfume and makeup; they're selling purity, spirituality, faith, virtue, and in some cases atonement.

If you're not a Muslim, and buying faith is what you're after, never fear: eBay has you covered. According to *Newsweek*, in 2008 the popular auction site offered strands of hair purportedly from the head of Saint Thérèse de Lisieux (bidding began at $40 per strand). Or you could purchase a fragment of bone supposedly from the thirteen-year-old saint Philomena, who, according to legend, was flogged, drowned, and finally beheaded for refusing to marry the Roman emperor Diocletian.[49] All of which prompted the author of the article to wonder whether it was really possible to purchase "a piece of God's grace and mystery with a credit card."[50]

That's not all. Among the strangest and arguably most ridiculous faith-based eBay offerings were a grilled cheese sandwich that appeared to be emblazoned with the face of the Virgin Mary (it was bought by an online casino for $28,000) and a Dorito that precisely resembled the Pope's miter, or signature hat (it was bought by the same casino for $1,209). But don't worry: those with more modest budgets need only shell out $3.26 for an item claiming to be "The Meaning of Life." What exactly would be arriving at your doorstep after purchasing such an item was unclear; the only picture the seller provided was a vista of a beautiful rainbow.[51]

I can't talk about selling faith without mentioning the phenomenon of the megachurch, which debuted in 1977 with Houston's First Baptist—seating capacity 3,300—and today is nothing less than a marketing machine. Concentrated mostly in the South, megachurches tend to look more like shopping malls than places of worship, outfitted with coffee bars, bookstores, video games, food courts, and even bowling alleys. Others more closely resemble cineplexes, as they've hired technological consultants to help them install multimedia screens on which the sermon is broadcast via the Web. With a high-velocity mixture of music, media, print, and Web, "the amount of technology . . . can rival a large concert hall," says Jack Duran, executive vice president of Turner Partners Architecture, LP.[52] Says another architect who has worked on transforming the look of American churches as well as theaters and entertainment complexes, including one at Universal Studios, "When you get the children to come back again and again, the parents will follow." [53] Yet other churches have embraced the more corporate side of the coin. According to *Forbes* magazine, World Changers Ministries "operates a music studio, publishing house, computer graphic design suite and owns its own record label," [54] while the New Birth Missionary Baptist Church not only has a CEO in place but offers a "special effects 3-D Web site that offers videos-on-demand." [55] And the Great Barrington, Illinois–based Willow Creek Community Church is famous for its marketing conferences and seminars and for its "buzz" events, featuring speakers ranging from business consultant Jim Collins to President Bill Clinton to former Washington Redskins coach Joe Gibbs. [56] Tickets can range anywhere from $25 to hundreds of dollars a pop.

Hope Floats

Whether the brand's promise is health, happiness, or enlightenment, what all the marketing ploys we've been talking about in this chapter have in common is that they tap into our very human desire to return to the earth. To reclaim an innocence untainted by money or by the stresses of contemporary life. They're all about selling us inner peace, spiritual fulfillment, and a better life.

And selling us hope, as well. This is nothing new; companies have been selling hope in one way, shape, or form for the past hundred years. Because hope works. We crave it. We need it. And we buy it. Charles Revson, the founder of Revlon, was clearly onto something when in 1967 he was quoted as saying: "In the factory, we make cosmetics; in the drugstore, we sell hope in a bottle."

Hope is the loan we take out for the perfect home—or the faraway city—we dream of living in someday. Hope is a bunch of camping gear we buy to feel closer to nature (even if we live in the middle of a siren-filled city); a kayak rack for a kayak we'll never paddle; boots intended to scale a mountain we will never climb; a tent to pitch under the stars we'll never sleep under.

Hope is joining a health club to get the body we've always wanted;

the local, grass-fed beef we eat in the service of leaving our children a better planet; the expensive outfit we buy just in case we someday have someplace fancy to wear it. It's any product that promises to make our life better in some small way.

I have a friend who recently found his sources of income drying up. One day I peered in his garage and saw his expensive Hummer, which was hooked to his speedboat. "Why don't you sell your car and your boat?" I asked. It seemed to make sense if he was hurting financially.

No, he told me. At first I thought he was being bullheaded, but then I realized that he was clinging to those objects—those *things*—because they represented hope. And that if he sold them, he would be selling his entire imagined future, that these objects represented a world in which he hoped he would someday live.

Whenever I do speeches across the world, I knock on wood, just for the hell of it. As far as I can tell, it's never brought me any spectacularly good luck, but I still do it. Hope may be an illusion, but we believe in it—and we're willing to spend our hard-earned money for it—all the same.

CHAPTER 9

Every Breath You Take, They'll Be Watching You

THE END OF PRIVACY

You're sitting at home, killing time at your computer, when an e-mail announces itself. No, it's not from a friend or from your boss; it's a notice from the chain drugstore you frequent down the street. "Joanne," it says, "save $5 off your next purchase of Neutrogena moisturizer!"—adding that this special offer expires in three weeks' time.

Now how, you wonder, did the drugstore know you were a Neutrogena user? Must be a coincidence, you think, and then promptly forget about it. That is, until the following week, when you're sorting through your snail mail and find another flyer from the same store. This time it's offering you discounts for your brand of laundry detergent (Tide), your preferred toothpaste (wintergreen Crest with extra whitening), and your guilty-pleasure snack food ("Hint of Lime" Tostitos). This is clearly not a coincidence.

The pieces start to come together as you flash back to your last drugstore visit.

"Will you be using your loyalty card?" the bored teenage clerk asked as you were paying for your purchases (which included, besides the aforementioned items, Band-Aids, vitamins, your husband's Head & Shoulders, and your family's various prescriptions).

As usual, unthinkingly, you handed over the red plastic card, watching impatiently as the clerk scanned the tiny bar code under her wand. After you paid up, the clerk pulled up a two-foot-long receipt, announcing without interest, "You've got four coupons today." One for half off a pack of Venus razors (funny, you did just switch to Venus from another brand), another for a six-ounce bottle of Purell (weird thing is, you just ran out), a third offering you a 10 percent discount on your next bottle of vitamin D tablets (how did they know that recently you'd been reading tons of articles about vitamin D?), and one for a dollar off the next time you develop a roll of digital photos (huh, you *do* have a family reunion coming up).

On the way out, you were struck by the music playing overhead: James Taylor's "Fire and Rain." Though you'd heard this song seven hundred million times in your life, you couldn't help but wonder: was it sheer coincidence the drugstore knew you're a sucker for this particular heart-tugging, late-baby-boomer lullaby? Did these people have a microchip implanted in your brain, or what?

Well, sort of.

As it turns out, thanks to the sophisticated techniques today's companies have for keeping track of your every move, this drugstore—and virtually every other place you shop, for that matter—probably knows more about your wants, your needs, your dreams, and your habits than even you do. And it's using this information to make money off you in ways you couldn't even imagine.

Welcome to the $100 billion world of data mining.

Save the Data

Data mining—euphemistically referred to in the marketing industry as "knowledge discovery" or "consumer insights"—is an enormous and rapidly growing global business devoted to tracking and analyzing consumer behavior, then categorizing, summarizing, and smoothing that data so it can be used to persuade and on occasion manipulate us to buy products. Data mining is how companies know not only your buying habits but also your race, gender, address, phone number, education level, approximate income, family size, pet's name, favorite movie, and much, much more, creating what one expert calls a "mirror world" of us.[1] The goal of "consumer insights," according to Stuart Aitken, the CEO of dunnhumbyUSA, a leading data-mining company based in Ohio, whose clients include Procter & Gamble, Macy's, PepsiCo, Coca-Cola, Kellogg's, Kraft Foods, and Home Depot? "We're looking for the motivations and the understanding behind what consumers do and buy."[2]

Being able to predict what a consumer is likely to buy next—and being the first company in line to perfectly target the offering to the consumer in question—is of paramount importance to companies of all stripes. Why? Because based on marketers' data, consumers who try a new product are likely to stick with it for an average of *a year and a half.* So if a store can figure out what new product you *might* like and offer a free sample or coupon or promotion persuading you to try it, it's potentially locked up your dollars for the next eighteen months.

Thanks to data-mining companies, or as I like to call them, Big Brother, every time we do a Google search, write on a friend's Facebook wall, swipe our credit card, download an iTunes song, look up directions on our cell phone, or shop at the local grocery store, an unseen data collector is shadowing us, recording every last bit of information, crunching and analyzing it, and then turning around and reselling it to retailers and marketing firms.

What's more, the data-mining industry is growing 10 percent a year, and why? Because thanks to technologies like the GPS tracking built into our smart phones, the license agreements we sign every time we download a new piece of software onto our laptops, commercial spyware (otherwise known as adware) that tracks and records every Web site we visit, and increasingly sophisticated algorithms and computer models to analyze all this information, today each and every move we as consumers make is producing reams more data than ever before. And you better believe companies are using this data to take our dollars in ways we don't even realize.

Code Blue

Don't you miss the good old days, when coupons showed up in the Sunday newspaper? You'd put down your steaming mug of coffee, get out your scissors, cut along the dotted lines, then contentedly file away that freshly clipped coupon in the handy little folder you kept in your desk drawer. Well, those days are over. Thanks to the Web, the coupon has now gone digital, and that digital coupon knows more about you than you can imagine.

Digital coupons: another sneaky yet little-known tool of the data-mining world. If you think digitizing coupons is merely about convenience and saving postage, you're wrong. Today the innocent-looking bar codes on those ubiquitous online coupons are encoded with a shocking amount of information about you—including your computer's IP address, everything written on your Facebook profile and posts, the date and time you both obtained and redeemed the coupon, the location of the store where you used it, whether you found the coupon online, and even the search terms you used to track it down in the first place. And if this wasn't bad enough, more and more retailers are cross-pollinating this data with other information their databank has about you, including estimates of your age, your gender, your income, your buying history, what Web sites you've visited recently, and your real-time whereabouts—creating a profile so intricate and detailed it would impress a CIA operative.

Here's how it works. Let's say you receive a coupon in your in-box from Macy's. You either print it on your computer or send it to your cell phone. Then, when you go into a store to redeem it, the clerk scans it, sending all the information I just noted to a company called RevTrax. RevTrax then analyzes this information and assigns you to a particular cluster or cross section, depending on the type of consumer the data indicate you are. By matching your online behavior with your in-store purchasing, the retailers can figure out which ads or online product promotions work best on *you*, what offers you are likely to jump at or ignore, and even how long after searching for something online you're likely to actually go to a store to chase it down. "Over time," says RevTrax cofounder Jonathan Treiber, "we'll be able to do much better profiling around certain I.P. addresses, to say, hey, this I.P. address is showing a proclivity for printing clothing apparel coupons and is really only responding to coupons greater than 20 percent off."[3] Adds Robert Drescher, chief executive of Cellfire, a mobile-coupon company that works with grocery chains including Safeway, Kroger, and ShopRite, "We can already tell if you are near or inside a store and can give you particular offers, but that's the kind of thing we're moving fairly cautiously on so that the user can get to know us and trust us first."[4]

If you use a coupon on your mobile phone, it's even worse. For example, Starbucks recently started a program that allows coffee drinkers to keep track of each purchase on our cell phones, rewarding us with a free drink for every fifteenth purchase. Yet what most unsuspecting customers don't know about this seemingly bighearted program is that it's actually pulling data from our phones and sending it straight into Starbucks' database, where it's then used to target us with personalized entreaties. "We've tried to build a program around recognition . . . and in some ways, that relevance comes from knowing about purchases from data collected from the loyalty program,"[5] Brady Brewer, the vice president of Starbucks overseeing brand loyalty and the Starbucks card, told the *New York Times*.

Similarly, last year Target rolled out bar-code coupons, scannable straight from your phone, at its nearly two thousand stores across the United States. But in exchange for receiving five coupons per month on various small items from lip balm to bubble gum, are you aware of what you're giving up? Check out the company's terms and conditions, which give Target permission to collect users' cell phone numbers, their carriers' names, and the date and the time users redeemed their coupons.[6] Worse, a Target spokesperson clarifies that the company may merge the information it pulls from people's phones with information "from other sources" before sharing that information with "carefully selected" third parties.[7] Target's spokespeople were naturally reluctant to discuss what kinds of data they collect, but one expert estimates that roughly fifteen pieces of information, ranging from what search term you typed in to your address and where you were when you downloaded the coupon (thanks to the fact that most smart phones are GPS equipped) could be relayed via the bar code of a simple mobile coupon.

That's right, even our closest friends—namely, our phones—are betraying our privacy. A mobile-phone security firm known as Lookout, Inc., analyzed roughly three hundred thousand free applications for the iPhone, as well as for Google's Android, and found that many of them "secretly pull sensitive data off users' phones and ship them off to third parties without notification"[8] (by third parties they mean advertisers and marketing firms). This information these apps are stealing from right under our noses? Everything from our contact lists to our pictures to our text messages to our Internet search histories to our real-time locations.[9] In fact, as the *New York Times* recently reported, when one German politician went to court to investigate just how much his cellphone company, Deutsche Telekom, kept track of his whereabouts, he discovered that within a six-month period the company had recorded and stored the actual coordinates of his location a total of thirty-five thousand times. "We are all walking around with little tags, and our tag has a phone number associated with it, who we called, and what we do with the phone," as Sarah E. Williams, an expert on graphic information at Columbia University, explained to the *New York Times*.

And in April 2011, a firestorm erupted when it was discovered that the iPhone, the 3G version of the iPad, and Google's Android phone all contain software that silently tracks and records the user's location—and has been doing so, unbeknownst to the vast majority of users, for a year or longer. In the case of the Android, the software records data about the user's location as frequently as every few seconds, then transmits that data back to the company, where it is stored in a database, as regularly as every few hours. In the case of the iPhone and iPad, two San Francisco programmers discovered, the data also gets stored in a file that is automatically copied onto the hard drive of any computer synced to the device. Meaning that if I charge my iPad on a colleague's or acquaintance's computer, he or she now possesses a permanent record of my whereabouts over the last year—in a file that could be easily hacked, copied, or disseminated via the cloud. And the worst part? Various reputable news outlets report that Apple has been loading up phones with this software—which can't, by the way, be turned off—without users' knowledge; it simply appeared one day, silently and invisibly, as part of a (seemingly) routine upgrade. Understandably, privacy advocates were outraged at this blatant attempt to capture what the *Wall Street Journal* cites as a "$2.9 billion market for location-based services."

The newest ploy to turn our own cell phones into data-mining tools? An iPhone app called shopkick, rolled out in November 2010, just in time for the holiday shopping season, which offers reward points for shopping. Redeemable everywhere from Macy's to Sports Authority to Best Buy, a few points are awarded for simply checking into a store, more points for scanning a product, and, of course, still more points for buying. But of course, that's not all you get. Each time you check in to a store, scan a product, or make a purchase, shopkick collects and crunches the data about your purchase and then uses it to send targeted deals and offers straight to your phone.

I don't know about you, but I'm starting to feel creeped out.

Charge It at Your Own Risk

It may not shock you to learn that Walmart, the biggest and most profitable retailer in the world, also operates one of the most massive databanks in the world. Capturing data on point-of-sale transactions from nearly three thousand stores in six countries, Walmart maintains a 7.5-terabyte Teradata warehouse[10]—a database many times the size of the federal government's. Because of its size, Walmart has unprecedented access to information about a staggering number of us. Which is why, at any given time, Walmart always knows what's selling and what's languishing, and with which specific customers, too (in fact, the chain store is famous for hoarding its data somewhat obsessively). And it knows how to use this information to make us spend. I talked earlier about how retailers like Walmart employ a company to help them predict and capitalize on extreme weather events like earthquakes and snowstorms. Well, it turns out they also use the data about past extreme weather events to figure out which products (beyond the obvious) to stock. For example, a few years ago, when a hurricane was approaching the Atlantic coast, Walmart crunched the numbers to figure out what hurricane victims had purchased during the previous hurricane. No, it wasn't flashlights. Instead, the top-selling prehurricane item was beer, while, oddly enough, sales of strawberry Pop-Tarts, of all things, had increased sevenfold. Accordingly, trucks bulging with toaster pastries and six-packs were soon speeding toward the site of the oncoming storm.

But the scariest thing about this isn't that it's making the giant retailer a lot of money (which it is, of course). It's that the typical shopper has *absolutely no idea* how closely she is being monitored. At Walmart there are no loyalty cards to swipe, no coupon bar codes to scan, just "everyday low prices." So without any loyalty program in place, how does Walmart capture information? Via our very own credit and debit cards.

It's amazing what a sophisticated data miner can learn from a credit card. In 2002, J. P. Martin, an executive at Canadian Tire (which, in addition to tires and car accessories, sells electronics, sporting goods, and kitchen appliances), began analyzing the data gleaned from the credit card transactions the company had processed the year before. Among the many things Martin found: people who bought carbon monoxide monitors practically never missed payments, and neither did people who bought those little soft pads that keep furniture legs from scratching up your floor. They also found that people who bought cheap, no-name automotive oil were much more likely to miss a credit card payment than people who got the expensive, brand-name stuff, and that if a person bought a chrome-skull car accessory, he "was pretty likely to miss paying his bill eventually."[11] From all this Martin concluded that the brands we buy are "the windows into our souls—or at least into our willingness to make good on our debts."[12]

This wasn't just an isolated experiment. Martin's methods are actually very common. Most credit card companies have (and in fact have always had, though they are getting far more sophisticated thanks to technology) systems in place that pore through all your data looking for clues that you might stop making payments. What kind of clues? Well, logging onto your online account in the middle of the night is one, as it bespeaks anxiety about your finances. If you use a card to buy essentials like groceries or prescriptions, it's another indication that you may have fallen on hard times. Have you all of a sudden charged a large expense to a credit card you seldom use? That's another red flag that you may be delinquent with your upcoming monthly payment, or even teetering toward financial insolvency. American Express has admitted it once used data about where its "members" shopped to set its credit limits, decreasing the limits if signs indicated a person was having money trouble. Though it has suspended the practice, not every company has; in 2008 it was revealed that one subprime credit card marketer had decreased credit limits on cardholders who frequented "pawnshops, massage parlors, tire retread shops, marriage counselors and bars and nightclubs."[13]

No matter which credit card you use, each and every time you charge something on it, the company records how much you spent and on what type of product. And while cagey company representatives refuse to reveal how they use this data, the least you should know is that every single credit card transaction (online or off) is assigned a "merchant category code," a four-digit number that indicates what kind of business or service the charge was for. The category codes include everything from "wig and toupee stores" to "packaged beer, wine and liquor stores" to "pawnshops" to "wholesale clubs" to "bail and bond payments,"[14] all of which, when you think about it, tell the credit card companies a whole lot about you and your lifestyle. Men: please note that if you happen to be among the 87 percent of males in the United States who buy less-spoken-about products or subscriptions on Web sites promising that some vague and discreet wording like "international trading company" will appear on your credit card statement (rather than, say, Carl's Adult Videos), that little merchant category code will still reveal the truth to the credit card company.

Have a lot of transactions in the "air travel" category? You may get an offer in the mail for either travel-related services or a rewards-equipped credit card from a major hotel chain. Says Paul Stephens, the director of policy and advocacy for the San Diego–based Privacy Rights Clearinghouse, "Depending on how extensively you use your credit card, they conceivably have a very clear, distinct picture of an individual."[15]

These kinds of tactics explain why a person in serious debt can expect to find a handful of new credit card offers proclaiming to be for individuals with "less-than-perfect credit" awaiting them in their mailboxes. Who's behind these offers, and how do they know so much about our finances that they show up when they do? Well, certain financial institutions—including the big-three credit rating agencies, Equifax, Experian, and TransUnion—pore through all kinds of documents, including bank and court records, to craft intricate profiles of the financial lives of over one hundred million Americans.[16] They then turn around and sell this detailed data, including names, addresses, Social Security numbers, marital statuses, recent family births, education levels, car makes, TV cable service providers, and even magazine subscriptions, to banks, credit card companies, and mortgage brokers, who then fiercely compete to find untapped customers—even those who would normally face an uphill battle getting credit in the first place! Yes, that's right: the companies responsible for maintaining and updating your credit scores are the very same ones turning around and selling your financial information to credit card companies and mortgage lenders.

Most people write it off as a timely coincidence when an offer for a new home equity loan arrives in the mail just as they've started struggling to make their mortgage payments. But it isn't. "We called people who were astounded," said Allan E. Geller, chief executive of Visions Marketing Services, a Lancaster, Pennsylvania–based company that carries out telemarketing campaigns for banks offering new terms of credit. "They said, 'I can't believe you just called me. How did you know we were just getting ready to do that?' " He adds, "We were just sitting back laughing." The goal of this incredibly devious tactic is to create "the appearance of almost irresistible serendipity,"[17] like a devil whispering into our ears at the precise moment our defenses are at their lowest and our needs are highest.

Thanks to data-mining practices, banks and lenders know enough about our finances to tailor the specific wording in unsolicited letters to our individual situations. Often they even go so far as to calculate, to the dollar, what we would save on a mortgage or a monthly credit card payment if we "took advantage" of the offer in question. A few years back, one bank took this personalization to an extreme. It actually took satellite snapshots of a particular neighborhood and then highlighted each homeowner's property on the envelope accompanying the personalized credit offer. Not surprisingly, most consumers were spooked, and the campaign was withdrawn.

Again, while neither banks nor credit card companies will confirm their precise internal methodologies, it's widely acknowledged that property deeds are one of their major sources of data. Since property deeds are public records, each time we buy a piece of property we get put on a list, known in the industry as a "trigger list," indicating that we've just moved or are about to move. Companies then purchase these "trigger lists" and use them to shower us not just with loan offers and credit card offers but also with decorating catalogs, magazine subscriptions, and more. Knowing that homeowners spend close to $12,000 furnishing their new digs within the first six months of moving into a new home, and a good percentage of that in the first weeks or days, a company known as ALC Milestones New Movers and New Homeowners, for example, sells companies and businesses—like Crate & Barrel and Pottery Barn—updates every twenty-four hours about who has just purchased a property and is in need of brand-new furnishings.[18]

Using a technique known as "predictive modeling" (which is essentially comparing your behavior to that of consumers who fit roughly the profile you do), data compilers and banks know whether you are likely to need new home credit before even you do. Equifax (yes, one of the companies that maintains your credit score) even offers lenders a brochure called "TargetPoint Predictive Triggers," whose "advanced profiling techniques" promise to help them sniff out consumers who show a "statistical propensity to acquire new credit."[19]

Naturally, the company declines to reveal its exact formula, but let's figure out how it might do it. Let's say a bank does a mail campaign offering new terms for home refinance. You receive the offer, check the box saying you might be interested and would like to learn more, and send the card in, complete with your name and address. Next, data crunchers proceed to pull together other information they have about you on file, including the value of your home, your outstanding credit card debt, and whatever savings you may (or may not) have. The bank then feeds all this into sophisticated statistical models that ferret out other consumers who match the profile you do (e.g., other consumers who have a good-sized property, shop at Williams-Sonoma, etc.), whom they then know to target with similar offers. In effect, the bank is getting us to unwittingly rat out one another.

In 2010, the U.S. Congress passed a bill designed to protect unsuspecting consumers (especially young consumers) from predatory credit card companies. Among the requirements of the new act was that colleges and universities publicly reveal the long-standing secret contracts they enjoy with credit card companies. That's how it was discovered that in 2007 hundreds of institutions of higher learning (including some very prestigious ones, like Yale University) had entered into a highly lucrative "affinity agreement" by which they were essentially selling Chase bank access to their alumni, staff, sports fans, and even students.[20] This is also how it was revealed that a staggering eight hundred of the United States' two-year colleges and seven hundred of the country's four-year colleges maintained similar agreements with various credit card companies or banks.

Under some of these agreements, the colleges received a cut of every new bank account a student opened; under others, they got a percentage of every retail purchase a student made with their new card; under still others, the schools actually earned money if an alumnus took on debt. Obviously, this was a huge incentive for these schools to encourage their students to rack up credit, which is why so many permitted credit card companies to advertise on campus, with some even granting the companies access to private campus events.[21]

Why were the credit card companies so aggressively going after these young customers? Simple. These students, with their meager incomes, irresponsible spending habits, and high credit limits (thanks to the fact that many of them opened joint accounts with their parents), are cash cows for these banks. According to student lending company Sallie Mae, in 2008 seniors graduated from college with a median credit card debt of more than $4,100, and six years ago, before the recession, the "collegiate affinity market" represented a more than $6 billion credit card debt portfolio.[22] Oh, and don't be fooled: credit card companies *love* it when students max out their cards; in fact, so long as students don't default on what they owe, this is most credit card companies' covert goal. Moreover, as Ohio State University researchers found, not only are first-time college-age cardholders eager to buy stuff on credit, but they're apt to hang on to that particular card for up to fifteen years. No wonder Bank of America's FIA Card Service Unit outspends its competitors by 288 percent to entice college students to sign up for its card, according to the Federal Reserve Board of Governors.

What's most valuable about these customers from a data-mining perspective is that, to prevent these young spenders from falling off the bank's radar once they graduate, every single one of these affinity agreements requires colleges to provide students' and graduates' personal data, including names, phone numbers, and addresses.[23]

What Your Shopping Cart Says About You

The loyalty card is another sneaky yet powerful tool companies use to turn every intimate detail about our lives into marketing gold. Today the average person carries around fifteen so-called loyalty cards, now being issued by every retailer under the sun, from your local drugstore to Staples to Best Buy to Starbucks. Yet most of us forget we've even signed up for all these loyalty schemes. In a study I once conducted in the UK, when I asked a group of middle-aged females how many loyalty programs they belonged to, most were able to recall only half (and when, to jog their memories, I asked them to empty their wallets, most were shocked by the number of cards that fell out). So what's so bad about loyalty cards, you might be wondering? Isn't the whole point of them to *save* me money? No, not exactly. Sure, the language and terminology that retailers use in talking about these programs—"reward card," "loyalty program," "preferred customer savings"—may make you feel sort of special, or may even lead you to believe that these programs are about rewarding you, loyal customer, with money-saving offers. Well, they aren't. The reason these clever programs exist isn't to save you fifty cents here, fifty cents there, as their marketers and advertisers would have you believe. Loyalty programs exist for one simple and rather shifty purpose: to try to persuade you to buy *more*. In fact, each time you sign up for a store's loyalty program, what you are actually doing is giving the store explicit permission to collect, aggregate, summarize, and crunch unparalleled amounts of information about you, your family, your habits, and your interests—all of which data miners then turn around and use to craft marketing and advertising entreaties too perfect, too persuasive, and too uncannily targeted to your individual psychology and lifestyle to resist. One study about Safeway, the supermarket chain, sums up the technique neatly: "Safeway . . . has turned itself into an information broker. The supermarket purchases demographic data directly from its customers by offering them discounts in return for using a Safeway savings club card. In order to obtain the card, shoppers voluntarily divulge personal information that is later used in predictive modeling."[24] In other words, each time we hand the clerk that colorful little card we keep on our key ring, we're swapping our privacy for a twenty-five-cent savings here, a dollar off there, maybe the occasional buy-two-get-one-free deal.

Have you ever found yourself standing behind someone in the checkout line at the grocery store, trying to figure out who she is based on her purchases? Let's say she's buying a package of garlic chicken Lean Cuisine and a six-pack of Diet Coke. *Okay,* you tell yourself, *she probably lives alone and is dieting.* Next she sets down a bottle of high-end shampoo and conditioner. *She's brand and beauty conscious,* you note, *and probably makes a good living.* Also in her basket are a can of Lysol with bleach and a bottle of Purell, so you figure she's germ-conscious. Then she surprises you by pulling out a home blood-pressure kit. *Does she have an elderly parent living at home?* you wonder. *Or is she in iffy health herself?* You file this last observation away, awaiting later confirmation.

This kind of speculation, in a nutshell, is what data miners do, only thanks to all the sophisticated data-tracking technology and computer models they have at their disposal, these few purchases tell them a whole lot more about this woman than the naked eye ever could. How? Every time you or I use our loyalty card in a store, a record of what we've bought, how much of it, at what time of day, and at what price is sent to a data warehouse, where it is added to our digital folder (most companies and retailers with loyalty programs amass data continuously, then parse it into chunks that sum up our weekly, monthly, and yearly behavior. Then algorithms so complex they would make a math major's head spin crunch all the data to come up with all kinds of interpretations of who we are and what we're likely to buy (based on our own buying habits and those of millions of consumers similar to us). For example, when we use a loyalty card to buy groceries, we are being pegged by at least one supermarket chain as one of six different customer profiles: a "Time Pressed Meat Eater," a "Back to Nature Shopper," a "Discriminating Leisure Shopper," a "No-Nonsense Shopper," a "One-Stop Socialite," or a "Middle of the Road Shopper,"[25] categories used to target us with specific deals and offers.

There's no end to what this data can tell companies about what we're likely to buy. If I buy yogurt and vitamins, the algorithms predict I am probably a good target for an invitation to join the new local gym that just opened up. If I buy ready-to-eat meals, the data shows it's a sign that I'm a busy guy and more likely to use a coupon that's delivered straight to my phone than one I have to clip from the newspaper or print from my in-box. If I suddenly start buying baby wipes and diapers, I've clearly recently experienced a life change that's likely left me run down and tired and am statistically likely to jump at a special offer for a day at the spa.

It is by crunching these kinds of numbers that the data-mining industry has uncovered some even more surprising factoids: Did you know, for example, that at Walmart a shopper who buys a Barbie doll is 60 percent more likely to purchase one of three types of candy bars? Or that toothpaste is most often bought alongside canned tuna? Or that a customer who buys a lot of meat is likely to spend more money in a health-food store than a non-meat-eater?

Or what about the data that revealed to one Canadian grocery chain that customers who bought coconuts also tended to buy prepaid calling cards? At first, no one in store management could figure out what was going on. What could coconuts possibly have to do with calling cards? Finally it occurred to them that the store served a huge population of shoppers from the Caribbean islands and Asia, both of whose cuisines use coconuts in their cooking. Now it made perfect sense that these Caribbean and Asian shoppers were buying prepaid calling cards to check in with their extended families back home.

This is all well and good, you might be thinking, *but how could that supermarket use this information to make more money off us?* Well, first and foremost, it could create what's known in retail parlance as an "adjacency." An adjacency is when a store positions two or more products next to each other that are seemingly unrelated but appeal to the same target customer. This way, after that Jamaican shopper has picked out a coconut to cook with, she need only glance to her left to find the strategically placed display of prepaid phone cards and be reminded she owes Mom a call.

Often adjacencies make stores and companies money by offering us solutions to problems we didn't even know we had. For example, imagine it's mid-August and recent incoming data shows that a lot of people are buying frozen strawberry shortcake. Now, typically the ingredients for fresh, homemade strawberry shortcake—local strawberries, bottles of whipped cream, and pound cake—are located in three discrete aisles of the store. However, gleaning from the data that this particular demographic has a weakness for strawberry shortcake, the supermarket installs a stand-alone display of strawberries, whipped cream, and pound cake at the front of the store. Thus, the shopper enters the store, murmurs to herself, *Instant fresh dessert? Why didn't I think of that?*, and swooshes all three into her basket—costing herself about three times as much as a box of Sara Lee.

Some businesses are using the adjacency technique to turn even bigger profits. Take Marks & Spencer, the upscale English department store chain. A few years back, by parsing the data taken from loyalty cards, its management noticed that more and more of its customers were buying Indian-style dishware, followed by ready-to-eat Indian meals. When management realized that a large number of first- and second-generation Indians must have started shopping there, a lightbulb went off. Why not open a currency exchange office right there in the store? Then another thought occurred: why not sell a service organizing travel to these countries? Which is why the retailer partnered with Thomas Cook, the UK's largest travel agency, to create the Marks & Spencer Travel Club, which offers holiday discounts as well as "loyalty points when you book your holiday using your M & S Credit Card."[26]

But this isn't all companies do with the information they compile from our loyalty cards. Not by a long shot. To truly see the volumes that even an innocent trip to the grocery store can tell a company about us, and what it then does with that knowledge, let's take a quick trip to a regional grocery chain we'll call Sparky's.

First off, mind if I note right off the bat here that Sparky's was smart to position its front door on the right? That's because data compiled from a study of two hundred stores reveals that shoppers who move counterclockwise spend two dollars more per trip than those who go in the opposite direction. Human beings are naturally more inclined to move to the left (because it's easier to reach out with our right arms to grab whatever it is we need), so a right-side entryway is a subtle yet effective way to ensure a counterclockwise shopping flow. I might add here that Sparky's was smart to outfit its store with oversize shopping baskets, as studies show that the bigger the shopping basket, the more likely we are to fill it to the brim.

After desperately making my way through the labyrinth of shelves, towers of products, and special displays looking for the apples, I find the Granny Smith apples and put five in my basket (I really only wanted three, but I saw the sign saying "buy four, get one free" and immediately fell for the classic ploy that author William Poundstone calls "nonlinear pricing," meaning the store has upped the price of those four apples by 20 percent so I'm actually paying the exact same amount per apple even though I think I'm getting a bargain). My choice of organic apples tells Sparky's database that I'm pretty well educated, make a good living, and am more likely to buy eco-friendly products. No surprises there.

Let's pause once again. Notice how I had to navigate around numerous displays before I chanced upon the apples? It's no coincidence. The more complex the navigation paths we're asked to walk, the slower we walk, and the slower we walk, the more *stuff* we are exposed to . . . and tempted to buy. In order to combat the increasing sophistication of shoppers, many of whom have learned to arm themselves with shopping lists and make a beeline for what they want, more and more supermarkets are mixing around groceries—or changing the location of items on a monthly basis—so it's harder for us to find what we're looking for. The result is that not only are we tempted by more products, but finding what we want becomes a game of sorts (remember the power of games?), at the end of which we often reward ourselves for our hard work by buying something that wasn't on our list.

Next, over by the pharmacy aisle, I pick up a package of Nicorette (even though I've never smoked; it's just part of my little experiment). By my buying the Nicorette, Sparky's is immediately able to establish that

I'm almost certainly between the ages of twenty-five and fifty-four and more likely to buy name-brand products over the generic or store-brand variety. Again, makes sense, right?

Next, just for fun, I buy a package of Jheri curl texturizer in the women's hair-care section and a small box of Dora the Explorer Band-Aids. Now the store will make two fairly good assumptions about me: that I'm an African American female and that I have a child under the age of five—and am thus a good candidate for coupons and offers on those particular brands of everything from juice to breakfast cereals to cosmetics that the data miners have found to appeal to my demographic.

Tucked away at the rear of the store, so the pharmacists can keep a close watch on teenage boys, the condom display takes up half a shelf. Just for fun, I pick up a pack of neon, ribbed ones. Now I'm *confirming* to the data miners that I'm a woman (who just happens to be named Martin). Why? Because most people who buy condoms are, in fact, female (note that the name of the section is "family planning," which subtly targets the female of the household by implying that this is the section for the person who is generally in charge of schedules, date books, doctors' appointments, and, yes, condom use). Incidentally, this is why nine tenths of the condoms for sale proudly exhibit the words "sensitive" and "thin," two adjectives guaranteed to strike a chord with the contemporary woman.

The one exception to the women-buy-condoms rule? It comes in a box similar to the others, except nowhere on its packaging does it mention the words "sensitive" or "thin." Instead, its packaging features what at first glance appears to be a Roman soldier's helmet, or, wait, could that actually be the engorged head of a penis? The words on the box say it all: "Extra Large Trojan Condoms." That's right, had I picked up a box of Extra Large Trojans, Sparky's data miners would have instantly revised their assumption about my gender, as swaggering (often hopeful) males, not females, are the ones who buy "extra-large" condoms (and I tip my hat to the marketing whiz who thought up *that* one).

At the cash register, I give the cashier my Sparky's card and pay, though not before grabbing a bag of those new pretzel M&Ms—a small impulse buy telling the data-mining company that I'm amenable to trying new products and therefore a good target for future coupons on newly rolled-out products.

Next, the second the cashier swipes my loyalty card, Sparky's database will know exactly what I've purchased and how much and will nail my demographic as an educated, health-conscious, sexually active African American ex-smoker between the ages of twenty-five and fifty-four who has a young daughter. Then the company will add my purchases to its databank, where its computers will crunch that data (and the data generated by every other card-wielding customer who walked into the store that day) to make all kinds of conclusions and predictions about who I am and what my preferences are. Then it will turn right around and sell the results not just to the companies that make the products that I bought but also to the companies that make the products my profile indicates I am *likely* to buy. It will do so for each and every subsequent visit, just as it will for the thousands of other shoppers in my particular zip code. And based on what the companies now know about me—and us—they will reformulate their marketing messages, rethink their inventory, and, sneakiest of all, start targeting each and every one of us with advertising so tailored, so personalized, that we're powerless to resist it.

Believe me, in the future supermarkets will get even smarter and more invasive. Recordant is an Atlanta-based in-store monitoring company that provides digital audio recorders to capture all customers' conversations with store employees. Sophisticated software then analyzes these recordings to isolate recurring words or phrases. Then there's Brickstream, whose clients include Toys "R" Us, Office Depot, and Walgreens and which uses dual-lens cameras to amass information about where and for how long people shop, as well as how they respond to various products.[27] And PathTracker is an electronic monitoring system that combines buying data with the paths of shopping carts through supermarkets. How? It wires carts and baskets with a location-tracking device that emits an inaudible signal every few seconds. At which point "an array of antennae around the store's perimeter captures the signal, which is then analyzed for individual shoppers as well as aggregated to provide composite views of shopping in the store."[28]

Yikes.

They're Playing My Song

But wait, that's not all that's going on at Sparky's. As I meander out of the store, I catch myself humming the Paul McCartney song that was playing overhead while I was shopping. Think this is just some random selection? It's not. It's actually a very carefully and deliberately selected track of Muzak, a type—and in fact a brand—of music that has expanded beyond the insides of elevators and today serenades some one hundred million people a day[29] inside Gaps, McDonald's, Barnes & Nobles, and countless other restaurants and stores. So how does a store decide what tune to play overhead? Well, first, one of Muzak's "audio architects"—a term for someone who's trained in the physiological and psychological applications of music—pays a visit to a retailer or restaurant and looks at the store's data-mining research to figure out what demographic shops or eats there. Then the audio architect carefully selects a playlist targeted at that demographic, a practice known in the biz as "narrowcasting."

It's in this way that Muzak has designed seventy-four music programs in ten categories, ranging from indie rock to hip-hop to classical. Mapped out in fifteen-minute cycles that rise and fall in intensity using a technique known as "stimulus progression," the speed and pacing of each individual playlist are carefully designed to have a certain psychological impact. Ever notice that the Muzak playing in supermarkets and grocery stores is much slower than the Muzak playing in restaurants? Well, again, it's because research shows that slow music makes us move more slowly, and the longer we hang around in a store, the more likely we are to buy something. According to Douglas Rushkoff, author of *Coercion: Why We Listen to What "They" Say*, in U.S. department stores, customers exposed to Muzak with a slow tempo shop 18 percent longer and make 17 percent more purchases, and in grocery stores, shoppers make a whopping 38 percent more purchases when slow Muzak is overhead. On the other hand, says Rushkoff, fast-food restaurants play Muzak with more beats per minute "to increase the rate at which a person chews."[30] Thus, they get us out of there sooner and can serve more customers and earn more money.

Thanks to narrowcasting, Muzak can even tweak its selections to subconsciously persuade us to buy different items depending on what day of the week it is. Saturdays? The music will be more romantic, suggesting, *Buy her something—like roses or jewelry.* This technique has been found to be so effective that some Japanese supermarkets have split their stores into zones, each one serenading consumers with sounds designed to optimize spending per minute. In the fresh-fruits-and-vegetables department, water drips, birds sing, and the wind blows from overhead speakers; in the confectionery department, childish songs are interspersed with the sounds of children giggling, while over at the butcher's a steak sizzles overhead.

As if that weren't enough, Muzak also offers retailers a more subtle service dubbed "atmospherics," designed to hit us on an even deeper level.[31] Imagine you're a sixteen-year-old girl walking into a clothing store in Middle America. The mood and the decor are silvery, sexy, and urban. The employees are uniformly hip and attractive. Now add the seductive beat of fast-paced electronic music. Does this environment create a fantasy for a starry-eyed young girl who's always dreamed of moving out of her small town and into the big city? I'll say. On a subconscious level, the music allows the girl to imagine herself as the cool, sophisticated city dweller she'd like to be—then buy those shirts and pants to complete the picture. Believe me when I tell you that stores do this deliberately. When the Gap was rolling out a new sweater line, for example, Muzak vice president Alvin Collis determined that since sweaters represented friendship, family, security, and protection, the stores should play music that evoked fuzzy, cozy feelings. Among the songs Muzak selected to create this "atmospheric"? Louis Armstrong's "It's a Wonderful World."[32]

A South American banking chain once tasked me to help it transform the widespread public perception of its having shoddy, second-rate customer service and long waiting times. When I analyzed the customer experience, including how long people had to wait, I realized that the wait wasn't actually that long; because people anticipated that their visit to the bank would be long and frustrating, they felt as if they were in line longer than they actually were. So using the data compiled by companies like Muzak, we carefully choreographed the rhythms of the music playing overhead and created what was essentially a three-act soundtrack. At the door of the bank, the music serenading consumers was slow and welcoming (in fact, it was a beat slower than the average human heartbeat). As they came closer to the counter, the music would gradually increase in tempo, culminating with a fast beat as they carried out their transactions. The result? Customers "perceived" customer service as being twice as good as before—and incidentally, the bank's revenue increased by 10 percent—all thanks to the speed of the music playing overhead. The good news? The service was already great—yet it took music to convince the customers of it.

I Know What You Bought Last Summer

Have you noticed that those traditional printed price tags on the shelves of supermarkets and big-box stores like Costco and Walmart are slowly being replaced by digital pricing displays? You probably assumed this was for the sake of efficiency; after all, why have employees waste time walking around the store changing those prices every day or week when it can be done electronically? And sure, there's some truth to this explanation . . . but it's far from the whole story.

Have you also noticed how, not unlike highways and commuter trains, supermarkets have their peak traffic times? Swing by the store at 5:00 p.m., and it will be jam-packed. Stop by at eleven in the morning, on a weekday, at least, and it will be nearly deserted (except for maybe that elderly couple buying a cantaloupe). No big shock here; everyone knows that the vast majority of people do their grocery shopping when they get off work, if not on Saturday or Sunday. But what you probably didn't know is that now these stores can, in keeping with the traffic metaphor here, change the price of the toll depending on what time of day you're driving. Have you ever felt that uncontrollable craving for an ice cream sundae at midnight and realized you were out of whipped cream? Such an urge is too powerful to be denied, so you gun your car to the nearest twenty-four-hour supermarket to buy some. I'm guessing that you're willing to pay more for that can of whipped cream than you would have paid at the 5:00 p.m. peak shopping time. Now you can!

Companies and retailers know full well that our price sensitivity varies across the day, week, month, and year. Sometimes we enter a store determined to find a bargain, while other times, like when we're in a pinch or a hurry, we couldn't care less. Well, guess what? Thanks to data-mining technology, in some countries supermarkets and other large retailers know exactly when we're willing to shell out more for products—and are altering their prices accordingly.

Enter digital signage! In Scandinavia, some supermarkets are already switching their prices daily, and across Japan some are even doing so on an hourly basis. The factors that currently determine the price of an item include weather (bad weather means that prices go up) and the density of customers in the store (lots of customers means prices decrease). I can promise you that this trend can lead to one thing and one thing only: in the future, prices will begin fluctuating like the stock market, creating a sort of game (remember the addictive quality of games) out of getting the lowest prices for your everyday stuff.

Companies are using data mining to play on our price sensitivities in other ways, too. Over the past year, a whole new data-mining tool has taken flight, and many Fortune 100 companies are embedding it into their Web sites as we speak. It's called Predicta.net, and its purpose is simple: Predicta allows Web sites to identify then segment shoppers based on what they do and where they go online, then direct highly specific advertising and marketing tailored to how much they're willing to spend.

Let's say that just this morning you were perusing a sale on Best Buy.com for a digital camera. If the Best Buy site is enabled with Predicta (whose clients include Visa, Philips, and Hewlett-Packard),[33] it immediately knows two things: that you're in the market for a digital camera and that you're a true bargain hunter. Thus it serves you up a "personalized" coupon that offers a shockingly good discount on—yes!—that very same camera you've been hunting down all morning. There's only one catch: you'll have to visit the store to buy it (where you may spot and be unable to resist that laptop you've had your eye on). In short, based on what online searches you have made or Web sites you've visited, Predicta will ensure that the entire home page of the store you coincidentally decided to visit is redesigned in a split second to feature—guess what?—the camera you've been checking out all morning. This is known as "behavioral targeting," and as data-mining technologies become cheaper and easier to use, it's becoming an increasingly popular tactic among marketers of all stripes.

Let's take a slightly different scenario: Say your friend spent the morning searching for a premium camera on the Canon or Nikon home page. This time the Predicta-enabled site realizes in a split second that a bargain offer isn't for her and that she's willing to pay a high price for all the bells and whistles, which is why it offers up its best-quality camera—along with a coupon that gives her a slight discount on an equally high-end leather carrying bag (though the camera itself is for full price, of course). The upshot is essentially what economists call price discrimination: you and your friend end up buying the same item, but at radically different prices.

An even newer software program known as Baynote (in use by companies including AT&T and apparel maker Anthropologie) not only tracks your online purchases, where you scroll on a page, what you click, and what search terms you use on any given site, but also refines its search results to recommend to you products based on what products have appealed to users who have browsed and searched similar products.[34] In one example, when AT&T noticed that people were plugging in a lot of searches for a new phone model known as Insight, Baynote was able to bump Insight up higher on the search results on the AT&T Web site in a matter of minutes. And AT&T is not alone. EBay has a team that buys Internet search terms in order to drive search traffic back to its site.

Predicta and Baynote are just two of the many variations on a new and increasingly widespread marketing tool called "personalized retargeting" or "remarketing" that is popular with retailers like Diapers .com, eBags.com, and the Discovery Channel, as well as companies that sell real estate, travel, and financial services online. These programs capture the "cookies" that your computer automatically deposits into your Web browser, creating an indelible imprint of every site you visit and every page you view, then use that information to send you personalized offers relating to anything you have read, viewed, or bought online. This, in fact, was the mysterious force behind a bizarre tale of a pair of stalkerish shoes. As the *New York Times* reported last year, one morning a Canadian mother of two saw and admired the pair of shoes on Zappos, the huge online shoe retailer. From then on, the shoes just wouldn't leave her alone. "For days and weeks, every site I went to seemed to be showing me ads for those shoes," the woman recalled.

"Cookies are used by virtually all commercial Web sites for various purposes, including advertising, keeping users signed in and customizing content," the article went on, adding, "Bad as it was to be stalked by shoes, Ms. Matlin said she felt even worse when she was hounded recently by ads for a dieting service she had used online. 'They are still following me around, and it makes me feel fat,' " she says.[35]

Last year researchers at the University of California at San Diego found that "a significant proportion of the 50,000 most-visited sites on the Web"[36] were engaging in some manner of behavioral tracking—with some even employing an analysis known as "history sniffing," which delves into our past browsing behavior to uncover what sites we've visited in past months or even years. (Note: as of writing this kind of tracking doesn't work on Apple's Safari, Google's Chrome, or Firefox, though it will work on Internet Explorer.) Similarly, sites like Perez Hilton, Wired, Technorati, and Answerbag employ an analytics service known as Tynt.com, which measures what articles users cut and paste, a spying protocol known as "behavior sniffing."[37]

Experiencing a recurrent pain in your abdomen? Having trouble sleeping? Concerned about a relative's depression? What do you do? I'm guessing you go straight to the Internet, where you quickly type in the symptoms. This is why some pharmacy chains are now monitoring our search patterns online. Imagine how valuable this data is for drugstores. Not only can they use it to send us offers related to our specific condition, but they know what health concerns are most prevalent in our geographic area or among our demographic and can alter their inventory or in-store signage accordingly. As of writing, a number of prominent consumer organizations are asking the FTC to investigate deceptive ads that pop up when we go online to hunt down medical or prescription drug information. Notes the consumer complaint, "Nearly $1 billion dollars will be spent this year by online health and medical marketers targeting the growing number of U.S. consumers who increasingly rely on the Internet for information about medical problems, treatments, and prescription drugs."[38] Among the companies named in the complaint are Google, Yahoo!, Microsoft, AOL, WebMD, QualityHealth, Everyday Health, and HealthCentral. What's more, as of writing, pharmaceutical and other health-oriented marketers are pressuring the FDA to grant them greater latitude to expand their online advertising, whether it's through data mining, Internet-search monitoring, or online behavioral profiling.

In short, even the most private details about our health aren't safe from data miners.

Gay or Straight? Advertisers Know.

Thanks to social media, our digital footprints have gone from a faint silhouette in the sand to a sprawling, multiclawed track that could easily belong to Bigfoot. One of the main culprits is the Web site everyone loves, loves to hate, and otherwise cannot live without, namely, Facebook. Ready to know what they know?

Although Facebook's much-maligned privacy policies have generated a lot of controversy, they are fairly straightforward—that is, if you bother to take the time to read them. The site claims it does not share personally identifiable information with advertisers "unless we get your permission." At the same time, Facebook does allow "advertisers to choose the characteristics of users who will see their advertisements"[39] and retains the right to use any attributes the site has collected—including information you may have opted to keep private, such as your birthday—"to select the appropriate audience for those advertisements." Scarier still, the site adds, "When (users) click on or otherwise interact with an advertisement there is a possibility that the advertiser may place a cookie in (their) browser and note that it meets the criteria they selected." Which is just a confusing way of saying that if you click on an ad, that advertiser reserves the right to pull up as much information as your Facebook account permits and use it to sign you up for months and even years of "conveniently personalized" ads.

In the fall of 2010, a *Wall Street Journal* article made waves when it revealed that nearly a dozen popular Facebook apps, including Texas HoldEm Poker, FrontierVille, and FarmVille, were sharing information (including users' names and the names of those users' friends) with at least twenty-five advertising and Internet-tracking companies, shattering all Facebook's privacy rules and compromising the privacy of 70 percent of all those who regularly use apps on Facebook, even those who maintained the most secure privacy settings. Though no one was able to prove that Facebook had any prior knowledge of this breach, the shocking affair "renew[ed] questions about [Facebook's] ability to keep identifiable information about its users' activities secure," the *Journal* reported.[40]

If this wasn't enough to make you want to sell your virtual farm, disband your Mafia crew, and deactivate your profile, a few weeks later the other shoe dropped. This time, it was the *New York Times* that broke the story, revealing that in some cases Facebook advertisers (or, as the article put it, "snoops posing as advertisers") could capture sensitive profile data, including users' sexual orientations and religions (even though, as a policy, Facebook does not trade this information with marketers).

As an experiment, researchers in India and Germany created six separate Facebook user accounts. These accounts were identical except for one difference: in two of the six the (fake) user checked off that he/she was interested in persons of the same sex. Not surprisingly, gay-specific ads (e.g., ads for gay bars) soon began to pop up on the sites of the individuals who had revealed themselves to be gay, as did other ads that had no link to users' sexual preferences. However, since these seemingly neutral ads appeared exclusively on gay men's pages, if the user clicked on one of them and was taken to that company's site, he would be dropping a "unique identifier" telling that company or advertiser that he was gay. And while the identifier, "typically a cookie or a computer's Internet address," does not necessarily disclose the identity of the person who clicked," the *Times* reported, "privacy experts said an advertiser could potentially obtain the name in other ways and link it to the user's sexual orientation, perhaps by asking the person to sign up for a newsletter or fill out a form."

In a related experiment, a Stanford researcher placed an ad on Facebook targeting users based on their location, age, gender, interests, and sexual orientation. She next placed a Facebook ad targeting those characteristics, including ads aimed at users interested in same-sex relationships. As the "advertiser" she was able to see whom Facebook had chosen to display that particular ad to—and could thus conclude that that person was gay. According to the *New York Times*, she concluded that someone could use this same technique to find other profile information supposedly protected by the privacy settings, including relationship status and political and religious affiliations, and that it could even be "on other social networks or Web sites, like Google and MySpace."[41]

True, no identifying names are involved, and true, Facebook doesn't directly or deliberately share your personal information with advertisers (or if it does, I can't prove it). Still, it doesn't make it all that difficult for probing advertisers to get around its privacy control, either. In fact, the site is notorious for constantly changing and tweaking its privacy policy—and each time it does, it's an excuse for the site to reset users' privacy controls to a default setting. And after all, what is Facebook if not an incomparably rich database of information about every detail of our lives, and what is Facebook's business model if not one of reliance on its partnerships with advertisers? Noting that someday soon Facebook will represent the "default single sign-on for the web," the *Financial Times* imagines a nightmarish future fantasy in which "a user shares information about their eating and exercise habits on Facebook, and this is paired with other information, such as web browsing history, by any number of so-called 'data mining' companies. These companies create a profile of the user that is sold to various parties, potentially including health insurers. Based on some of this unflattering information, the insurer decides to deny the user coverage."[42]

Every Step You Take

If you want to keep your personal information away from data miners, I also suggest you stay away from Foursquare, which not only stores any information you provide, including your IP address, browsing history, phone number, birthday, and more, each time you "check in" somewhere but also reserves the right to "draw upon this personal information in order to adapt the services of our community to your needs, to research the effectiveness of our network, and to develop new tools for the community," as well as to "provide aggregate information to our partners about how our customers collectively use our site."[43] Of course, Foursquare claims, "We share this type of statistical data so that our partners also understand how often people use their services and our Service, so that they, too, may provide you with an optimal on-line experience," but this really means it reserves the right to share any of your information with third-party search engines, businesses, and advertisers—and in real time, too. And what happens if you broadcast your Foursquare location to all your buddies on Facebook, as most people do? Well, uh, then, "such information is no longer under the control of Foursquare and is subject to the terms of use and privacy policies of such third parties."[44] In other words, it's fair game for all.

But perhaps the biggest thorn in privacy advocates' paw is Google, the king of the Internet, which has made it a corporate mission to "organize the world's information." Known for having the most sophisticated and predictive algorithms and data-tracking capabilities of any site on the Web, Google not only knows what you search for and links our accumulated search patterns to the computers we use, it knows what online videos you watch, what music you stream, what articles you read, what files you download, and more. It also knows what's in your e-mails—which it scans automatically for the purpose of serving you up "contextual advertising," that is, targeted advertising for products somehow related to something you've just e-mailed about. And of course, thanks to Google Maps, it also knows where you live, what books are on your shelves, what car is parked in your driveway, and whether or not there's a wisp of smoke coming out of your chimney.

If you sign up for Google Buzz, an online service that's also available via your smart phone, Google will know even more. Google Buzz works by bringing together all the information you post on various social media—including Facebook, Twitter, Flickr, Foursquare, and Picasa—in one place. If you subscribe, Buzz not only will know who appears in your photos, what topics you tweet about on Twitter, and what you "like" on Facebook; it will "geo-tag" your Buzz post so it will also know exactly where you are at all times. And since what Google Buzz does differently from other social media services is filter the information from people you've signed on to follow so that only the most popular content shows up in your in-box, Google will also know which individuals are the most valuable or influential members of your circle—in other words, which individuals are the most irresistible marks for advertisers.

Still, if you thought this was bad, wait until you find out how advertisers and data miners will use social media to brandwash you in the future. Software company SAS recently rolled out a product that can analyze the "chatter" across social media, including Facebook and Twitter, and identify those who post the most influential comments and are therefore the best marketing targets. Last year a broad array of companies, including Amazon, joined forces with Facebook. Now, if you opt into this particular alliance, not only will Amazon be able to see what books and music you—and any of your friends who have also opted in—deem cool and market to you accordingly, but if you view a product on Amazon, a little icon will tell you how many of your friends "like" it on Facebook. It's data mining meets peer pressure at its finest.

Surrendering Our Immortal Souls

As if this digital spying weren't enough, companies also have a lot of tricks up their sleeves for getting us to *voluntarily* divulge a whole lot of data. If you want to cash a paycheck at a Walmart, for example, you must surrender both your Social Security number and your driver's license information, and quite often your e-mail address. Guess where that information ends up? You guessed it, in Walmart's headquarters in Bentonville, Arkansas. And if Walmart were working with a "data enhancement company" (which, as of writing, it's not), merely divulging your e-mail address could reveal not just your name and address but also additional information about the value of your house and even the size of your mortgage.

Often we unwittingly give companies permission to share our personal information with other companies and advertisers by blindly agreeing to "terms of service" or "license agreements" on sites like the iTunes store. It's no secret that companies bury all kinds of privacy waivers in pages and pages of writing so complex, tedious, and confusing only a member of Mensa using a microscope could decipher it. But take a guess how many people read these disclaimers, known in industry circles as "EULAs" (end-user license agreements)—before clicking "yes" or "I agree"? According to a 2009 study conducted by the New York University School of Law, of the 45,091 households tracked over a thirty-day period, only one or two per every thousand shoppers (that's about 0.01 percent) spent longer than a single second reading a product's EULA,[45] and what's more, the 2005 National Spyware Study by Ponemon Institute found that only 13 percent of people bother to read EULAs before they download free software.

Did you bother to read the latest Apple iTunes user agreement? Me neither—so let's review what it says. Included are new terms and conditions in which Apple asks—or rather, requires—that iTunes users consent to let Apple know where their iPhone, iBook, or MacBook is at any time. In other words, if you want to use the Apple iTunes store (and it won't let you in until you click "I accept"), you have to agree to let Apple track your computer in real time 24/7 *and* share that information with third parties. (Don't forget that Apple knows a lot about you already, including all your past purchases and your credit card number, which it keeps on file.) No wonder Germany responded to Apple's demands with the country's federal justice commissioner insisting that Apple without delay "disclose the details of the location data it is collecting from handhelds," and that in the United States the House Bipartisan Privacy Caucus has demanded that Steve Jobs explain the sudden appearance of this new policy and how, precisely, he intends to guarantee users' anonymity.[46]

A few years ago a neat little April Fool's joke revealed just how little attention we pay to this kind of fine print. Gamestation, a British online video game retailer, playfully buried a clause in its terms and conditions that read, "By placing an order via this Web site on the first day of the fourth month of the year 2010 Anno Domini, you agree to grant us a non transferable option to claim, now and for ever more, your immortal soul. Should we wish to exercise this option, you agree to surrender your immortal soul, and any claim you may have on it, within 5 (five) working days of receiving written notification from gamestation.co.uk or one of its duly authorized minions."[47] How many souls did the company capture? Roughly 7,500, or 88 percent of all the people who bought stuff from the site on that April 1. April Fool's!

A Postprivacy Society

Yes, it's true that we as consumers are partly to blame for all that companies know about us. We place way too much information online. We blog. We chat. We tweet. We play Foursquare. We post our favorite YouTube videos. We enter our credit card numbers every time we want to buy a book, a T-shirt, a plane ticket, and more. We announce to our Facebook friends where we're going on vacation, that we like Pink Floyd, Cold Stone ice cream, Pixar, and *House*. And each time we do, we're playing right into the hands of the data miners.

It's no huge surprise, given how much of their lives the younger generation spends on Facebook and Twitter, that when I gathered groups of teenagers from across the country to talk about privacy (in conjunction with the recruitment firm Murray Hill Associates), the word "privacy" appeared to mean nothing to them; either they were completely indifferent to the subject or they'd completely given up on it. It was a little chilling.

It should also come as no surprise, given how much time today's kids spend online, that data miners are collecting information about children as young as four or five. Some do this via online questionnaires that pop up on kid-friendly sites, asking kids their age, favorite toys and cartoon characters, and buying behavior, and sometimes even the buying behavior of their parents. Your kid wants to register for the Warner Bros. Looney Tunes kids' Web site? Well, he'll have to *join* first, by giving his first name, answering a security question, and offering up his parents'—i.e., your—e-mail address. Once you've answered with a confirming e-mail, Warner Bros. will ask for your child's e-mail address, followed by his zip code and year of birth, and then will require you to check a box agreeing to the terms of agreement on his behalf. What *are* those terms of agreement? According to the Web site, "We may ask them to provide us with their first name, hometown, and e-mail address. On some pages of our sites, such as where children can send electronic postcards to their friends, we also may ask your child to provide personal information about other people."[48]

Then again, even if your kids don't sign up for the Looney Tunes Web site, it's not too difficult for marketers to mine data about them given the fact that, according to Internet security firm AVG, *92 percent of American children have a digital footprint before the age of two,*[49] 7 percent of babies exit the womb to find they already have an existing e-mail address, and 5 percent have a social network profile (and almost a quarter of all newborns already have a photographic presence online, too, as 23 percent of parents upload their sonogram photos online). And as social networking becomes even more ubiquitous, there's no question in my mind that these numbers will continue to grow. Remarks J. R. Smith, the CEO of AVG, "It's shocking to think that a 30-year-old has an online footprint stretching back 10–15 years at most, while the vast majority of children today will have online presence that will continue to build throughout their whole lives." He also cautions parents to be mindful of the privacy settings on Web sites where parents "share" photos and information about their children, including YouTube and Flickr.[50]

Still, while many of us are fully aware that all these details about our likes, dislikes, habits, and personal lives are out there floating around in the ether, most of us are ignorant of the *extent* to which every movement we make, every step we take, every item we buy is being recorded and transcribed onto an indelible digital footprint that stays with us for the rest of our lives (and in fact will outlive us long after we're gone). As the *New York Times* notes, all of us are members of "the post-privacy society, where we have lost track of how many entities are tracking us. Not to mention what they are doing with our personal information, how they are storing it, whom they might be selling our dossiers to and yes, how much money they are making off them."[51]

It's true. We *are* living in a postprivacy society. Nothing drove this point home more for me than a poignant irony IBM boss Sam Palmisano noted in a recent speech: that today, some thirty-two closed-circuit cameras sit within two hundred yards of the London flat where author George Orwell wrote *1984*, his dystopian book about the prying eyes of Big Brother.

So yes, we all know that every time we tweet our whereabouts on Twitter, update our Facebook profiles, buy something online with our credit card, or swipe our reward card at a drugstore, we're letting information about ourselves out into the world. But we don't fully realize that every time we do, we're essentially giving companies and marketers permission to record, store, compile, and analyze every last bit of information we choose to share—and many pieces of information we don't—and then turn around and use it to trick, manipulate, and seduce us into buying more stuff. The fact is, as our world becomes increasingly networked, digitized, and hyperconnected and we inevitably conduct even more of our lives online, it will become harder and harder to escape the prying gaze of the data miners. Sure, we could toss out our cell phones, deactivate our Facebook profiles, and cancel our credit cards, but let's get real. We're far too brandwashed to do anything as drastic as that.

I'll Have What Mrs. Morgenson Is Having

THE MOST POWERFUL HIDDEN PERSUADER OF THEM ALL: US

It was close to midnight, Pacific Standard Time, as one truck after another crept down a quiet, gated village road in the heart of Laguna Beach, one of the most beautiful oceanside communities in Southern California (as well as one of the most affluent and most expensive: the median income for a family is $146,562, and the average home price easily tops $1 million). Most of the ornate, sprawling stucco houses were in shadows, their owners asleep—with the exception of the very last house on the block. Considering the time of night, it was unusual to see one, let alone several, vehicles on the road. Yet five or six trucks stood silhouetted in the driveway and along the front curb, as workers silently unloaded camera equipment and cardboard boxes, then carried them inside the house.

What was about to take place over the next eight weeks was among the most risky and unconventional operations my team and I had ever concocted. If a single person in the neighborhood had found out what we were up to, the entire project (which we'd been planning and preparing over the past six months) would be jeopardized. Why? Because the families in this upscale neighborhood could have no idea they were about to become unwitting participants in a massive, $3 million social experiment whose results would reveal a side of consumer behavior few of them would have believed.

Inspired by the 2010 Hollywood movie *The Joneses*, about a family of stealth marketers who move into an upper-middle-class neighborhood to peddle their wares to their unsuspecting neighbors, my scheme was both simple and ambitious: to test the power of word-of-mouth marketing. I would create a real-life version of the film, taking a real-life California family, dropping them in a real-life California neighborhood, and then film them in every waking moment as they went about covertly persuading friends, colleagues, and loved ones to buy a number of carefully selected brands.

First step: I hired one of America's top reality-show casting directors (Marcy Tishk, who has worked on shows ranging from *Jersey Shore* to *Paris Hilton's My New BFF*) and producer Andy McEntee (whose credits include *The Millionaire Matchmaker* and *Extreme Makeover: Home Edition*) to narrow a large field of candidates to select our perfect all-American family. If our experiment was to succeed, the Morgenson family had to represent a perfect mix of ages, styles, interests, and aspirational values. After a lengthy search, Marcy and Andy found their ideal candidates in Eric and Gina Morgenson and their three sons, Jack, Sam, and Max—a successful, good-looking, picture-perfect Southern California family who agreed to make it their life's mission (well, for at least a month) to discreetly persuade their neighbors to buy a broad array of products.

Let's meet them.

Eric Morgenson: In his midforties, with a degree from an East Coast college, Eric is a successful, compassionate, funny, sports-obsessed, and involved father (with a latent party-hearty streak).

Gina Morgenson: Sophisticated, charming, and popular, Gina is politically and environmentally aware, as well as a fashion trendsetter among her friends.

Jack, Sam, and Max Morgenson: As sports-crazy and outdoorsy as their father, Jack, Sam, and Max are hip, handsome Justin Bieber–esque Southern California adolescents (ages sixteen, fourteen, and twelve), smitten with music, skateboarding, technology, and, like most teens and tweens, the latest brands and styles.

Now I want you to picture the scene that took place several days later.

In the Morgensons' spacious yard (complete with heated in-ground swimming pool, Toro-mowed and impeccably landscaped lawn, and three-car garage housing a 2005 Ford Expedition Eddie Bauer edition, a 2008 BMW 750Li, and a 2008 Nissan Altima coupe), Eric Morgenson shows off his grilling techniques and new Frontgate and T.J.Maxx barbecue tools to a handful of male buddies. Two hundred feet away, Gina Morgenson is entertaining a group of female friends in her state-of-the-art kitchen (containing an array of top-of-the-line KitchenAid appliances, including a combination microwave-oven, induction cooktop, ice maker, trash compactor, toaster, immersion blender, and water filter), gushing about how hard she's fallen for a beautiful new jewelry line. Upstairs, Jack, Sam, Max, and a few school friends play the newest game on Xbox while showing off the hip new Vans and etnie sneakers they've recently picked up on a family shopping spree.

The point of this multimillion-dollar experiment was to test the seductive power of word-of-mouth marketing. By filming a "real" family in spontaneous, unscripted situations and scenarios like these, from barbecues to champagne brunches to shopping expeditions, we would document how the Morgensons' circle of friends responded to specific brands and products the Morgensons brought into their lives. When put face-to-face with another family's "enviable" lifestyle—and the brands and products that sustain it—would they want all the things that family has? And more important, would this influence be so powerful as to make them actually go out and buy those things?

With the help of thirty-five video cameras (seventeen hidden from view) and twenty-five microphones tucked away inside the furniture and fixtures, providing us with a 360-degree view of every room in the house, so we could follow the Morgensons wherever they went, the results of this clandestine operation would ultimately reveal something shocking: that the most powerful hidden persuader of them all isn't in your television set or on the shelves of your supermarket or even lurking in your smart phone. It's a far more pervasive influence that's around you virtually every waking moment, brandwashing you in ways you don't even realize: your very own friends and neighbors.

You Run Your Mouth and I'll Run My Business

Over these past pages, we've learned that few, if any, accidents take place in the marketing and advertising world. We've looked at many of the tricks, machinations, untruths, and manipulations that marketers and advertisers use to pressure, cajole, and entice us. We've seen how they use fear, sex, celebrity, New Age promises, insecurity, nostalgia, data mining, and more to prey on our most deeply rooted fears, dreams, and desires in the service of selling us their products. We've witnessed up close the alarmingly young age—often before we've even left our mothers' wombs—at which they begin to target us and the sometimes surreal lengths they'll go to in order to secure us as lifelong customers. We've even looked at the role peer pressure can play in shaping our buying habits. But this chapter goes well beyond that.

In a world where roughly 60 percent of all Americans are members of Facebook (and some 175 million people worldwide log in to Facebook *each day*) and Twitter has around 190 million users (who tweet approximately 65 million times during a twenty-four-hour period), I believe I've only just scratched the surface in exploring how vulnerable and susceptible we are to the advice, recommendations, and subconscious influence of our friends, neighbors, and peers.

The seed of the idea for the reality TV show we dubbed *The Morgensons* occurred to me almost eighteen months before I started writing this book, when I'd been unknowingly lured into a covert marketing ploy that prompted me to doubt my own ability to separate reality from advertising spin. As I pulled up to a gas station in Sydney, Australia, the guy across from me, who'd just finished filling up his own tank, approached me. "Hey, mate, love your car," he said. "Oh, thanks," I said politely. "But mate," he went on (yes, Australian men *do* love to use this endearing term), "you really should consider using superoctane ninety-eight gas." He proceeded to tell me he had the same model of car as mine at home in his garage, adding, "You can't believe the difference in your car's performance—it's amazing."

I thanked him, then promptly forgot his advice. Yet over the next few weeks, every time I needed to gas up my car, I couldn't get his words out of my mind. Whenever I drove into a gas station, the same internal dialogue—*Should I buy the octane or the superoctane 98?*—rolled around in my brain. *What the hell?* I'd begun thinking. *It couldn't hurt, and it costs less than ten cents more.* And sure enough, from then on, each time I needed gas, I'd fill up with the superoctane 98.

Then, a few months later, with the needle of my gas gauge close to empty, I pulled into the very same gas station. I was filling up when I heard an extremely familiar voice.

It was *him*, the superoctane 98 man! This time, though, he wasn't addressing me but another car owner who was filling his tank with the cheapest brand of gas. "Hey, mate," he called over, "love your car." "Thanks," the guy replied in the same polite tone as I had. "But mate," the man went on, "you really should consider using superoctane ninety-eight. Thing is, I have the same model of car at home, and once you've tried it, you won't believe the difference—it's *amazing*."

I'd been completely punked. Either this guy owned every brand of car ever manufactured and knew only two sentences in the English language, or the gas station had planted him to ramp up sales of its higher-priced gas. At the same time, I couldn't help wondering, *Martin, how could you fall for it? You—who work day in and day out in the marketing industry—have been duped into changing your whole buying behavior thanks to five seconds of covert marketing?*

But it wasn't until a year later, when the film *The Joneses* hit the big screen, that I was inspired to hatch my own marketing experiment—to test the effects, over an eight-week period, of that same tactic I had succumbed to in the suburbs of Sydney.

A month later, after screening literally hundreds of hours of videotape, the results from *The Morgensons* came in. But anecdotal evidence like this, no matter how many hours of it, isn't always the most scientific, which is why I decided to conduct an additional fMRI study to confirm our findings. The results proved beyond any doubt whatsoever that marketers, advertisers, and big businesses have nothing at all compared to the influence we consumers have on one another.

Mrs. Morgenson Goes Shopping

Picture this. Gina and a gaggle of friends are going shoe shopping at DSW, the giant retail chain. (DSW, for the uninducted, stands for Designer Shoe Warehouse.) En route to the giant shoe mecca, Gina ingenuously asks a carful of her friends, "Has anyone been to DSW before? I just love the whole concept. You're just *bound* to find the shoe you want there." Two hours later, she's managed to "convince" (subtly, of course) five of her friends to buy multiple pairs; some, in fact, have walked out of the store armed with as many as five new pairs of boots, heels, and flats. Not only that, but I discovered later that following their trip, three of Gina's friends visited DSW's Web site, "liked" the store on Facebook, and, as of writing, had bought several more pairs of its shoes online.

How did I know this? Well, because I called upon ChatThreads, a company that specializes in capturing data on how, when, and where consumers notice specific brands in their day-to-day lives, then analyzing how these encounters impact buying behavior. Both before and after the experiment, the ChatThreads team interviewed Gina's friends about their buying behavior (the "before" interviews were under the guise of a random survey) and were thus able to analyze exactly how exposure to the brands they'd encountered had influenced their subsequent buying behavior. Plus, once the experiment had wrapped up, Gina's friends were asked to text-message whenever they came across the brand, saying how they felt about and interacted with it. DSW came up *numerous* times. Perhaps even more telling, in later scenes, two of Gina's friends showed up at the Morgensons' house wearing the shoes they'd bought on the expedition, and on hidden camera, one of the friends even boasted about her $30 shoes, adding, "I love them—they are the most comfortable heels I own."

What else did I observe on that shopping trip? Well, for one thing, that Gina's friends seemed very reluctant to buy an item unless their friends approved of their purchase beforehand. At one point, two of the friends opted to buy the same style of shoes as the other (whereupon one of the women was heard to gleefully use the word "samesies")—another testament to the power of peer influence, especially given that there are hundreds of different shoe styles in the store. In addition, I noticed that a woman's friends could sway or change her choice up until the very last second; at one point, Gina talked a friend into changing her purchase *while* the clerk was scanning the product behind the cash register.

We saw similar effects of peer pressure again and again. At one point during our filming, Gina invited a dozen or so friends over for a champagne brunch (more like one long infomercial disguised as a champagne brunch). First everyone was served Taltarni, a sparkling wine from Australia. "Isn't it *yummy*?" Gina asked at one point, repeatedly dropping the name of the brand (which her friends continued to describe as "yummy" for the rest of the evening). Then she went on to show her friends the amazing new Pandora brand jewelry she was wearing—"Isn't it spectacular?" she asked. Gina explained that Pandora's Web site allowed her to customize her new charms and that she especially loved the breast cancer charm that the company had created in honor of National Breast Cancer Awareness Month. Gina was so skilled at pushing this particular jewelry line on her friends that one even asked her to write down the name of the brand so she could visit the Web site once she got home. Bingo!

But Gina wasn't done. After all, she needed to tell her friends that she'd recently replaced every single one of her beauty soaps and lotions with a brand of natural products called Kiss My Face, which sells everything from toothpaste to mouthwash to shaving cream. She even loved the brand so much, she told them, that she'd decided to give every single one of her guests a gift bag that included Kiss My Face soaps and lip balms. Later on, she popped open a few bottles of Clos Du Val wine—from a Napa winery "known for their fantastic reds," she told her guests.

Oh, and by the way, had everyone seen her exquisite new bag, created by the London company knomo—a "stylish, modern briefcase that would be perfect for all you corporate girls"?

So how did Gina's friends respond? Well, we first witnessed the impact of Gina's influence two weeks later, when three of her friends showed up at a Laguna Beach party newly adorned in bracelets, charms, and earrings all created by the jewelry company Gina had trumpeted.

Later on, ChatThreads' interviews revealed that after the brunch a handful of Gina's friends had gone out and actually bought knomo bags, along with a whole bunch of Kiss My Face products. In subsequent interviews one friend actually stated that using these products at Gina's house made her "really impressed at how great the products are. I thought because they are so low-priced that they would not be so great. Now I love the products and because of the low price and accessibility, I will definitely start using them." Clos Du Val, our branded California wine, too, had caught on—the women started buying it in bulk, and in later scenes several women told Gina how much they liked the taste. One stated later in an interview, "I really enjoy wine. I am reluctant to purchase wine that I have not tasted—I have not had a 'tasting' of that particular brand—but I was happy to hear that a friend I trust has given her seal of approval . . . so I would be more apt to purchase it when I come across it."

Turned out the power of word of mouth extends even beyond footwear and jewelry choices. Among women, at least, it seemed that a preference for even the most personal of personal products can spread like wildfire. At one point during our filming, Gina brought out a box of Libresse, a Swedish brand of tampons unavailable (as of writing) in the United States (which allowed us to ensure that Gina's friends didn't have prior knowledge of the product). What's so amazingly different about Libresse? Among other things, it's hard to tell at first glance what the box contains. Gina's friends went crazy for the brand, also proving that as far as certain products are concerned, subtle packaging is an irresistible selling point.

What else did this experiment reveal about the power of guerrilla marketing, particularly among women? Well, it seems if a female is actually *wearing* or *using* the brand or product in question—a new line of jewelry, a brand of skin-care products, a pair of boots, or a stylish new bag—her influence over her peers is that much more formidable. What's more, if a friend is impressed enough to write down the name of a brand on a piece of paper, it's pretty much a slam-dunk certainty that she is going to later buy the thing.

"Now I'm Going to Get Fat"

So what about Mr. Morgenson? Was he able to sway his friends' and neighbors' brand choices as effectively as his wife was?

Here's where the genders go their separate ways a little. It turns out that Eric's male buddies were actually more likely to come right out and challenge him when he recommended a brand or a product. *What makes you the expert?* was the unspoken and default male response. (In one scene, for example, a friend visibly bristled when Eric suggested he try a certain brand of barbecue marinade.) My guess? Many men experience these kinds of suggestions as an assault on their authority—as if Eric was implying he knew better.

Yet we did come across some exceptions to this rule. Turns out Eric's male friends were happy to accept a word-of-mouth recommendation about a brand or a product that was aspirational and that signaled money, power, and worldly success—say, a new Jaguar or a state-of-the-art grill or an expensive bottle of wine. That said, they would *only* accept this kind of word-of-mouth recommendation if it came from another male whose opinion and expertise they respected: like Eric. Without that, as our footage clearly showed, another man's recommendation carries no impact whatsoever. In our experiment, we saw evidence of this in the mere words people used to describe a product. In one scene, when one neighbor, who was clearly not a member of Eric and his friends' inner circle, used the word "super-cool" to describe one of the Kiss My Face products, the gang was visibly dismissive of his recommendation. But when one of Eric's other friends who clearly *was* in the inner circle used the term "funky," the term caught on among the group like wildfire.

Another surprising thing I noticed from the Morgensons' footage was that the *men* in the Morgensons' circle seemed to be more easily influenced by their peers' food and dietary choices than the women. At one point during the filming, Eric went so far as to change his drink order when a friend reminded him of the drink's caloric content (and *not* because he was scripted this way, either—remember, there was no script). "There's a ham sandwich in a glass of dark beer," Eric remarked after his friend suggested he switch to a vodka and cranberry juice, adding, "Now I'm going to get fat."

The Junior Morgensons

Earlier we talked about how susceptible teens and tweens are to peer pressure—and the Morgenson sons' friends were no exception. Part of their influence over their peers had to do with the aura of confidence Jack, Sam, and Max exuded; the Morgenson boys always seemed to know exactly what they were talking about (and it helped that they were cool and handsome). At one point Jack was telling his friend about an environmentally friendly snowboard he was trying out and planned to buy. His friend was clearly impressed and immediately wanted one. "Hey, I'll look into it when I get my own board," he said, completely unprompted.

It seemed that the boys' influence persisted even across ages and genders; when Jack told his college-age female cousin (who was not in on the experiment) about Stinky Stink (the brand of body spray marketed to teen boys that I mentioned in chapter 1) and gave her a whiff, she commented that the young men in her dorm should use the stuff.

Interestingly, though, it turned out that as much brandwashing power as the Morgenson kids had on their friends and peers, the people they ended up having the most persuasive power over were their own parents. At one point during our filming, forgetting the cameras were running, Eric and Gina took their three sons shoe shopping. Over and over again, Eric approached his sons with one brand of sneaker after another. "Would you ever wear something like this?" he would ask. It should come as no surprise, given how brand-obsessed most teenagers are, that Jack, Sam, and Max made it clear that unless the sneaker was made by Nike, Vans, or etnie, they weren't interested. In the end? In an obvious (and somewhat sweet) attempt to gain their children's approval, Eric and Gina ended up buying exactly those brands.

The Sounds of Science

After watching the hundreds of hours of footage, I could come to only one conclusion: whether it's shoes, jewelry, barbecue tools, or sports equipment, there's nothing quite so persuasive as observing someone we respect or admire using a brand or product. Still, as convincing as the

Morgensons footage was, I wasn't completely satisfied with this anecdotal data. I wanted to empirically measure and validate our findings. So we had ChatThreads analyze the data. This revealed a couple of interesting trends.

The first was that whether Gina was telling her friends about a great spa where she'd just spent a week or simply drinking a new brand of coffee in front of them, the Morgensons' friends were by a long shot most likely to be susceptible to guerrilla advertising in the mornings, specifically between the hours of eight and ten. Why? Because in the wake of our dreams, mornings are when we tend to be most vulnerable to influence, persuasion, and suggestion. My guess is that mornings are also the time when we haven't yet been exposed to marketing messages. Thus, our "filters" haven't yet been activated.

At the same time, it's worth noting that not a single person we spoke to in the show recalled even one TV commercial they'd seen over the past month. Not one! Yet when we asked the Morgensons' friends to reel off a few random brand names, practically everyone came up with the brands that Eric and Gina had recommended. It was as though they'd stored these "Morgenson-approved" brands in an easily recallable "personal" place in their brains (as opposed to a "corporate" or "commercial" region that usually puts our brains on the defensive).

The brands the Morgensons advocated had another effect, as well: they went viral faster. Perhaps more important, they also carried a "halo effect" (meaning they became safe, preapproved, and inured to any possible criticism). Consequently, roughly one third of the Morgensons' friends began promoting and even flaunting these same brands to *their* friends and acquaintances. (It even reached the point that when several of Gina's friends came home raving at such length about the brands the Morgensons had recommended, the location producer suspected he was the victim of a setup. These women sounded like walking, talking TV commercials! Later, he discovered that the women were simply enthusiastically repeating what Gina had said to them, even using her exact same phrases and words.)

Might I take a moment here to add that during our four-week shoot, none—I mean, *not one*—of the Morgensons' friends ever suspected *anything*, even when Gina drove an hour and a half out of her way to go shoe-shopping? (Gina later told me she'd never driven this far to *any* store.) At times, Eric and Gina both felt they were pushing the products too hard—that is, until they realized just how much many people's natural, everyday conversations actually do revolve around brands.

Perhaps not surprisingly, ChatThreads also found that the brands the Morgensons' peers were most likely to go out and buy at the Morgensons' subtle suggestion were the bigger and better-known ones. Which confirmed my theory that conventional marketing and the more covert variety work best together, that the most persuasive of advertising strategies become that much more so when *amplified* by word-of-mouth advertising.

In the end, even I was genuinely flabbergasted by the power of word-of-mouth marketing. Going in, my paranoid fear had been that perhaps I'd overestimated the power of peer pressure. What if no matter how much the Morgensons promoted this or that brand, none of their friends actually went out and bought anything—or at best, just bought a single brand now and again? Turns out I needn't have worried. The fact that *the Morgensons' friends actually ended up buying an average per person of three brands recommended by the Morgensons* blew my mind. More amazing still? The impact the experiment had on the buying habits of the Morgenson family themselves. *Once our reality show wrapped, Eric, Gina, and their boys continued using and buying six out of the ten brands they'd spent the last month touting.*

A few more things took me aback. I was surprised to learn that, according to ChatThreads' analysis, even off-camera, more than 50 percent of people's everyday conversations revolve around brands. I was surprised by the extent to which people "show off" brands in their homes (both consciously and unconsciously). As one woman told me, "I guess I wanted to display the brand because it gave me something to talk with all my friends about." Finally, I was surprised that when we told Eric and Gina's friends and acquaintances that the whole thing was a hoax, and a reality show, no one was angry or upset or cared even slightly that they had been duped.

Let me reiterate this last point. When I finally revealed the truth about the reality-show experiment, the Morgensons' friends were at first disbelieving—come on, who wouldn't be? But when I asked them if they minded that two of their closest friends had betrayed them in order to convince them to buy brands, it was *my* turn to be shocked. *It was okay,* they said. *If the Morgensons told us a brand was good, it was totally okay.* "But what if the brands the Morgensons recommended *weren't* ones they liked?" I asked. The answer? *Even if the Morgensons recommended brands they disliked, I'd still buy them.* And what's more, not one person felt that our reality-show experiment had been unethical or wrong.

Strange, huh?

I kept asking questions. When asked if they could measure how influenced they were by the Morgensons' recommendations on a scale of one to ten, Eric and Gina's friends unanimously answered, "Ten out of ten." What's more, when I asked one man, a corporate speaker, whether he had ever mentioned the Morgenson-approved brands onstage, he told me he'd probably passed on the names of the brands to "thousands" of audience members. Assuming I'd misheard him, I asked him to repeat the figure. "Thousands," he repeated, adding, "I just happen to love the shoes they recommended."

In some instances, the persuasive effect was unconscious. In these cases it was only after multiple promptings that the Morgensons' friends did admit that yes—come to think of it—they'd altered their purchase patterns by buying precisely the products the Morgensons had recommended. More than once, one of Gina's friends volunteered that her favorite cosmetics brand was Kiss My Face, and that she'd heard about it, well, seems she couldn't remember where. When asked to recall the date she first started using the brand, it turns out it was the day after she'd had dinner at the Morgensons.

At another point, that same woman mentioned how thrilled she was that her twelve-year-old had picked up his childhood LEGO obsession. "Why did he suddenly start playing with LEGO again?" I asked. The woman confessed she had no idea, but finally revealed that something had (literally) snapped into place "after we had dinner at the Morgensons." Talk about unconscious! Eric and Gina had never even promoted the brand by name. But upstairs, while the adults were at dinner, this woman's son had spent a half hour playing LEGO with the Morgenson boys.

Clearly, the Morgensons had exerted a very powerful influence—on both conscious and subconscious levels.

Still, I wanted to learn more. So now it was time to measure precisely just how much guerrilla marketing can amplify the persuasive power of a marketing or advertising strategy by carrying out an fMRI research study.

My goal? To compare the power and effectiveness of personal, word-of-mouth recommendations to the blizzard of other media pushing and persuading us to buy stuff, whether it's a TV commercial, an Internet campaign, or a fashion-magazine spread touting the latest miracle cosmetic.

Six weeks later, after analyzing millions of pieces of fMRI data, the research team sent me the results—allowing me to put into words finally why the Morgensons held in their hands the most irresistible tool of persuasion there is.

You see, in contrast to conventional TV or magazine advertising, a very surprising event takes place in our brains the moment other people recommend a car, a book, a band, a makeup, or a wine. The rational, executive regions of our brains close down while a fireball of activity occurs in the insula—a brain region that is responsible for "social emotions" such as lust, disgust, pride, humiliation, guilt, empathy, and even love. In addition, the brain scans showed, our friends' recommendations stimulate the sensory regions of our brains, causing a sensation not dissimilar to the biological cravings I described in the chapter on addiction. In other words, it's as though word-of-mouth endorsements are "recorded" on multiple brain tracks—and I know from my experiments in *Buyology* that the more "tracks" of the brain a brand or a product affects, the more engaged and attuned we are with it—and the more likely the recommendation is to stick.

Once again, the inner workings of the brain explain why word-of-mouth advertising lingers in our memory for weeks, whereas we can't even recall the TV commercials we saw just this morning. More interesting still, it explains why we seem to have an innate tendency to spread these word-of-mouth endorsements to others. Recent research into the evolutionary roots of gossip (itself a form of word-of-mouth marketing, when you really think about it) has found that whenever someone tells us something good (like, "This is a delicious wine," or "This makeup makes you look five years younger"), and we go on to repeat it, our brains reward us with a shot of dopamine, that "feel-good" neurotransmitter associated with everything from addiction to sensation-seeking. In short, whenever we hear about a brand from people we like and admire, then spread the secret along to others, not only are our brains emotionally engaged, they are also doused with a chemical reward that, as the expression goes, keeps on giving.

In short, if you can get word-of-mouth influence behind your brand, that influence multiplies the power of your brand exponentially.

Which is why I predict the premise behind the Morgensons will soon become a reality—that in the future, companies will hire and plant thousands of Morgenson-like families in communities everywhere, tasking them with the mission of promoting a brand or even an entire family of brands. We may even reach the point where certain households begin to accept salaried positions as stealth marketers. (Think of these thousands of households as "marketing sleeper cells" that will come to life once a company releases a new product or, conversely, when a brand endures a bout of bad publicity.) Sure, there may be resistance at first, but quite simply, companies have too much to gain. So consumers, when you receive product recommendations and advice from that affluent, attractive family who lives down the block from you, beware. Remember that to companies, their words are worth roughly $10,000 a month in marketing power.

And companies won't have to look hard to find these covert marketers, either. According to our incredible casting director Marcy Tishk and producer Andy McEntee, when they began their search to find the perfect family to play the Morgensons, countless auditioning families were all but begging to be cast in the experiment. "So let's say that a show like *The Morgensons* morphs from experiment to reality," I said to Marcy, "and I tasked you to identify families who would be willing to carry out a similar job of secretly promoting brands to their friends and acquaintances—how difficult would that be?" "Oh, it would be pretty easy," Marcy replied. "Could you recruit, say, tens of families like the Morgensons?" I pressed. "Martin," Marcy said patiently, "yes. But not tens—*thousands*."

Whenever I meet up with executives around the world, I remind them that today the most powerful force in marketing is not a corporation. It's not a CEO. It's not a big-budget marketing department. And that with all apologies to Don Draper, the *Mad Men* days of sneaky, one-way-mirror marketing are over. Today and in the future, the people who hold the *real* power are hyperconnected, mouse-clicking consumers and their wide circles of virtual and real-life friends and acquaintances. In other words, the people who hold the real power are *us*.

As consumers, we may think that brands own us—but in reality it's the other way around. So the good news I want to leave you with is this: In our hyperconnected world of Twitter and YouTube and WikiLeaks—a world in which a single trick or deception or secret can be immediately broadcast to the world with the click of the mouse—the consumer is more empowered than ever. As a result, brands of the future simply *must* be transparent and live up to their promises. Trust me (and you marketers out there take note), any brand that doesn't will be instantly and painfully exposed and reviled. That, in the end, is what this book is all about.

Mountain Greenery

At this point in the experiment I began to wonder something: if covert marketing could be used to persuade us to buy all sorts of luxury brands and products, could it also be used for a more noble purpose, like nudging us to buy more socially and environmentally friendly products and even live "greener," more ecologically conscious lives? And, after all, if Toyota can peer-pressure us into buying environmentally friendly Priuses, the Morgensons could peer-pressure their friends into buying environmentally friendly soap.

As of writing, according to the World Meteorological Organization, the past decade has been the hottest ever, a trend that many scientists attribute to man-made pollutants trapping heat in the atmosphere. In 2010, as you may recall, eleven thousand people in Moscow died heat-related deaths; floods overran Pakistan, Thailand, and Vietnam; heavy rains saturated Australia; and Indonesia and parts of China endured droughts—all tragic events that are at least in part attributable to the major climate changes sweeping our planet.

Which is why one of the goals with which I tasked the Morgenson family was to increase awareness within their circle of friends of the crucial importance of going green, and to try to covertly persuade their friends and neighbors to buy more environmentally friendly products. Which they succeeded in doing in small yet meaningful ways.

But before the Morgenson family embarked on this last mission, I brought in an environmental coach known locally as the Green Goddess. Sophie Uliano, the author of the book *Gorgeously Green: 8 Simple Steps to an Earth-Friendly Life*, is a leading expert who has built a career around helping consumers begin living greener lives.

Following Uliano's advice, the Morgenson family began using the same tactics they used to persuade their friends to buy those beautiful bracelets and those bottles of California bubbly to persuade them to live in more ecologically mindful ways. For example, the Morgenson boys began showing up at school with GreenSmart bags— eco-conscious backpacks, messenger bags, and lunch boxes that are created entirely from recycled materials. And sure enough, a number of their classmates soon started doing the same. Gina introduced these same bags to her friends as great picnic tote bags—"perfect for keeping hot things hot and cold things cold," she told them. This little mini-experiment within my experiment worked better than even I anticipated. In the sixty days following the Morgensons' ecological mission, ChatThreads found that the number of "green" activities the Morgensons' friends and neighbors engaged in increased by an astonishing 31 percent. Moreover, the influence seemed to stick; according to ChatThreads' analysis, these same friends and neighbors showed a strong likelihood of performing at least one "green" behavior or activity—or making an eco-friendly purchasing decision—each day over the *next* thirty days as well.

The fact of the matter is that peer pressure is the *only* way to make people go green. The most powerful persuader, for better or for worse? Guilt. Naturally, most people recognize the importance of living environmentally mindful lives. We've read the articles and watched the TV documentaries. But in this era of media overload and instant amnesia, the influence of our peers ends up being far, far more powerful. I couldn't help but notice that when Eric took center stage to announce to his friends what green products he was using, everyone in the room not only listened intently to what he was saying—they later actually changed their habits.

It's easy enough to imagine. A woman mentions to a friend in passing that she just bought a GreenSmart bag. That second woman goes out and buys it, mentions it to six of her friends, several of whom go out and buy it and then talk about it to their friends. Or a businessman is aboard an airplane, his laptop enclosed in a GreenSmart bag, when his seatmate asks, "Where'd you get that bag?" That passenger happens to be a popular blogger who buys it and gives it a plug in his widely read weekly column. A day or so later, 250,000 readers are aware of GreenSmart and its products and are "liking" the GreenSmart Facebook page—and remember, if our Facebook friends "like" a product, we perceive it as preapproved and "like" it more ourselves. From there, buzz about the brand—and what it stands for—spreads virally, and in no time at all it has a worldwide following that's stronger, deeper, and far more loyal than any big-budget campaign that even the savviest marketer, advertiser, or corporation could ever concoct.

In 2011, Bharat Anand of Harvard University, and Aleksander Rosinski, a former visiting researcher there, found that we are far more likely to be persuaded by a product recommendation when it comes from a source we trust and respect. When they placed the exact same ad in two different publications (one a respected print publication, the other an online news site), they found that the more respected the publication, the more that people would trust the ad. I would argue that when it comes to word-of-mouth recommendations (which we expect to be authentic and genuine rather than paid for by a company), the source matters even more. Which brings me back to the Morgensons. The Morgensons embody the American dream. They are successful, wealthy, attractive, the picturesque harmonious family living a life we all want to live. In short, we not only respect them, we aspire to be them. And in turn, we trust them.

We all have the equivalent of the Morgenson family in our own social circle. Because they've created a life we all somehow would like to have, we believe (consciously or not) that buying the things they buy and doing the things they do just might give us a whiff of their success, or their happiness. Just as with a beloved celebrity, our respect and admiration for the Morgensons (or the equivalent in our neighborhood) gets transported onto every brand they recommend.

So yes, while companies and marketers have all kinds of sneaky ways of tricking us into buying their products, at the end of the day we're not *just* being brandwashed by companies—the fact is, we're also being brandwashed (and sometimes in a good way) by *one another.*

Here I will leave you with just one final reflection: for better or for worse, a year after my Brand Detox, I'm still coming to terms with how completely hooked I was (and still am) on the brands I love and use—from my Gillette Fusion razor, to the Clarins moisturizer I slather over my face after a long plane flight, to the Pepsis in my fridge at home.

At the same time, my failed detox helped open my eyes to the fact that I may be a marketer, but I'm also a consumer, just like the rest of us. It helped me realize that there are simply a handful of brands I cannot live without, brands that define who I am and who I wish to become. I hope this book has similarly helped you to understand your own complicated relationship with brands, and that it's educated and empowered you to be able to recognize when you're being manipulated—and when you're not (and, for those advertisers and marketers reading this who want to continue the conversation about the ethical issues addressed in *Brandwashed* or receive more information on what your brand or company can do to become more consumer-friendly, please visit my website at www.martinlindstrom.com).

And by the way, I still ❤ Cyprus.

ACKNOWLEDGMENTS

In my experience, we all have three bank accounts. As most of the world knows, the first is where you stash your money. The second—our "personal brand account"—is a place where we actively innovate or enhance our brand. Just as critical is our third account, which I dub our "exploration account," a time, period, or state of mind when we learn, improve ourselves, or just plain evolve . . . or enhance our personal brand. When did you last set aside time to strengthen the skills you were born with? It's pretty hard to remember, right?

The point is, a deposit into our brand and exploration accounts takes place only with the help, support, encouragement, and talent of others. And without them, this book would never have hit the bookstores, or made it into your hands in the first place.

First, a huge thanks goes to all the sponsors of *Brandwashed*—in particular Julia Steerman and the Murray Hill Center, one of the top focus-group companies in the United States, who have not only helped support some of the fascinating results you've just read about, but helped confirm many of my hypotheses and theories.

Headed up by Ruth Stanat, SIS International made our nationwide study on kids and parents become a reality by exploring millions of data points, which led to a host of intriguing conclusions. A big thank-you also goes to Ashan Khan, John Nuding, and John Spadaro of Zenith Media, for giving me access to some rather spectacular media habits across the U.S.

Without Anne-Marie Kovacs, who forwarded me the trailer to the film *The Joneses* months before its theatrical release and helped craft the experiment's hypothesis and outline, the inspiration for *The Morgensons* would never have taken place. Anne-Marie also co-ran focus groups in Chicago related to many of the topics in this book. I owe you one (or several), Anne-Marie.

Which brings me back to my sponsors, without which this project would never have become a reality. I'd like to thank my number one favorite brand: LEGO. (If you've read my previous books, you probably know about my lifelong love affair with that company.) A special thank-you goes to LEGO senior vice president Mads Nipper, with whom I've worked since the birth of the Internet—that's sixteen years, Mads, if you're counting. Also a big thank-you to Chris Sellers from StinkyStink. You're really an amazing guy, and I'm grateful for all your support.

Let's pause for a moment because here comes without any doubt the most important part of my thank-you speech—the editorial team.

First of all, Peter Smith, my favorite ghostwriter. Peter and I worked together on *Buyology*—the success of *Buyology* can without any doubt be credited to his amazing work. Peter and I have worked on *Brandwashed* for close to two years. He's more than a ghostwriter (Peter, we really need to re-brand that stupid term, eh?); he's a mentor, creative genius, and amazing writer. Traveling as much as I do means impossible working hours and constant jet lag (can you imagine what it's like to work with me?). Peter coped with it all, and did so with brilliance. Thanks for everything, Peter.

Close behind Peter is the team behind *Buyology* and now *Brandwashed*. First, my extraordinarily talented editor, Talia Krohn. The truth? I didn't invent the concept for this book, and neither did I come up with the title. Both were Talia's doing, which I think says it all. Talia has worked extraordinarily hard on this book, and performed magic. My gratitude to her skills and patience is enormous. I'd also like to thank a truly essential member of the Crown team, senior editor Roger Scholl, who has kept a critical, objective eye on this project over the past two years. Among the biggest champions of this book from the get-go were Senior Vice President and Publisher Tina Constable and Crown Deputy Publisher Michael Palgon. Tina, you did a great work in guiding the entire publication of *Brandwashed*—making everyone believe this was something special. Amy Boorstein—thank you for your guiding hand—and a special thanks to the Random House sales team, which in my mind is an essential reason why *Brandwashed* became what it is today.

Okay—let's get this in writing once and for all—you are my favorite publisher (but you all know that).

Another big thank-you goes to my hardworking agent, Jim Levine, and his foreign-rights director, Elizabeth Fisher. Jim was one of the forces behind *Brand Sense* and *Buyology*, and I know our professional relationship will only flourish in the future.

What is a book without marketing? By now you probably know the answer: not a lot. First of all a big thank-you goes to Melissa Hobley at LINDSTROM Company in New York. Melissa oversaw the entire marketing machine—a team of more than ten people in and out of house. Melissa not only made our *Morgensons* experiment a reality, she did an amazing job overseeing the fMRI studies, the SIS studies, and all our promotion and marketing plans. Supporting Melissa is Kate Ferfecka, who worked day and night to craft online strategies and make our online visibility a reality.

Much of our online presence—our marketing concepts, graphics, and viral videos—was overseen by Jonathan Greenstein and Lara Greenstein at Juice, my favorite marketing company operating out of Canada. They know how to create magic, and I'm deeply in debt to them for sharing their amazing skills and talents with me. A huge debt of gratitude also goes to Random House's amazing marketing and publicity team. In particular, I'd like to thank Meredith McGinnis, Jennifer Robbins, Katie Conneally, Tara Gilbride, Jacob Bronstein, and Dennelle Catlett.

But I've also had to learn—a lot—and in order to do so, there are a ton of people I need to thank.

Mark Fortier has been a cornerstone behind all the publicity for *Brandwashed*. Mark and I have now worked together on two books, and Mark—you are without any doubt one of the top PR people not just in the U.S. but in the world. Period.

As you've probably noticed, marketing and psychology go together—which is why I'd like to thank psychologist Dr. Belisa Vranich, a *Today* show contributor (and a just plain amazing person). Belisa not only oversaw many of the psychological behaviors taking place in Los Angeles, she also contributed with amazing observations and interpretations during *Brandwashed*'s journey. Belisa, you're a true (also sexy as hell) star! Thank you. (Oh, and Krista Brunson from the *Today* show—you're quite literally a star as well!)

I'd also like to thank Dr. Greg Dillon; Dr. Hawk Smith; Dr. Jorge

Petit; Dr. Isabelle Souffront; Dr. Gertie Quintandon; Rose Garcia; John Dulworth; and Ron Mitchell, who helped shape some of my thoughts and clarify some of my hypotheses.

Among my goals in a book is to share observations, fascinating statistics, and of course access to people who my readers never thought existed. Making all this possible is my number one researcher, Bobbie7—yep, that's really her name. Bobbie7 has worked for me for over ten years—together we've worked on four books—yet we've never met. (Part of her brand is to be mysteriously unknown.) Thank God I found you, Bobbie7. Joining our research effort were the talented Risa Sacks and Amelia Kassel, who ran some of the primary and secondary research jobs for almost one year. They've interviewed and screened hundreds of people and helped me verify hard-to-track-down data. I'm so proud to have worked with both of you—thanks heaps for all your hard work. Frank Foster—thanks for your friendship and thanks for your guiding hand turning the last chapter around in the eleventh hour.

All of which leads me to the hundreds of people we've interviewed worldwide. A special (and enormous) thank-you goes to Unilever's David Cousino, a shining star in the field of consumer insight. Thank you so much for sharing the most amazing insights about a fascinating project led by a fantastic company. Howard Roberts and Richard Huntington, both from Saatchi & Saatchi, also contributed amazing insights. I'd also like to thank Isabel Lopes, MSLIS, Assistant Librarian, Center on Media and Child Health, Children's Hospital, Harvard Medical School, Harvard School of Public Health; and Sally J. Persing, Center on Media and Child Health (CMCH), Children's Hospital Boston. Also a special thank-you to Linda Ackerman and Beth Givens, Privacy Activism, for their insight into online practices. Steven Pray, PhD, DPh, Professor of Nonprescription Products and Devices at College of Pharmacy, Southwestern Oklahoma State University, helped me understand the addictive qualities of products.

Thanks also go to Dr. Charles Lynde, past president of the Canadian Dermatology Association, Assistant Professor at the University of Toronto; Giselle Whitwell—music therapist—a pioneer in music therapy, especially for prenatal and early childhood; Peter Hepper, Fetal Behavioral Research Center, Queens University, Belfast, Northern

Ireland; Catherine Lynch and Joanne Irwin; and Jenny Saffran, Distinguished Professor, Psychology, University of Rochester, Group Coordinator, Communication and Cognitive Sciences Group. Thank you to Janet DiPietro, Associate Dean for Research, Professor, Department of Population, Family and Reproductive Health, Johns Hopkins Bloomberg School of Public Health; Claire Lerner, Director of Parenting Resources, ZERO TO THREE; and David Chamberlin, PhD, author of *Prenatal Memory and Learning* and *The Mind of Your Newborn Baby*, among other books.

I'd also like to thank Marcy Axness of Quantum Parenting for help understanding the uses of data mining; Bryan Pearson, President and CEO, Alliance Data and LoyaltyOne Air Miles Reward Program; Michael Berry, Data Miners; Peter Fader, Wharton School of Business; Herb Sorensen, TNS Global; and Wendy W. Moe, Associate Professor of Marketing, Robert H. Smith School of Business, University of Maryland.

For help with early childhood issues I'd like to thank Emily Korns, Nestlé Infant Nutrition; and Abigail Tuller, Editor in Chief, *Pregnancy* magazine and Pregnancy360.com. Thank you both for all your amazing insight.

Last, but certainly not least: thanks to the talents of our incredible casting director, Marcy Tishk, we searched for months for a beautiful, kind, outgoing, smart, beautiful family—and boy, were Eric and Gina Morgenson and their children, Jack, Sam, and Max, ever up for it. A very significant and major thank-you to the Morgenson family, who couldn't have made this project more interesting, easier, or more exciting, and to all their lovely friends in Laguna, who allowed us to observe their consumer habits. We are forever grateful.

Enormous thanks also go to our TV producer, Andy McEntee, who made this project so successful and provocative, and without whose expertise, ideas, and warmth this project would never have happened. Finally, ChatThreads, a company that captures data on how, when, and where consumers notice individual brands in their day-to-day lives, then analyzes how these encounters impact purchase behavior, helped measure the profound impact of word-of-mouth marketing. I truly believe no other company can perform better than they did.

NOTES

Introduction

1. See the organization's Web site, www.enough.org.uk.

Chapter 1. Buy Buy Baby

1. Minna Huotilainen, "Foetal Learning: A Bridge over Birth" (available at http://www.edu.helsinki.fi/lapsetkertovat/lapset/In_English/Huotilainen.pdf).

2. P. G. Hepper, "Fetal Memory: Does It Exist? What Does It Do?" *Acta Paediatrica Supplement* 416:16–20 (available at http://www.cirp.org/library/psych/hepper1/#n29).

3. "Children Whose Mothers Smoked During Pregnancy and Early Childhood More Likely to Smoke as Adults," *Science Daily*, May 21, 2009 (available at http://www.sciencedaily.com/releases/2009/05/090519134657.htm).

4. Emily Oken, Elsie M. Taveras, Ken P. Kleinman, Janet W. Rich-Edwards, and Matthew W. Gillman, "Weight Gain in Pregnancy Linked to Overweight in Kids," *American Journal of Obstetrics & Gynecology*, April 2007.

5. "Pregnant Mother's Diet Impacts Infant's Sense of Smell, Alters Brain Development," *Science Daily*, December 6, 2010 (available at http://www.sciencedaily.com/releases/2010/12/101201095559.htm).

6. "Children Whose Mothers Smoked."

7. J. A. Mennella, C. P. Jagnow, and G. K. Beauchamp, "Prenatal and Postnatal Flavor Learning by Human Infants," *Pediatrics* 107(2001), no. 6: E88.

8. Annie Murphy Paul, *Origins: How the Nine Months Before Birth Shape the Rest of Our Lives* (New York: Free Press, 2010).

9. Dani Veracity, "Child-Centered Marketing Causing Kids to Carry Unhealthy Food Habits into Adulthood," *Natural News*, October 30, 2006 (available at http://www.naturalnews.com/020920.html).

10. F. J. Zimmerman, D. A. Christakis, A. N. Meltzoff, "Television and

DVD/Video Viewing in Children Younger Than Two Years," *Archives of Pediatric & Adolescent Medicine* 161, no. 5 (2007): 473–79.

11. J. McNeal and C. Yeh, "Born to Shop," *American Demographics*, June 1993, pp. 34–39.

12. Lina Perez and Victoria Vasile, "Kids' Opinions Hold Sway," *Kids Today*, March 1, 2007 (available at www.kidstodayonline.com/article/518854 -Kids_opinions_hold_sway.php).

13. Andrew Meltzoff, "Imitation of Televised Models by Infants," *Child Development* 59 (1998): 1221–29(available at http://ilabs.washington.edu/ meltzoff/pdf/88Meltzoff_TVimit_ChildDev.pdf).

14. Alan Mozen, "Cartoon Characters Sell Kids on Unhealthy Foods," *U.S. News and World Report*, June 21, 2010 (available at http://www.health .usnews.com/health-news/diet-fitness/diet/articles/2010/06/21/ cartoon-characters-sell-kids-on-unhealthy-foods.html).

15. Thomas N. Robinson, Dina L. G. Borzekowski, Donna M. Matheson, and Helena C. Kraemer, "Effects of Fast Food Branding on Young Children's Taste Preferences," Stanford Archives of Pediatric and Adolescent Medicine 161, no. 8 (2007): 792–97 (available at http://www.ncbi.nlm .nih.gov/pubmed/17679662).

16. Douglas Rushkoff, *Coercion: Why We Listen to What They Say* (New York: Riverhead Press, 2000), p. 197.

17. Julie Schor, *Born to Buy* (New York: Scribner, 2007).

18. "What Kids Know: McDonald's, Toyota, Disney," *ABC News*, April 12, 2010 (available at http://abcnews.go.com/Business/kids-mcdonalds -toyota-disney/story?id=10333145).

19. Matt Richtel, "In Online Games, a Path to Young Consumers," *New York Times*, April 21, 2011.

20. Tralee Pearce, "Cashing In on Preteen Puberty" *Globe and Mail*, November 13, 2007 (available at http://www.theglobeandmail.com/life/ article797684.ece).

21. Douglas Quenqua, "Graduating from Lip Smackers," *New York Times*, April 28, 2010 (available at http://www.nytimes.com/2010/04/29/ fashion-29tween.html).

22. Peggy Orenstein, *Cinderella Ate My Daughter* (New York: HarperCollins, 2011), p. 82.

23. Ibid.

24. Andrew Adam Newman, "Depilatory Market Moves Far Beyond the Short-Shorts Wearers," *New York Times*, September 14, 2007 (available at

http://www.nytimes.com/2007/09/14/business/media/14adco.html
?_r=1&ref=media).

25. Allan D. Kanner, "Globalization and the Return of Childhood," *Tikkun*,
September/October 2005 (available at http://www.tikkun.org/article
.php/Kanner-Globalization).

26. Valerie Baulerine, "Gatorade's 'Mission': Sell More Drinks," *Wall Street
Journal*, September 13, 2010 (available at http://online.wsj.com/article/
SB10001424052748703466704575489673244784924.html).

27. Ibid.

28. Ad Tunes, "BP British Petroleum 'Say Hey' TV Commercial Music,"
http://adtunes.com/forums/showthread.php?t=87309.

29. Porsche 911 commercial, available at http://www.youtube.com/watch?v=
7sWPHKU1XZU.

30. Chris Reiter, "BMW Sleds, Mercedes for Kids Battle $13,000 Audi on
Santa List," *Bloomberg News*, November 20, 2010 (available at http://www
.bloomberg.com/news/2010-11-23/bmw-sleds-mercedes-for-kids-battle
-13-000-audi-toy-on-luxury-santa-list.html).

31. Allison Linn, "Starbucks Rethinks Stance on Young Customers," msnbc
.com, September 10, 2007, http://www.msnbc.msn.com/id/20608492/
ns/business-consumer_news.

32. Ellen Ruppel Shell, *The Hungry Gene* (New York: Grove Press, 2003),
pp. 192–93.

33. Elizabeth S. Moore, William L. Wilkie, and Richard J. Jutz, "Passing the
Torch: Intergenerational Influences as a Source of Brand Equity," *Journal
of Marketing* 66 (April 2002): 17–31 (available at http://warrington.ufl.edu/
mkt/docs/lutz/PassingtheTorch.pdf).

34. Banwari Mittal and Marla B. Royne, "Consuming as a Family: Modes of
Intergenerational Influence on Young Adults," *Journal of Consumer Behaviour*
9, no. 4 (July/August 2010): 239–57.

35. Bruce Temkin, "Apple's Newest Strategy: Influential Bundling," *Consumer
Experience Matters*, August 25, 2008 (available at http://experiencematters
.wordpress.com/2008/08/25/apples-strategy-influential-bundling).

Chapter 2. Peddling Panic and Paranoia

1. "Report: U.S. Hand Sanitizers Market to Exceed $402M by 2015,"
Occupational Health and Safety, June 14, 2010 (available at http://ohsonline
.com/articles/2010/06/14/us-hand-sanitizers-market-will-grasp-millions
.aspx).

2. Susan Todd, "Hand Sanitizer Brings Big Profit for Johnson and Johnson," *Star-Ledger*, February 14, 2010 (available at www.nj.com/business/index .ssf/2010/02/hand_sanitizer_brings big_prof_ htm).

3. Melly Alazraki, "Swine Flu Lifts Sales of Purell Sanitizer, Clorox Wipes, Other Consumer Products," *Daily Finance*, November 5, 2009 (available at http://www.dailyfinance.com/story/company-news/swine-flu-boosts -sales-of-purrell-santizer-clorox-wipes-other/19222737/).

4. See the "Know the Facts" page on Purell's Web site, http://www.purell .com/page.jhtml?id=/purell/include/facts.inc.

5. Jennifer Whitehead, "UK Brands Lag Behind US Counterparts in Response to Swine Flu," *Brand Republic*, April 30, 2009 (available at http:// www.brandrepublic.com/bulletin/brandrepublicnewsbulletin/article/ 902174/UK-brands-lag-behind-US-counterparts-response-swine-flu/ ?DCMP=EMC-DailyNewsBulletin).

6. See the Kleenex Web site, http://www.kleenex.com/FacialTissues.aspx.

7. "Marketers Already Aiming at Swine Flu Ads," *Radio Broadcast News*, April 30, 2009 (available at http:www.rbr.com/media-news/advertising/ 14311.html).

8. See the ReStockIt Web site at http://www.restockit.com.

9. Shane Starling, "Kellogg's Settles Rice Krispies Immunity Claims Dispute," *Nutra Ingredients USA*, January 5, 2010 (available at http://www .nutraingredients-usa.com/Regulation/Kellogg-s-settles-Rice-Krispies -immunity-claims-dispute).

10. Press release, Kellogg Company, November 3, 2009 (available at http:// www.reuters.com/article/pressRelease/idUS199098+04-Nov-2009 +PRN20091104).

11. See the SafeEggs Web site at http://www.safeeggs.com.

12. Mandy Hougland, "Forecast Calls for Sales," *Retailing Today*, October/ November 2007 (available at http://www.wxtrends.com/files/ retailnews15.pdf).

13. "Wal-Mart Praised for Hurricane Katrina Response Efforts," *NewsMax*, September 2, 2005 (available at http://archive.newsmax.com/archives/ ic/2005/9/6/164525.shtml).

14. Max Read, "Americans: Afraid of Freemasons, Canada, Alex Rodriguez," Gawker, March 24, 2010, http://gawker.com/5500661/americans-afraid -of-freemasons-canada-alex-rodriguez.

15. Brandon Keim, "That Nearly Scared Me to Death! Let's Do It Again,"

Wired, October 31, 2007 (available at http://www.wired.com/science/discoveries/news/2007/10/fear_neurology).

16. Lou Dzierzak, "Factoring Fear: What Scares Us and Why," *Scientific American*, October 27, 2008 (available at http://www.scientificamerican.com/article.cfm?id=factoring-fear-what-scares).

17. "The Four-Letter Word in Advertising: Fear," *Ai InSite*, January 27, 2010 (available at http://www.insite.artinstitutes.edu/the-fourletter-word-in-advertising-fear-20072.aspx).

18. Dzierzak, "Factoring Fear."

19. Sharon Begley, "The Roots of Fear," *Newsweek*, December 24, 2007.

20. Ibid.

21. "Political Fear Mongering and Why It Works," *Daily Kos*, October 24, 2010, http://www.dailykos.com/story/2010/10/24/75819/005.

22. Kim White, "Putting the Fear Back into Fear Appeals: The Extended Parallel Process Model," *Communication Monographs* 59 (December 1992): 329–49 (available at https://www.msu.edu/~wittek/fearback.htm).

23. Aquafresh toothbrush ad, 1994 (available at http://www.youtube.com/watch?v=V42QI4r8fWU).

24. Press release, University of Bath, "Fear Is Stronger Than Hope for Worriers Trying to Get Fit, Says Researchers," November 27, 2007 (available at http://www.bath.ac.uk/news/2007/11/27/gym-fear.html).

25. Libby Copeland, "The Cure for Your Fugly Armpits," *Slate*, April 14, 2011, http://www.slate.com/id/2291205/.

26. Robert Klara, "Caution: Fear Mongering May Be Hazardous to Your Brand," *Brandweek*, December 9, 2009 (available at http://www.brandweek.com/bw/content_display/current-issue/e3i75b60f5d014806b03410001d22a9e74e).

27. Rich Thomaselli, "Fear Factor Gets Brink's Buzz—and a Sales Boost," *AdAge*, April 13, 2009 (available at http://adage.com/article?article_id=135944).

28. *Saturday Night Live*, season 35, episode 17 (available at http://www.hulu.com/watch/134720/saturday-night-live-broadview-security).

29. " 'I Want More Time,' Saddest Commercial Ever," http://www.youtube.com/watch?v=UvYb4BLIAQw.

30. Kirsten A. Passyn and Mita Sujan, "Self-Accountability Emotions and Fear Appeals: Motivating Behavior," *Journal of Consumer Research*, March 2006.

31. Fiona Macrae, "From Cheating Golfers to MPs on the Fiddle: Why

Men Really Do Feel Less Guilt Than Women," *Daily Mail*, January 27, 2010.

32. Peter Sells and Sierra Gonzalez, "The Language of Advertising," Unit 7: Words and Phrases Used in Advertising, http://www.stanford.edu/class/linguist34/.

33. Marc-André Gagnon and Joel Lexchin, "The Cost of Pushing Pills: A New Estimate of Pharmaceutical Promotion Expenditures in the United States," *PLoS Medicine*, January 3, 2008.

34. "Method Products, Cleaning and Growing!" EcoSherpa, October 17, 2006, www.ecosherpa.com/uncategorized/method-products-cleaning-and-growing/.

Chapter 3. I Can't Quit You

1. Brad Stone, "Breakfast Can Wait. The Day's First Stop Is Online," *New York Times*, August 9, 2009.

2. Ibid.

3. Shelley DuBois, "How Pepsi's Crowd-Sourced Ads Beat the Super Bowl Beer Spots," *Fortune*, February 10, 2011.

4. "Shopaholic Granny Stole More Than £150,000 from Her Employers to Fund an Addiction," *London Evening Standard*, May 6, 2007 (available at http://www.thisislondon.co.uk/news/article-23399529-shopaholic-granny-stole-150000-to-feed-her-addiction.do).

5. Amy S. Clark, "Shopping Addiction: A Serious Problem," *CBS Evening News*, December 9, 2006 (available at http://www.cbsnews.com/stories/2006/12/09/eveningnews/main2243936.shtml).

6. Merriam-Webster online dictionary, http://www.merriam-webster.com/medical/addiction.

7. Pandelis Pazarlis, Konstantinos Katsigiannopoulos, Georgios Papazisis, Stavroula Bolimou, and Georgios Garyfallos, "Compulsive Buying: A Review," *Annals of General Psychiatry* 7 (2008) (Supp. 1): S273.

8. Shulman Center for Compulsive Theft & Spending, "Compulsive Shopping and Spending Disorders: The Next Frontier of Addiction Treatment!" February 28, 2007, http://blog.theshulmancenter.com/2007/02/28/compulsive-shopping-and-spending-disorders-the-next-frontier-of-addiction-treatment.aspx.

9. "Estimated Prevalence of Compulsive Buying Behavior in the United States," Lorrin M. Koran, M.D., Ronald J. Faber, Ph. D., Elias

Aboujaoude, M.A., M.D., Michael D. Large, Ph.D., and Richard T. Serpe, Ph.D. *American Journal of Psychiatry* 163:1806–12, October 2006. doi: 10.1176/appi.ajp.163.10.1806

10. "New Test Identifies Shopaholics," United Press International, September 16, 2008 (available at http://www.upi.com/Health_News/2008/09/16/New_test_identifies_shopaholics/UPI-71811221540181/).

11. Ibid.

12. Ibid.

13. "Shopaholics Are Addicted to Attention, German Researchers Find," *Deutsche Welle*, January 8, 2008 (available at http://www.dw-world.de/dw/article/0,2144,3530317,00.html).

14. Jennifer Berry Hawes, "Researchers Hunt Biological Sources of Drug Cravings," Medical University of South Carolina Web site, http://research.musc.edu/news/kalivas.html.

15. Sarah Klein, "Fatty Foods May Cause Cocaine-Like Addiction," CNN.com, March 30, 2010, http://www.cnn.com/2010/HEALTH/03/28/fatty.foods.brain/index.html.

16. Paul M. Johnson and Paul J. Kenny, "Dopamine D2 Receptors in Addiction-Like Reward Dysfunction and Compulsive Eating in Obese Rats," *Nature Neuroscience* 13 (2010): 635–41.

17. France Bellisleb, "Effects of Monosodium Glutamate on Human Food Palatability," *Annals of the New York Academy of Sciences* 855 (1998): 438–41 (available at http://onlinelibrary.wiley.com/doi/10.1111/j.1749-6632.1998.tb10603.x/abstract).

18. Shannon Bell, "Red Bull Cola Cocaine Report in Germany," Rightpundits.com, May 25, 2009, http://www.rightpundits.com/?p=3985.

19. Joy Victory, "Studying the Sweet Tooth," *ABC News*, May 25, 2006 (available at http://abcnews.go.com/Health/Diet/story?id=2001298&page=1).

20. Nicole M. Avena, Pedro Rada, and Bartley G. Hoebel, "Evidence for Sugar Addiction: Behavioral and Neurochemical Effects of Intermittent, Excessive Sugar Intake," *Neuroscience Biobehavioral Review* 32, no. 1 (2008): 20–39 (available at http://www.ncbi.nlm.nih.gov/pmc/articles/PMC2235907/?tool=pmcentrez).

21. Ibid.

22. "What Is Lip Balm Addiction?" WiseGeek, http://www.wisegeek.com/what-is-lip-balm-addiction.htm.

23. "Are You Addicted to Lip Balm?" Beautiful with Brains, June 30, 2009,

http://www.beautifulwithbrains.com/2009/06/30/are-you-addicted-to
-lip-balm/.

24. "Boy's Daily 15-hour Xbox Habit," *The Sun*, August 25, 2010 (available at
http://www.thesun.co.uk/sol/homepage/news/3111299/Boys-daily-15
-hour-Xbox-habit.html#ixzz12x4kfqX5).

25. Braden Quartermaine, "Stress over Teen's 'Addiction,' " *Sunday Times*,
July 13, 2007 (available at http://www.perthnow.com.au/news/western
-australia/stress-over-teens-addiction/story-e6frg13u-1111113958526).

26. NPD Group, press release, "Extreme Gamers Spend Two Full Days per
Week Playing Video Games," May 27, 2010 (available at http://www.npd
.com/press/releases/press_100527b.html).

27. "Video Game Addiction: Is It Real?" *Harris Interactive Online*, April 2,
2007, http://www.harrisinteractive.com/NEWS/allnewsbydate.asp
?NewsID=1196.

28. Panel on Game Addiction, International Game Developers Association,
Austin chapter, January 2003 (available at http://archives.igda.org/
articles/austin_addiction.php).

29. Elizabeth Landau, "In Gambling, Brain Explains Attraction of Near-
Misses," CNN Health, May 7, 2010, www://pagingdrgupta.blogs.cnn
.com/2010/05/07/in-gambling-brain-explains-attraction-of-near-misses/.

30. Jeffrey C. Friedman, "Understanding, Assessing and Treating Online
Role-Playing Game Addiction," *Counselor*, May 27, 2010 (available at
http://www.counselormagazine.com/feature-articles-mainmenu-63/
113-video-game-addiction).

31. "Gaming Addiction: An Epidemic for a Growing Technological
Generation," *Everything Addiction*, April 10, 2010 (available at http://www
.everythingaddiction.com/addiction/video-game/gaming-addiction-an
-epidemic-for-a-growing-technological-generation/).

32. Elizabeth Olson, "For Farmville Players, a Crop from a Real Organic
Farm," *New York Times*, July 14, 2010 (available at http://www.nytimes
.com/2010/07/15/business/media/15adco.html).

33. DICE 2010, "Design Outside the Box" Presentation (available at http://
g4tv.com/videos/44277/DICE-2010-Design-Outside-the-Box
-Presentation/).

34. Peter Kafka, "Facebook, Farmville Now Wasting a Third of Your Web
Time," All Things Digital, August 2, 2010, http://mediamemo.allthingsd
.com/20100802/facebook-farmville-now-wasting-a-third-of-your-web
-time/.

35. Bryan Morrissey, "Zynga Offering 'On Game' Ads," *Brandweek*, May 3, 2010 (available at http://www.brandweek.com/bw/content_display/ news-and-features/digital/e3ie1921c607ec2b9abf2c8f961922a11b3).

36. Olson, "For Farmville Players, a Crop."

37. Dan Fletcher, "How Facebook Is Redefining Privacy," *Time*, May 20, 2010.

38. Simone S. Oliver, "Who Elected Me Mayor? I Did," *New York Times*, August 18, 2010 (available at www.nytimes.com/2010/08/19/fashion/ 19foursquare.html).

39. Ibid.

40. Sarah Lolley, "Shopping Sample Sales . . . Recessionista Style," *Pittsburgh Post-Gazette*, March 28, 2010 (available at http://www.post-gazette.com/ pg/10087/1045669-314.stm).

41. Heather Dougherty, "Weekly Share of Market Visits—Online Sample Sales," Hitwise, June 12, 2009, http://weblogs.hitwise.com/heather -dougherty/2009/06/online_sample_sales_1.html.

42. Ty McMahan, "Groupon: Deals for Members, but What About the Investors?" *Wall Street Journal* Venture Capital Dispatch, May 27, 2010, http://blogs.wsj.com/venturecapital/2010/05/27/groupon-deals-for -members-but-what-about-the-investors/.

43. Jonah Leher, "Swoopo," The Frontal Cortext, July 10, 2009, http:// scienceblogs.com/cortex/2009/07/swoopo.php.

Chapter 4. Buy It, Get Laid

1. "Finally, Some Actual Stats on Internet Porn," Gizmodo, June 1, 2010, http://gizmodo.com/5552899/finally-some-actual-stats-on-internet-porn.

2. John Tierney, "Message in What We Buy, but No One Is Listening," *New York Times*, May 18, 2009 (available at http://www.nytimes.com/2009/ 05/19/science/19tier.html?_r=1&th&emc=th).

3. "An Attractive Revenue Producer," *Spray*, May 2007 (available at http:// www.precision-valve.com/assets/2446/article_spray_technology_200705 .pdf).

4. Sam McManis, "Amusing or Offensive, Axe Ads Show That Sexism Sells," *Seattle Times*, December 4, 2007 (available at http://seattletimes.nwsource .com/html/living/2004050655_axeads03.html).

5. Josh Loposer, "Minnesota Educators Want to Ban Axe Body Spray," *Stylist*, March 27, 2009 (available at http://www.stylelist.com/2009/03/27/ minnesota-educators-want-to-ban-axe-body-spray/2).

6. "Body Spray Banned from N.B. School," *CBC News*, December 5, 2005

(available at http://www.cbc.ca/canada/story/2005/12/05/body-scent
-051205.html).

7. "Naughty," YouTube, http://www.youtube.com/watch?v=0g3sYR7fBl8,
   accessed February 28, 2011.

8. Finlo Rorher, "How Do You Make Children's Films Appeal to Adults?"
   BBC News, December 16, 2009 (available at http://news.bbc.co.uk/2/hi/
   8415003.stm).   ·

9. Emily Bryson York, "Quiznos Throws Subway Curve with 'Sexy'
   $4 Foot-Long," *Advertising Age*, March 25, 2009 (available at http://
   www.freerepublic.com/focus/news/2214960/posts).

10. Claire Suddath, "How the Internet Made Justin Bieber a Star," *Time*,
    May 17, 2010.

11. Jan Hoffman, "Justin Bieber Is Living the Dream," *New York Times*,
    January 31, 2009 (available at http://www.nytimes.com/2010/01/03/
    fashion/03bieber.html).

12. Beth Tietell, "Never Too Old to Swoon," *Boston Globe*, May 13, 2010
    (available at http://www.boston.com/community/moms/articles/2010/
    05/13/why_are_so_many_moms_smitten_with_todays_teen_idols
    ?mode=PF).

13. "Despite Recession, Overall Plastic Surgery Demand Drops Only 2
    Percent from Last Year," press release, American Society for Aesthetic
    Plastic Surgery, March 9, 2010 (available at http://www.surgery.org/
    media/news-releases/despite-recession-overall-plastic-surgery-demand
    -drops-only-2-percent-from-last-year).

14. Susan Reda, "Guess What? Men Shop, Too!" *Stores*, April 2010 (available
    at http://www.stores.org/stores-magazine-april-2010/guess-what-men
    -shop-too).

15. Barbara Kiviat, "Swaying Shoppers: The Power of Product Specs," *Time*,
    December 22, 2008 (available at http://www.time.com/time/business/
    article/0,8599,1868275,00.html).

16. "Vanity Sizing: Are Retailers Making Clothes Bigger So Customers Feel
    Better?" *Huffington Post*, April 19, 2010, http://www.huffingtonpost.com/
    2010/04/19/vanity-sizing-are-retaile_n_542830.html.

17. "Vanity Sizing Plagues MEN'S Stores," *Huffington Post*, September 8, 2010,
    http://www.huffingtonpost.com/2010/09/08/vanity-sizing-mens-pants
    _n_709004.html.

18. Ibid.

19. Ibid. ·

20. Michael Quintanilla, "H-E-B Aisle Is for Guys Only," *San Antonio Express-News*, January 27, 2010 (available at http://www.chron.com/disp/story .mpl/headline/features/6838384.html).

Chapter 5. Under Pressure

1. Pierre-Paul Grasse, *Termitologia*, vols. 1–3 (Paris: Masson, 1982–1986). See also http://www.forteantimes.com/strangedays/science/382/hive_minds .html.

2. Ibid.

3. Kevin Smith, "Are You a Termite or a Squasher?" NextWave Performance, the Executive Intelligence Report, September 3, 2007, http://www.nextwaveperformance.com/the-executive-intelligence-rep/ are-you-a-termite-or-a-squasher.html.

4. John R. G. Dyer, Christos C. Ioannou, Lesley J. Morrell, Darren P. Croft, Iain D. Cousin, Dean A. Waters, and Jens Krause, "Consensus Decision Making in Human Crowds," *Animal Behavior* 75 (2008): 561–470 (discussed at http://www.leeds.ac.uk/news/article/397/sheep_in_human _clothing_scientists_reveal_our_flock_mentality).

5. Smith, "Are You a Termite."

6. Clare Elsley, "Sheep in Human Clothing—Scientists Reveal Our Flock Mentality," University of Leeds, February 14, 2008, http://www.leeds.ac .uk/news/article/397/sheep_in_human_clothing_scientists_reveal_our _flock_mentality.

7. Peter Miller, *The Smart Swarm: How Understanding Flocks, Schools, and Colonies Can Make Us Better at Communicating, Decision Making, and Getting Things Done* (New York: Avery Books, 2010), p. 213.

8. Gene Weingarten, "Pearls Before Breakfast," *Washington Post*, April 8, 2007 (available at http://www.washingtonpost.com/wp-dyn/content/ article/2007/04/04/AR2007040401721.html).

9. Jan Faull, "Your Clever Toddler in Week 59: The Onset of Peer Influence," BabyZone, http://www.babyzone.com/toddler/toddler_development/ toddler-week-by-week/article/clever-toddler-weeks-59-60.

10. Olivia Barker, "Meet 'Top Secret Elmo,' " *USA Today*, February 1, 2006 (available at http://www.usatoday.com/life/2006-02-01-tickle-me -elmo_x.htm).

11. "Across the Zhu-Niverse Twitter Party," *Resourceful Mommy*, July 5, 2010, http://resourcefulmommy.com/3102/zhu-zhu-pets-giveaway/.

12. Martin Eisend, "Explaining the Impact of Scarcity Appeals in

Advertising: The Mediating Role of Perceptions in Susceptibility," *Journal of Advertising*, September 22, 2008.

13. Kit Yarrow, "Explaining the Why Behind the Buy," *Psychology Today*, December 9, 2009 (available at http://www.psychologytoday.com/blog/ the-why-behind-the-buy/200912/how-consumer-psychology-created-the -zhu-zhu-hamster-craze).

14. Robert Cialdini, *The Psychology of Persuasion* (New York: Harper, 2006).

15. "H1N1 Vaccine Shortage Fabricated to Create Hysteria, Boost Demand?" Health Freedom Alliance, November 6, 2009, http://blogs.healthfreedom alliance.org/blog/2009/11/06/h1n1-vaccine-shortage-fabricated-to-create -hysteria-boost-demand.

16. Ibid.

17. David Lieberman, "The Juicy Details Behind the Viacom-YouTube Lawsuit," *USA Today*, March 19, 2009 (available at http://content.usatoday .com/communities/technologylive/post/2010/03/media-morning-the -juicy-details-behind-the-viacom-youtube-lawsuit/1).

18. Ibid.

19. David Kravets, "Google Wins Viacom Copyright Lawsuit," *Wired*, June 23, 2010 (available at http://www.wired.com/threatlevel/2010/06/ dmca-protects-youtube/).

20. Kim Hart, "Peer Pressure in Online Shopping," *Washington Post*, July 9, 2008 (available at http://blog.washingtonpost.com/posttech/2008/07/ peer_pressure_in_online_shoppi.html?nav=rss_blog).

21. Ibid.

22. Sidney Frank, "How I Did It," *Inc.*, September 1, 2005 (available at http:// www.inc.com/magazine/20050901/qa.html).

23. G. S. Berns, "Natural Mechanisms of Social Influence in Consumer Decisions," University of Oregon, April 10, 2009.

24. Berns, "Natural Mechanisms of Social Influence."

25. Mark Buchanan, "Social Networks: The Great Tipping Point Test," *New Scientist*, July 26, 2010 (available at http://www.newscientist.com/article/ mg20727701.100-social-web-the-great-tipping-point-test.html).

26. Jonah Berger, "In Pursuit of the 'It' Gift at the Holidays," Oregon Live, December 20, 2009, http://www.oregonlive.com/opinion/index.ssf/ 2009/12/in_pursuit_of_the_it_gift_at_t.html.

27. David Pogue, "For Those Facebook Left Behind," *New York Times*, July 7, 2010 (available at http://www.nytimes.com/2010/07/08/technology/

personaltech/08pogue.html?pagewanted=2&adxnnl=1&ref=general
&src=me&adxnnlx=1278849675-D3KlidM/7ANbaohmVO7CJA).

28. Dan Fletcher, "Friends Without Borders," *Time*, May 31, 2010.

29. "Facebook: Facts and Figures for 2010," Digital Buzz, March 22, 2010.

30. Dan Fletcher, "How Facebook Is Redefining Privacy," *Time*, May 20,
    2010 (available at http://www.time.com/time/business/article/
    0,8599,1990582,00.html).

31. Ibid.

32. Fletcher, "Friends Without Borders."

33. Ibid.

34. Maja Beckstrom, "'Tweens Want Hip Stuff, but Self-Esteem Is the Real
    Need," *Twin Cities Pioneer Press*, January 28, 2008 (available at http://www
    .twincities.com/allheadlines/ci_7558230).

35. Ibid.

36. Kevin Rawlinson, "Coming Soon to a Wrist Near You . . . the Craze That's
    Sweeping America," *Independent* UK, August 4, 2010 (available at http://
    www.independent.co.uk/news/uk/this-britain/coming-soon-to-a-wrist
    -near-you-the-craze-thats-sweeting-america-2042599.html).

37. Emmi Kuusikko, "Teens Prefer Buying Brands," VVWarc, June 5, 2009,
    http://www.warc.com/News/TopNews.asp?ID=25231&origin.

38. Wray Herbert, "The Psychology of Knock-Offs: Why 'Faking It' Makes
    Us Feel (and Act) Like Phonies," *Huffington Post,* April 7, 2010.

39. Ibid.

40. Amanda Lenhart, Kristen Purcell, Aaron Smith, and Kathryn Zickuhr,
    "Social Media and Mobile Internet Use Among Teens and Young
    Adults," Pew Internet & American Life Project, the Pew Research Center,
    February 3, 2010 (available at http://pewinternet.org/Reports/2010/
    Social-Media-and-Young-Adults.aspx).

41. See http://www.apple.com/education/mac-for-school/.

42. Mike Adams, "Laughter Is Good Medicine for Reducing Stress,
    Enhancing Brain Chemistry," Natural News, April 28, 2005, http://
    www.naturalnews.com/007551.html.

43. Young Lee, James Moon, and Michael Lin, "Levi Strauss & Co.: An
    Analysis," http://www.docstoc.com/docs/18141871/Levis-Strauss
    -Marketing-Plan.

44. N. Ravindran, "Asia's Love for Luxury Brands," *Entrepreneur,* February–
    March 2007.

Chapter 6. Oh, Sweet Memories

1. See http://www.groundreport.com/Media_and_Tech/Largest-TV
   -Audience-In-History-Super-Bowl-XLIII_2/2883568,

2. Jochen Gebauer and Constantine Sedikides, "Yearning for Yesterday,"
   Scientific American Mind, July/August 2010.

3. Ibid.

4. Ibid.

5. T. R. Mitchell, L. Thompson, E. Peterson, and R. Cronk, "A Theory of
   Temporal Adjustments in the Evaluation of Events: Rosy Prospection &
   Rosy Retrospection," in *Advances in Managerial Cognition and Organizational
   Information-Processing*, vol. 5, eds. C. Stubbart, J. Porac, and J. Meindl
   (Greenwich, CT: JAI Press, 1994), pp. 85–114.

6. K. A. Braun-LaTour, M. S. LaTour, J. E. Pickrell, and E. F. Loftus, "How
   and When Advertising Can Influence Memory for Consumer Experience,"
   Journal of Advertising 33, no. 4 (December 2004): 7–25.

7. Robert M. Sapolsky, "Open Season," *New Yorker*, March 30, 1998, p. 57
   (available at http://www.newyorker.com/archive/1998/03/30/1998_03
   _30_057_TNY_LIBRY_000015234#ixzz0hnCIoX3R).

8. Ibid.

9. See http://en.wikipedia.org/wiki/List_of_McDonald's_ad_programs.

10. Jennifer L. Aaker and Melanie Rudd, "If Money Doesn't Make You
    Happy, Consider Time" (research paper, Stanford University, Graduate
    School of Business, November 2010).

11. See http://brontosbrain.blogspot.com/2010/10/im-no-longer-lovin-it
    .html.

12. "Nostalgia Brands Make a Comeback in China," Red Luxury,
    September 7, 2010, http://red-luxury.com/2010/09/07/nostalgia-brands
    -make-a-comeback-in-china/.

13. Laura M. Holson, "A Little Too Ready for Her Close-Up?" *New York
    Times*, April 23, 2010 (available at http://www.nytimes.com/2010/04/25/
    fashion/25natural.html).

14. Iain Murray, "Nostalgia Is Just the Comfort Blanket We Need Against
    Today's Cold Reality," *Marketing Week*, February 5, 2009 (available at
    http://www.marketingweek.co.uk/opinion/nostalgia-is-just-the-comfort
    -blanket-we-need-against-todays-cold-reality/2064185.article).

15. "Brand Nostalgia," VGroup: Marketing Branding Design Interactive,
    http://blog.vgroup.com/post/brand-nostalgia/.

16. Zoe Wood, "Milky Bar Kid Rides Out Again as Tough Times Send

Shoppers on Nostalgia Trip," *Guardian*, May 12, 2009 (available at http://www.guardian.co.uk/media/2009/may/12/nostalgic-advertising -milky-bar-kid-persil-hovis).

17. Matthew Gorman, "Blast from the Past," *Marketing Week*, February 14, 2007 (available at http://www.marketingweek.co.uk/home/blast-from -the-past/2055016.article).

18. See http://great-ads.blogspot.com/2009/01/allstate-insurance-back-to -basics.html.

19. "Hey Marketers, Need a Quick Way to Improve Sales? Listen to Your Customers," Point to Point, http://www.pointtopoint.com/2010/01/ hey-marketers-not-sure-what-to-do-to-improve-sales-listen-to-your -customers/.

20. Jeffrey Zaslow, "Get Back to Where You Once Belonged," *Wall Street Journal*, January 20, 2010 (available at http://online.wsj.com/article/ SB10001424052748704561004575012964067490650.html?mod=WSJ _newsreel_lifeStyle).

21. Ibid.

22. Stuart Elliott, "Vintage Brand and Corporate Names to Be Auctioned," *New York Times*, November 8, 2010 (available at http://mediadecoder .blogs.nytimes.com/2010/11/08/vintage-brand-and-corporate-names -to-be-auctioned/).

23. Diane Cardwell, "A Vision of the City as It Once Was," *New York Times*, May 19, 2010 (available at http://www.nytimes.com/2010/05/20/ nyregion/20nostalgia.html?scp=1&sq=west%20village&st=cse).

24. See http://www.quotationspage.com/quote/839.html.

Chapter 7. Marketers' Royal Flush

1. Neil Tweedie, " 'Footman' Exposes Tupperware Secret of the Queen's Table," *Telegraph*, November 20, 2003 (available at http://www.telegraph .co.uk/education/3323191/Footman-exposes-Tupperware-secret-of-the -Queens-table.html).

2. Professor John M. T. Balmer, "Comprehending the Constitutional Monarchies of Britain and Sweden: Issues of Trust and Corporate Brand Management" (working paper no. 05/35, Bradford School of Management) (available at http://www.bradford.ac.uk/acad/ management/external/pdf/workingpapers/2005/Booklet_05-35.pdf).

3. Peggy Orenstein, *Cinderella Ate My Daughter* (New York: HarperCollins, 2001), p. 14.

4. "10 Facts About Collecting Barbie Dolls," ArticlesBase, August 27, 2008, http://www.articlesbase.com/hobbies-articles/10-facts-about-collecting-barbie-dolls-538678.html.

5. "Star Power," *NPD Insights*, no. 42 (May 2006) (available at http://www.npdinsights.com/archives/may2006/cover.story.html).

6. "Celebrity Endorsement 'Alters Brain Activity,'" *BBC News*, July 13, 2010 (available at http://www.bbc.co.uk/news/10615182).

7. "Fame Matters More Than Beauty in Consumer Behavior," *Innovations Report*, August 13, 2008 (available at http://www.innovations-report.de/html/berichte/studien/fame_matters_beauty_consumer_behaviour_115992.html).

8. R. Bruce Money, Terence A. Shimp, and Tomoaki Sakano, "Celebrity Endorsements in Japan and the United States," *Journal of Advertising Research*, March 1, 2006 (available at http://www.accessmylibrary.com/coms2/summary_0286-16345940_ITM).

9. Jo Bowman, "Wishing on a Star," *CNBC Magazine*, July 2010.

10. "Logo Can Make You 'Think Different,'" *Science Daily*, March 30, 2008 (available at http://www.sciencedaily.com/releases/2008/03/080328085918.htm).

11. John King and Ed Henry, "Bill Clinton Awaits Heart Surgery Next Week," CNN.com, September 4, 2004 (available at http://www.cnn.com/2004/ALLPOLITICS/09/03/clinton.tests/index.html).

12. See http://search.barnesandnoble.com/South-Beach-Diet-Cookbook/Arthur-Agatston/e/9781579549572.

13. "Victoria Beckham Draws Attention to the 'Skinny Bitch' Diet," *Belfast Telegraph*, June 11, 2007 (available at http://www.belfasttelegraph.co.uk/lifestyle/victoria-beckham-draws-attention-to-the-skinny-bitch-diet-13449352.html).

14. See http://cleoparker.com/dogmarketing/2009/04/20/dog-product-placement-masterdog/.

15. Samantha Jonas-Hain, "'Saw It on Maddox': Jolie's Kids Set Trends," *Fox News*, September 30, 2005 (available at http://www.foxnews.com/story/0,2933,170834,00.html).

16. Ibid.

17. Ibid.

18. Deidre Woolard, "Cynthia Rowley Works with Pampers on Designer Diapers," Luxist, June 30, 2010, http://www.luxist.com/2010/06/30/cynthia-rowley-works-with-pampers-on-designer-diapers/.

19. Social Security Administration, "Popular Baby Names," Social Security Online, http://www.ssa.gov/oact/babynames/index.html.

20. See http://www.sephora.com/browse/section.jhtml?categoryId=C22220.

21. See http://answers.sephora.com/answers/8723/product/P247523/ questions.htm.

22. See http://www.dgskincare.com/aboutus_drgross.cfm?cat=3&CFID =2286718&CFTOKEN=89d9b63c4700105b-641166E7-E5F5-74FB -D4032C1B3ADBC884.

23. See http://www.physiciansformula.com/en-us/default.html.

24. See http://www.philosophydirect.com/about-philosophy.html.

25. Steve Hargreaves, "Trump: The Fragrance," CNN.com, September 23, 2004 (available at http://money.cnn.com/2004/09/23/news/ newsmakers/trump_fragrance/index.htm).

26. Zac Bissonnette, "Donald Trump Fragrance on Clearance at TJ Maxx— The End of an Era," BloggingStocks, November 26, 2007, http://www .bloggingstocks.com/2007/11/26/donald-trump-cologne-on-clearance -at-tjmaxx-the-end-of-an-er/.

27. Denise Winterman, "Eau de Bruce—What Does Die Hard Smell Like?" *BBC News*, July 1, 2010 (available at http://news.bbc.co.uk/2/hi/uk _news/magazine/8772076.stm).

28. Julie Boorstin, "The Scent of Celebrity," *Fortune*, November 14, 2005 (available at http://money.cnn.com/magazines/fortune/fortune_archive/ 2005/11/14/8360679/index.htm).

29. Lauren Sherman, "Best-Selling Celebrity Scents," *Forbes*, October 9, 2007 (available at http://www.forbes.com/2007/10/08/scent-perfume-celeb -forbeslife-cx_ls_1009style.html).

30. See http://www.classicbands.com/bowie.html.

31. Karen Richardson, "Bankers Hope for a Reprise of 'Bowie Bonds,' " *Wall Street Journal*, August 23, 2005 (available at http://online.wsj.com/public/ article/SB112476043457720240-Tvpthd07S8mCqCxLFNKIPnWWY9g _20060823.html).

32. Jock McGregor, "Madonna: Icon of PostModernity," Facing the Challenge, 1997, Url: http://www.facingthechallenge.org/madonna.php.

33. See http://www.lifegem.com/secondary/MichaelJacksonLifeGem.aspx.

34. Associated Press, "Michael Jackson Glove Fetches $330,000 at Auction," *Orange County Register*, December 6, 2010 (available at http://www .ocregister.com/news/auction-98978-ocprint-jackson-brought.html).

35. Lauren Sherman, "How Much Brands Pay for Celebs to Sit in Their Front

Rows," Fashionista, http://fashionista.com/2010/02/how-much-fashion
-brands-pay-for-celebrities-to-sit-in-their-front-rows/.

36. Emilie Boyer King, "Does Royalty Lead to Brand Loyalty?"
    Brandchannel, December 13, 2004, http://www.brandchannel.com/
    features_effect.asp?pf_id=242.

37. Jan B. Engelmann, C. Monica Capra, Charles Noussair, and Gregory S.
    Berns, "Expert Financial Advice Neurobiologically 'Offloads' Financial
    Decision-Making Under Risk" (Department of Psychiatry & Behavioral
    Sciences, Emory University School of Medicine, Atlanta).

38. Andy Coghlan, "Brain Shuts Off in Response to Healer's Prayer," *New
    Scientist*, April 27, 2010.

39. Ibid.

40. Vasily Klucharev, Ale Smidts, and Guillen Fernandez, "Brain
    Mechanisms of Persuasion: How 'Expert Power' Modulates Memory
    and Attitudes," *Social Cognitive and Affective Neuroscience* 3, no. 4
    (December 2008): 353–366 (available at http://scan.oxfordjournals.org/
    content/3/4/353.full).

41. See http://www.quotationspage.com/quotes/Andy_Warhol/.

42. Bruce Horovitz, "Buy a Pair of Socks, Become a Star in Times Square,"
    USA Today, November 6, 2009 (available at http://www.usatoday.com/
    money/industries/retail/2009-11-02-american-eagle-times-square_N
    .htm).

Chapter 8. Hope in a Jar

1. "XanGo, MonaVie, TNI Keep Squeezing Sales Out of Super Fruits,"
   Nutrition Business Journal (available at http://webcache.googleusercontent
   .com/search?q=cache:fz-uhasY6hwJ:subscribers.nutritionbusinessjournal
   .com/xango-monavie-tni-0501/index1.html+goji+sales+million+site:
   nutritionbusinessjournal.com&cd=2&hl=en&ct=clnk).

2. Cathy Wong, "What Are Goji Berries?" About.com, August 1, 2006,
   http://altmedicine.about.com/od/completeazindex/a/goji.htm.

3. O. Potterat, "Goji (*Lycium barbarum* and *L. chinense*): Phytochemistry,
   Pharmacology and Safety in the Perspective of Traditional Uses and
   Recent Popularity," *Planta Medica* 76, no. 1 (January 2010): 7–19 (available
   at http://www.ncbi.nlm.nih.gov/pubmed/19844860).

4. V. E. Reeve, M. Allanson, S. J. Arum, D. Domanski, and N. Painter,
   "Mice Drinking Goji Berry Juice (*Lycium barbarum*) Are Protected
   from UV Radiation-Induced Skin Damage via Antioxidant Pathways,"

Photochemical and Photobiological Sciences 9, no. 4 (April 2010): 601–7 (available at http://www.ncbi.nlm.nih.gov/pubmed/20354657).

5. "How Goji Berries Work," TLC, http://recipes.howstuffworks.com/goji-berry2.htm.

6. See http://www.vosgeschocolate.com/product/goji_exotic_candy_bar/exotic_candy_bars.

7. Rob Walker, "Consumed," *New York Times*, July 21, 2009.

8. " '09 Sales Growth Sputters in Every Nutrition Category as Economy Takes Its Toll," *Nutrition Business Journal*, February 9, 2011 (available at http://webcache.googleusercontent.com/search?q=cache: XeGdnJnhuhAJ:subscribers.nutritionbusinessjournal.com/supplements/sales_growth_sputters/+%3FGoji%3FJuice%3FSales+million+OR +billion+site:nutritionbusinessjournal.com&cd=4&hl=en&ct=clnk).

9. Sandra Young and Madison Park, "Group Challenges Acai Berry Weight-Loss Claims," CNN.com, March 23, 2009, http://articles.cnn.com/2009 -03-23/health/acai.berries.scam_1_advanced-wellness-research-acai -weight-loss-claims?_s=PM:HEALTH.

10. Ibid.

11. Mark Stibich, "Acai Berry's Anti Aging Properties—Fact or Marketing Fiction?" About.com, May 8, 2009, http://longevity.about.com/od/antiagingfoods/a/acai_aging.htm.

12. Arlene Weintraub, *Selling the Fountain of Youth: How the Anti-Aging Industry Made a Disease Out of Getting Old—and Made Billions* (New York: Basic Books, 2010), pp. 215–16.

13. H. M. Park, E. Moon, A. J. Kim, M. H. Kim, S. Lee, J. B. Lee, Y. K. Park, H. S. Jung, Y. B. Kim, and S. Y. Kim, "Extract of *Punica granatum* Inhibits Skin Photoaging Induced by UVB Irradiation," *International Journal of Dermatology* 49, no. 3 (March 2010): 276–82 (available at http://www.ncbi .nlm.nih.gov/pubmed/20465664).

14. P. Mirmiran, M. R. Fazeli, G. Asghari, A. Shafiee, and F. Azizi, "Effect of Pomegranate Seed Oil on Hyperlipidaemic Subjects: A Double-Blind Placebo-Controlled Clinical Trial," *British Journal of Nutrition* 104, no. 3 (August 2010): 402–6 (available at http://www.ncbi.nlm.nih.gov/pubmed/20334708).

15. Ibid.

16. See http://www.fda.gov/ICECI/EnforcementActions/WarningLetters/ucm202785.htm.

17. Ibid.

18. Meredith Melnick, "FTC and FDA to POM: You're Not So Wonderful," *Time*, September 27, 2010 (available at http://healthland.time.com/2010/09/27/ftc-and-fda-to-pom-youre-not-quite-so-wonderful/).

19. Melissa Bell, "Nutrition Buzzwords Make Hay Out of Grains of Truth," *Washington Post*, May 27, 2010 (available at http://www.washingtonpost.com/wp-dyn/content/article/2010/05/25/AR2010052504622.html).

20. Ibid.

21. Ibid.

22. Rachel Saslow, "Are Claims About Beauty Creams Only Skin Deep?" *Washington Post*, May 12, 2009.

23. Bryant Urstadt, "Lust for Lulu," *New York*, July 26, 2009 (available at http://nymag.com/shopping/features/58082).

24. Louise Story, " 'Seaweed' Clothing Has None, Tests Show," *New York Times*, November 14, 2007.

25. Ibid.

26. Ibid.

27. "Anti-Ageing Face Creams 'Don't Work'—Exercise and Eat Sensibly Instead, Say Scientists," *Daily Mail,* December 1, 2008, http://www.dailymail.co.uk/health/article-1090752/Anti-ageing-face-creams-dont-work-exercise-good-diet-do.html.

28. Darren McBride, "The Dietary Supplement Health and Education Act of 1994," *Proceedings of the Amazing Meeting* 4 (January 26, 2006) (available at http://www.csufresno.edu/physics/rhall/jref/tam4p/06_DM_tam4.pdf).

29. See http://she-conomy.com/report/facts-on-women/.

30. GfK Roper Yale Survey on Environmental Issues, "Consumer Attitudes Toward Environmentally-Friendly Products and Eco-Labeling," Yale School of Forestry and Environmental Studies, July 2008 (discussed at http://environment.yale.edu/news/5720).

31. Ibid.

32. Constance Casey, "The Spin Cycle," *Slate*, September 22, 2010, http://www.slate.com/id/2268089/.

33. Peter Korchnak, "Green as a Luxury? Premium Pricing and Conspicuous Consumption," Semiosis Communications, December 14, 2009, http://www.semiosiscommunications.com/green-as-luxury/.

34. "Why Toyota Is Afraid of Being Number One," *Bloomberg BusinessWeek*, March 5, 2007 (available at http://www.businessweek.com/magazine/content/07_10/b4024071.htm).

35. Nyasha-Harmony Gutsa, "Marketing Mix in Action: Toyoya Prius," Yahoo

Associated Content, June 8, 2009, http://www.associatedcontent.com/
article/1804334/marketing_mix_in_actiontoyota_prius.html?cat=35.

36. Micheline Maynard, "Say 'Hybrid' and Many People Will Hear 'Prius,' "
New York Times, July 4, 2007 (available at http://www.nytimes.com/2007/
07/04/business/04hybrid.html?_r=1).

37. Jacquelyn Ottman, "Marketers, Follow That Prius," *Advertising Age*, May 28,
2008 (available at http://adage.com/cmostrategy/article?article_id=127344).

38. "Starring Role: Hollywood's Love Affair with Toyota Prius Continues,"
GM Inside News, October 13, 2005, http://www.gminsidenews.com/
forums/f12/hollywoods-love-affair-toyotas-prius-continues-21170/.

39. Douglas Kenrick, "Sex, Murder, and the Meaning of Life," *Psychology Today*,
February 15, 2010 (available at http://www.psychologytoday.com/
blog/sex-murder-and-the-meaning-life/201002/want-show-your-wealth
-and-status-buy-hybrid).

40. Maynard, "Say 'Hybrid' and Many People."

41. Arnie Cooper, "The Highway to Enlightenment," *Mother Jones*, January 1,
2002.

42. Stephen Prothero, "Buddha Chic," *Salon*, May 24, 1997, http://www.salon
.com/may97/news/news970524.html.

43. See http://lasermonks.com.

44. "Cistercian Monks' Jesus Ink Business," Unusual Business Ideas That
Work, April 10, 2006, http://uncommonbusiness.blogspot.com/2006/04/
cistercian-monks-jesus-ink-business.html.

45. See http://www.intentionalchocolate.com/.

46. See http://www.ehalal.org/quranverses.html.

47. Carla Power, "Halal: Buying Muslim," *Time*, May 25, 2009.

48. Ibid.

49. Lisa Miller, "4 Sale: Bones of the Saints," *Newsweek*, February 11, 2008.

50. Ibid.

51. See http://webupon.com/services/you-bought-what-10-extraordinarily
-peculiar-ebay-purchases.

52. "Evolution of the Megachurch," *Houston Business Journal*, January 26, 2009
(available at http://www.bizjournals.com/houston/stories/2009/01/26/
focus1.html??b=1232946000%5e1766246).

53. Ibid.

54. Jesse Bogan, "America's Biggest Megachurches," *Forbes*, June 26, 2009.

55. Ibid.

56. Ibid.

Chapter 9. Every Breath You Take, They'll Be Watching You

1. "Your Own Private Matrix," *Economist,* November 4, 2010 (available at http://www.economist.com/node/17388382).
2. "Data Mining Is Big Business for Kroger & Getting Bigger All the Time," *KY Post*, May 27, 2010 (available at http://www.kypost.com/dpp/news/region_central_cincinnati/downtown/data-mining-is-big-business-for-kroger-%26-getting-bigger-all-the-time).
3. Stephanie Clifford, "Web Coupons Know Lots About You, and They'll Tell," *New York Times*, April 16, 2010 (available at http://www.nytimes.com/2010/04/17/business/media/17coupon.html?ref-general&src=me&pagewanted=print).
4. Ibid.
5. Ibid.
6. Ariana Eunjung Cha, "Digital Coupons Help Stores Get More Info About You," *Houston Chronicle*, July 4, 2010 (available at http://www.chron.com/disp/story.mpl/business/7094186.html).
7. Ibid.
8. Jordan Robertson, "Apps Secretly Sharing Personal Data with Third parties—Without Telling You," *Huffington Post*, July 28, 2010, http://www.huffingtonpost.com/2010/07/29/apps-secretly-sharing-per_n_662886.html.
9. Ibid.
10. Ibid.
11. Ibid.
12. Charles Duhigg, "What Does Your Credit Card Company Know About You?" *New York Times*, May 12, 2009 (available at http://www.nytimes.com/2009/05/17/magazine/17credit-t.html).
13. Ibid.
14. Connie Prater, "What You Buy, Where You Shop May Affect Credit," CreditCards.com, http://www.creditcards.com/credit-card-news/how-shopping-can-affect-credit-1282.php.
15. Ibid.
16. Brad Stone, "The Debt Trap," *New York Times*, October 21, 2008.
17. Ibid.
18. See http://www.alcmilestones.com/new-movers-homeowners-lists.php.
19. Ibid.
20. Rob Varnon, "Bank Pays Millions to Yale to Market Its Credit Cards,"

Connecticut Post, June 7, 2010 (available at http://www.ctpost.com/local/article/Bank-pays-millions-to-Yale-to-market-its-credit-514988.php).

21. Ibid.

22. Ibid.

23. "Inside the Deals: Contracts Allow Credit Card Marketing to Students," Huffington Post Investigative Fund, June 8, 2010, http://huffpostfund.org/stories/pages/inside-deals-contracts-allow-credit-card-marketing-students.

24. Kenneth Collier, Bernard Carey, Ellen Grusy, Kurt Marjaniemi, and Donald Sauter, "A Perspective on Data Mining," Center for Data Insight at Northern Arizona University, July 1998 (available at http://insight.nau.edu/downloads/DM%20Perspective%20v2.pdf).

25. Jean D. Kinsey, Paul Wolfson, Nikolaos Katsaras, and Ben Senauer, "Data Mining: A Segmentation Analysis of U.S. Grocery Shoppers" (working paper 01/01, Food Industry Center, University of Minnesota, 2001 (available at http://purl.umn.edu/14335).

26. See http://www.thomascookmands.com/.

27. "Watching as You Shop," *Economist,* December 6, 2007 (available at http://www.economist.com/node/10202778?story_id=10202778).

28. See http://www.tns-sorensen.com/documents/11.3b1MKT_Retail%20PTBroch.pdf.

29. Barbara Hagenbaugh, "Musak Thinks Outside the Box," *USA Today,* August 5, 2004 (available at http://www.usatoday.com/money/media/2004-08-05-muzak-cover_x.htm).

30. David McRaney, "Musak," You Are Not So Smart, October 26, 2009, http://youarenotsosmart.com/2009/10/26/muzak/.

31. Ibid.

32. "The Infinite Mind: Music and the Mind," Lichtenstein Creative Media, December 28, 2002, http://www.lcmedia.com/mind250.htm.

33. See http://www.predicta.net/home_html.php.

34. Erica Naone, "Software Helps Websites Predict Users' Tastes," *Technology Review,* November 2, 2010 (available at http://www.technologyreview.com/web/26664/?nlid=3714).

35. Ibid.

36. Christopher Mims, "Wired.com and Huffington Post Amongst List of Privacy-Invading Websites," *Technology Review,* December 3, 2010 (available at http://www.technologyreview.com/blog/mimssbits/26098/?nlid=3846).

37. Ibid.
38. Center for Digital Democracy, "CDD, U.S. PIRG, Consumer Watchdog, and World Privacy Forum Call on FTC to Investigate Interactive Marketing of Pharmaceuticals and Health Products and Services to Consumers and Health Professionals," November 23, 2010, http://www .democraticmedia.org/2010-11-16-press-release.
39. See http://www.facebook.com/policy.php.
40. Emily Steel and Geoffrey A. Fowler, "Facebook in Privacy Breach," *Wall Street Journal,* October 18, 2010 (available at http://online.wsj.com/article/ SB10001424052702304772804575558484075236968.html).
41. Miguel Helft, "Marketers Can Glean Private Data on Facebook," *New York Times,* October 22, 2010.
42. David Gelles, "Facebook's Grand Plan for the Future," *Financial Times Magazine,* December 3, 2010 (available at http://www.ft.com/cms/s/2/ 57933bb8-fcd9-11df-ae2d-00144feab49a.html#axzz18cUiyVDF).
43. See http://foursquare.com/legal/privacy.
44. Ibid.
45. Yannis Bakos, Florencia Marotta-Wurgler, and David R. Trossen, "Does Anyone Read the Fine Print? Testing a Law and Economics Approach to Standard Form Contracts" (working paper, New York University Law and Economics Working Papers, December 1, 2009) (available at http://lsr .nellco.org/cgi/viewcontent.cgi?article=1199&context=nyu_lewp).
46. "Germany Calls on Apple to Expose Location Data Policy," iPod News, http://www.ipodnn.com/articles/10/06/28/company.failing.to.live.up.to .openness/.
47. "7,500 Online Shoppers Unknowingly Sold Their Souls," *Fox News,* April 15, 2010, http://www.foxnews.com/scitech/2010/04/15/online -shoppers-unknowingly-sold-souls/.
48. See http://www.kidswb.com/privacy.
49. Mark Millan, "82 Percent of Kids under 2 Have an Online Presence," CNN.com, October 2010, http://www.cnn.com/2010/TECH/social .media/10/07/baby.pictures/index.html.
50. Ibid.
51. Natasha Singer, "Shoppers Who Can't Have Secrets," *New York Times,* May 1, 2010 (available at http://www.nytimes.com/2010/05/02/ business/02stream.html).

Abercrombie and Fitch, 22, 80, 123, 143
acai products, 184–87
addiction, 57, 58; to gaming, 71–73; to shopping, 57–60, 73–78; to smart phones, 54–57. *See also* brand obsession
addiction-based marketing: advertising games, 20, 73–78; cravings, 56, 60, 61, 63–66; food and drink, 66–69; lip balm, 69–71
Adidas, 88
adjacencies, 217–18
adolescents. *See* children and teens
Agatston, Arthur, 163
Allianz, 38
Allstate, 145–46
Amazon, 116, 232
American Apparel, 80, 88, 143
American Eagle, 178–79
American Express, 37, 167, 211
antibacterial products, 29–30, 40
antioxidants, 188
Apple, 26–27, 124, 208–9, 233. *See also* iPhone
Aquafresh, 51
Armani, Giorgio, 171–72
Asian consumers and marketing, 13, 16, 38–39, 127–28
atmospherics, 223–24
authenticity, 142–44
Axe, 82–87, 101

babies, 17–18, 108
baby names, 166–67
Badger, Madonna, 88
banks, 212–13, 214–15, 223–24
Barbie, 158–59
Baynote, 226
Beckham, Victoria, 165
behavior tracking. *See* data mining
Berns, Gregory, 177–78
best-seller lists, 114–15, 176

beverage marketing: cravings and addictiveness, 62, 63–64, 68–69; fear-based, 48, 49–50, 51; health beverages, 181–84; nostalgia in, 146, 147–48, 150–52; peer approval in, 115–16. *See also specific brands*
Bieber, Justin, 94–97
blockbuster effect, 115
body sprays, 23, 82–87, 101, 246
body wash, 98–99
books, 113, 175–76
Borrman, Brandon, 25
Bowie, David, 173
brand awareness/preferences: children, 10–11, 16–21, 25–27; nostalgia and, 16, 17, 26, 27, 150–52; parental influence on, 11–16, 25–27, 150
brand obsession, 60–63, 127–30. *See also* peer pressure
British royal family, 153–57, 177
Brunson, Krista, 179–80
burglar alarms, 37
Buyology (Lindstrom), 61, 183

caffeine, 68, 69
Calvin Klein, 88, 90–92
Cameron, Rose, 99
Canadian Tire, 210
Carmex, 70–71
cars, 24, 80–81, 195–96, 197, 198
celebrities, 157, 161–62, 175, 179–80; baby names and, 166–67; Bieber phenomenon, 94–97; as brands, 154–55, 156–57, 159–60, 171, 172–75; children of, 166, 167; pixie-dust phenomenon, 154–55; royalty, 153–54, 155–57, 177
celebrity doctors, 169–70, 178
celebrity-driven marketing, 157–58, 160, 161, 162–70, 176–78; fragrances and fashion, 163, 171–72; Toyota Prius, 196

Cellfire, 207
Cepia, 110–11
cereals, 31, 147, 189
CEW France, 9–10
ChatThreads, 242, 243, 247
children and teens, 9–27; advertising games, 20, 73–74; age-inappropriate marketing, 21–25; brand awareness and preferences, 10–11, 16–21, 25–27; celebrities' children, 166, 167; child safety products, 40; data mining, 234–35; fantasy-based marketing, 157–59; food preferences, 14–16, 19; gaming addiction, 71–73; generation lap, 125–27; girls' princess aspirations, 154, 158; influence on parents' purchases, 25–27, 246; media exposure, 18; peer pressure and word of mouth, 108, 116–17, 121–27, 246; pre-birth experiences, 11–16; social media addiction, 75; as target market, 17, 20–25, 124
children's products, marketing to adults, 92–97, 110
Chin, Toyna, 21
China, 128, 141–42
Christmas toy fads, 109–11
churches, 200–201
cigarettes, 18, 24, 61, 65, 69–70
Cinderella Ate My Daughter (Orenstein), 21, 158, 162
cleaning products, 39–40, 44–45
Clinton, Bill, 164
Clinton, Hillary, 164
clothing, 22, 80, 88, 142–43; celebrity fashion, 171–72; knockoffs, 123, 144; peer pressure and, 123–24, 125–26; vanity sizing, 101
Club Penguin, 73–74
Coca-Cola, 63–64, 136, 181
cocaine, 67
coffee, 16, 24–25, 68
Cohen, Marshal, 160
colleges, credit card lenders and, 214–15

Collis, Alvin, 223
condoms, 112, 220
conformity. *See* peer pressure
consumer insights. *See* data mining
convenience foods, 40–41, 148
cookies, 226–27, 228
coolness, 118, 122–23, 125–27
Cosby, Bill, 178
cosmetics, 21–22, 51, 201; celebrity-driven marketing, 163, 168–70; health-driven marketing, 186, 191–93; lip balm, 69–71; for men, 100–101, 102, 103; spiritually driven marketing, 198, 199
coupons, 204, 206–9
Cousino, David, 81–82, 83, 84, 91, 92
cravings, 56, 60, 61, 63–66
credit cards, 210–15
credit reporting agencies, 212, 213
customer reviews, 113–14
Cyrus, Miley, 159

Danone, 150–52
data mining, 6, 116, 140, 204–5, 215–16; children and teens, 234–35; credit cards and, 209–15; digital coupons, 206–9; Facebook, 228–30; in-store monitoring, 221; loyalty cards, 203–4, 215–21; mobile phones and, 207–9; Muzak narrowcasting, 222–23; online behavior tracking, 225–28, 230, 232, 234–35, 236; targeted pricing and, 224–25; terms of service and license agreements, 232–34
Davidson's, 31
DeGeneres, Ellen, 165
digital footprint, 235
digital price signage, 224–25
disease, fear of, 28–31
Disney, 158
doctors, celebrity, 169–70, 178
Dolce & Gabbana, 88, 163
dopamine, 56, 59–60, 66, 68, 72–73, 250–51
Dove, 35–36, 98

drinking games, 111–12, 129–30
DSW, 242–43

eBay, 200, 226
end-user license agreements, 232–34
entertainment, 93–97, 115, 117,
    144; advertising as, 20; nostalgia,
    139–40; television, 93, 139–40,
    144, 159, 161, 165–66
environmental responsibility, 194–97,
    252–54
EULAs, 232–34
Euphoria, 90–92
Evian, 150–52
exclusivity, 167–68
expert advice/recommendations,
    169–70, 177–78

Facebook, 74–76, 146, 148–49, 228–
    30; apps and games, 74–75, 229;
    brand pages, 119–20, 146, 242, 254
Factorygate, 48
fads, 109–11. *See also* viral marketing
fame, 161–62, 178–80. *See also*
    celebrities
Fanselow, Michael, 34
fantasy-based marketing, 158–59, 223
Farmgate, 48
FarmVille, 74–75, 229
FDA, 188–89, 190, 193–94
fear, 32–34
fear-based marketing, 34–36, 39,
    51–52, 111; foods, 31, 41, 46–52;
    health and safety products, 28–32,
    37, 39–41, 44–47, 98; life insur-
    ance, 37–39; pharmaceuticals,
    41–44; shopping addiction and, 59
Fey, Tina, 96, 167
50 Cent, 165
finishing touch, 41
fish, 51–52
food marketing, 94; addictive
    substances in foods, 66–69; fear-
    based, 31, 41, 46–52; health claims
    and buzzwords, 31, 182, 189–91;
    nostalgia in, 140–43, 145, 147–48;

packaging, 46–47, 49–50; spiritual
    associations, 197–98
food preferences, children's, 14–16, 19
food safety, 31, 46–47
Foursquare, 76, 120, 230–32
fragrances, 88, 90–92, 98, 198–99,
    246; Axe, 82–87, 101; celebrity-
    driven marketing, 163, 171–72
Frank, Sidney, 115–16
freshness, of food, 46–52, 141
fruit, 49, 50–51, 181–89, 191

Gagner, Amy, 58
gambling, 72
games, 148, 219; icing, 111–12; on-
    line, mobile, and video games, 20,
    71–78, 120, 228, 230–31
Gamestation, 233–34
Gatorade, 23
generation lap, 125, 126
Gillette, 23, 100
Girls Intelligence Agency, 22–23
goji products, 181–84
Google, 112–13, 208, 227, 231–32
Gorgeously Green (Uliano), 253
GPS tracking. *See* location tracking
Grasse, Pierre-Paul, 105
Grey Goose vodka, 115–16
Gross, Dennis, 169, 178
Groupon, 77
Grum, Amanda, 122
guerrilla marketing, 22–23, 118–20.
    See also The Morgensons; word of
    mouth
guilt, 39, 253

hair removal, 22, 99–100, 103
halal products, 199–200
Hamill, Dorothy, 42
hand-me-down influence, 25–27, 150
hand sanitizers, 29–30, 40
Hannah Montana, 159
health and safety products, 28–32,
    39–41, 44–47; online search track-
    ing, 227–28; pharmaceuticals,
    41–44

health benefits, as marketing tool,
184, 186, 189–90, 201; acai, 184–
87; cosmetics and supplements,
191–94; goji, 181–84; label buzzwords, 189–91; pomegranate,
187–89
health claims, 31, 186, 188–94
H-E-B, 102
Heinz, 49, 145
Hepper, Peter, 12
herd mentality. *See* peer pressure
The Hidden Persuaders (Packard), 6
Hofer, Johannes, 133
Hollister, 123, 143
Hollywood Stock Exchange, 117
hope-based marketing, 201–2
Huotilainen, Minna, 11, 15
hybrid cars, 195–96
hygiene, 29–30, 40, 44–47, 98. *See also*
personal care products

icing, 111–12
ideeli, 76, 77
Intentional Chocolate, 198
International Flavors & Fragrances,
9, 90–92
Internet. *See* online *entries;* social
media; YouTube
Internet celebrities, 161
iPad, 208
iPhone, 27, 54–55, 57, 123, 208. *See
also* smart phones
iPod, 124
iTunes, 114–15, 233

Jackson, Michael, 174
Japan, 127–28
Jolie, Angelina, 166
The Joneses, 8, 238
junk food, 14, 66–67

Kalivas, Peter, 60
Kellogg's, 31, 189
Kleenex, 30
knockoffs, 123, 144
Kodak, 137

Kool, 24
Krause, Jens, 106

label terminology, 189–91, 193,
194–95, 199–200, 220
Lacoste, 123–24
La Prairie, 191–92
LeDoux, Joseph, 33
LEGO, 24, 157
Levi's, 112, 125–26
Lewis, Michael, 33
license agreements, 232–34
licensed characters, 18, 19
LifeGem, 174
life insurance, 37–39
lip gloss and lip balm, 21, 69–71
loan offers, 212–13
location tracking, 205, 207, 208–9,
221; Apple, 233; Foursquare, 76,
120, 230–31; Google Buzz, 231–32
logos, 18
Longmead, Carolyn, 57–58
Lopez, Jennifer, 172
Louis Vuitton, 117–18, 127–28, 146
loyalty cards, 203–4, 215–21
LPs, 148–49
Lululemon, 192
Lysol, 30

Madonna, 173–74
Mafia Wars, 74, 75
Martin, J. P., 210
Mattel, 158–59
McCain, John, 194
McDonald's, 17–18, 19, 49, 138
McEntee, Andy, 238, 251
McNeal, James, 25
megachurches, 200–201
men: changing consumer habits, 97–
103; grooming and hygiene prod-
ucts, 82–87, 98–103; suggestive
advertising and, 79–80, 81–82, 87–
90; word-of-mouth influence, 246
Menella, Julie, 15
Men's Health, 88
menthol, 69–70

Method, 44–45
Millennials, 97
Mirzayantz, Nicolas, 15
Moleskine notebooks, 118
monosodium glutamate, 67
Morgenson, Eric, 238, 239, 245, 248, 253–54
Morgenson, Gina, 238, 239, 242–44, 247–48, 253
Morgenson, Jack, 238, 239, 246, 253
Morgenson, Max, 238, 239, 246, 253
Morgenson, Sam, 238, 239, 246, 253
The Morgensons, 8, 237–49; actors and setup, 237–39, 251; data analysis, 247–49, 253; environmental responsibility experiment, 252–54; implications of, 251–52; neighbors' responses, 242–46, 247, 248, 249
Moskvin, Alex, 90
Moss, Kate, 88
movies, 93, 117, 124
MSG, 67
Mueller, Astrid, 59
music, 11–12, 24, 115; celebrity branding, 173–75; consumer behavior and, 140, 222–24; nostalgia and, 135–36, 148–49. *See also* sounds
Muzak, 222–23

narrowcasting, 222–24
network marketing, 187
New Age spirituality, 197–99
Newman, Paul, 172
Newman's Own, 172
nonconformity, 126–27
nonlinear pricing, 219
nostalgia, 122, 131–36, 149–50; Bieber phenomenon and, 96–97; brand loyalty and, 16, 17, 26, 27, 150–52
nostalgia marketing, 135, 136–40, 150–52; authenticity strategies, 140–45; revivals of old ads, 139, 145–49
nutraceuticals, 169, 193–94, 199

Ogilvy, David, 123
online auctions, 72, 77, 111, 200
online behavior: data mining and, 205, 225–28, 230, 232, 234–35, 236. *See also* social media
online games, 71–78, 228, 230–31
online marketing, 23, 225–28; Facebook ads, 229–30; Facebook brand pages, 119–20, 146, 242, 254
online pornography, 80
OnStar, 38
Orenstein, Peggy, 21, 158, 162
Osmond, Donny, 94

packaging, 101, 144; food products, 46–47, 49–50; health-associated products, 183–84, 185, 187–88, 192; soft drinks, 65–66. *See also* label terminology
Packard, Vance, 6
peer pressure, 19–20, 106–8; in Asia, 127–28; children and teens, 108, 116–17, 121–27, 246; fads and viral marketing, 109–13; influence of peer recommendations, 240–46, 247–52; network marketing, 187; popularity phenomena, 113–18; Russian drinking rituals, 129–30; social media and, 118–20. *See also The Morgensons*
PepsiCo, 146, 181
Perricone, Nicholas, 169, 178
personal care products, 21–22, 23, 35–36, 50–51; hand sanitizers, 29–30, 40; for men, 82–87, 97–103, 246. *See also* cosmetics
pharmaceuticals, 41–44, 227–28
Philip Morris, 61, 62, 66
Pitt, Brad, 166
Pollan, Michael, 194
pomegranate products, 187–89
Porsche, 24
Pray, W. Steven, 70–71, 193
Predicta, 225–26
predictive modeling, 213

prescription drugs, 44. *See also* pharmaceuticals
pricing, 219, 224–28
princess aspirations, 154
privacy, 234, 235–36; on Facebook, 228–30; in-store monitoring, 221. *See also* data mining
Procter & Gamble, 102, 195
product recommendations: by celebrities/experts, 169–70, 177–78; by peers, 240–46, 247–52. *See also* word of mouth
property deeds, 213

Quiznos, 94

reality TV, 161, 165–66. *See also The Morgensons*
Red Bull, 62, 67–68, 68–69
religion and spirituality, 182–83, 194, 197–201
ReStockIt.com, 30
Revson, Charles, 201
RevTrax, 206–7
Ritts, Herb, 88
rosy retrospection, 133–34, 149–50
royalty, 153–57, 177
Rudolph, Larry, 175
Rushkoff, Douglas, 19, 222
Russia, 128–30

Safeway, 216
salicylic acid, 70–71
salmonella, 31
salt, 67
Sandberg, Sheryl, 120
Sapolsky, Robert, 135–36
SARS, 28, 29
Scent Analysis, 92
Schor, Juliet, 19
SCVNGR, 76
Sellers, Chris, 23
Selous, Edward, 104
Sephora, 168–70
sexually suggestive marketing, 79–81, 103; to adults buying for children,

92–97; Axe campaign, 82–87; homoeroticism, 87–90
shampoo, 51
shaving, 99–100
shopkick, 209
shopping addiction, 57–60; games to develop, 73–78
Shrek, 93
The Simpsons, 93
skin-care products, 186, 191–93, 198
slogans, 137–38; revivals of, 139, 145–49
smart phones, 27, 54–57, 123; data mining and, 207–9; game apps, 76, 120; GPS tracking, 205, 207, 208–9
smells, 9–10, 13, 15
Smirnoff, 111–12
Smyth, Erika, 90
soap, 98, 99
social media, 23, 118–20, 240, 252; addiction to, 55, 56; games, 74–75, 76, 120, 228, 230–31; privacy and data mining, 228–32; viral marketing, 111–13, 146. *See also* Facebook
social responsibility, 194–97, 252–54
somatic markers, 183, 185–86, 199
sounds, 11–13, 56, 64–66. *See also* music
South Beach Diet, 163–64
Spears, Britney, 175
spirituality, as marketing tool, 182–83, 194, 197–201
Starbucks, 24–25, 207
Stewart, Martha, 178
Stinky Stink, 23, 246
student credit offers, 214–15
sugar, 68
Super Bowl advertising, 132
superfruits, 181–89
superheroes, 157, 158
supermarkets, 218–21; digital coupons, 207; in-store monitoring, 221; loyalty cards, 216–21; music in, 222–23; product placement in, 102–3, 217–18, 219; time-sensitive pricing, 224–25; Whole Foods,

47–48, 51–52, 140–42. *See also* food marketing
supplements, 169, 193–94, 199
sweat, 48, 64
swine flu, 28–31
Swoopo, 77
symbolics, 47–51, 63–66, 141–44. *See also* packaging

Target, 148, 207
taste preferences, 15
Taylor, Elizabeth, 171
teens. *See* children and teens
television, 93, 139–40, 144, 159, 161, 165–66; *Today* show book club, 175–76. *See also The Morgensons*
termites, 104–5, 106
terms of service, 232–34
Tesco, 22
Thai Life Insurance, 38–39
time, in ads, 137–38
Tishk, Marcy, 238, 251
tobacco and cigarettes, 18, 24, 61, 65, 69–70
Today show book club, 175–76
Toyota Prius, 195–96, 197
toys, 109–11, 148, 158–59
Toy Story, 93
trans fats, 191
transference, 162–64, 167–68, 254–55
Trojan, 112, 220
Trump, Donald, 171
tweens, 21–23, 121. *See also* children and teens
Twitter, 120, 231, 232, 240

U.S. Food and Drug Administration, 188–89, 190, 193–94
Uliano, Sophie, 253
Underhill, Paco, 92–93

Unilever, 81–82, 99; Axe, 82–87; Euphoria, 90–92
universities, credit card lenders and, 214–15

VandenBiesen, Dean, 174
vanity sizing, 101
Viacom, 112–13
video games, 71–73
viral marketing, 110–13, 146
Vitaminwater, 164–66
vodka, 111–12, 115–16, 128–30
Vranich, Belisa, 89

wabi-sabi, 143
Wahlberg, Mark, 88
wallet carriers, 92–93
Walmart, 31–32, 209–10, 232
Warhol, Andy, 178
Web browsers, 226–27, 228
Weber, Fabrice, 171
Web sites. *See* online *entries*
Weintraub, Arlene, 187
Whole Foods, 47–48, 51–52, 140–42
Williams, Evan, 120
women, 194–95; Bieber phenomenon, 94–97; emotional decision making, 100; environmentally responsible products and, 194–95; fear-based marketing and, 37, 39–41; pregnancy and new mothers, 11–16, 39–41; suggestive advertising and, 79; word-of-mouth influence, 242–44, 246
word of mouth, 240–41, 247–48, 254. *See also The Morgensons*

YouTube, 112–13, 144, 146

Zhu Zhu pet hamster, 110–11
Zynga, 75

About the Author

When he was a kid growing up in Denmark, MARTIN LINDSTROM had but one thought in his life: LEGO. He was, to put it simply, obsessed with LEGO. He hand-built and slept on a LEGO bed. He dressed in LEGO's colors. He even turned the family garden into his very own LEGOLAND creation, a miniature village complete with bonsai trees, scooped-out canals, and dozens of houses and ships constructed entirely out of LEGO.

Then one bright summer's day in 1981, ambitious 11-year-old Martin Lindstrom opened the doors to his own LEGOLAND, optimistically anticipating hordes of visitors from near and far. Not a single person showed up.

Aware that something more than mere brilliant design was needed to attract visitors, young Martin suddenly had a flash of inspiration: he would advertise! He promptly persuaded the local newspaper to run an ad, and sure enough, the following week 131 people streamed through the garden gate. Including two lawyers from LEGO, who very politely informed Martin that if he persisted in using the name LEGOLAND he would be guilty of trademark infringement. *That's when he first realized the seductive power of marketing and advertising.*

So Martin decided to open his own advertising agency, which he did a couple of months later, at the ripe age of 12. And thus began a lifelong relationship with marketing and brands.

After selling his agency in 1988, Lindstrom attended the Academy of Advertising before joining international giant BBDO. By age 30, Lindstrom had become one of the most respected names in the industry.

He has since spent 300 days on the road annually sharing his wisdom and pioneering methodologies through his role as a speaker and trusted adviser to countless CEOs, celebrities, and royal families.

In 2009, amid the rubble of the economic meltdown, Lindstrom opened a new chapter. Disheartened by much that he had observed on the front lines of the branding wars for the past two decades, he decided to turn the spotlight inward and reveal all the tricks and traps he'd seen along his journey from 11-year-old LEGO enthusiast to one of the globe's foremost marketing experts. His goal? By opening our eyes to all the ways in which we, as consumers, are being manipulated and deceived, he would help us resist the siren song of advertising and make smarter, more informed decisions about how we spend our money. Thus, *Brandwashed* was born.

Lindstrom has been featured in the *Wall Street Journal, Newsweek, Time, The Economist, New York Times, BusinessWeek, Washington Post, USA Today, Fast Company, Forbes, Harvard Business Review, The Guardian, New York Post, Vogue,* and *People.* He also frequently appears on ABC News, *CNN Money,* CBS, Bloomberg, *Fox & Friends,* Discovery Channel, and NBC's *Today* show, as an expert on consumer awareness and advocacy. He also pens a weekly column for *Fast Company.*

His previous book *Buyology* (February 2010 paperback by Crown Publishing) was voted "Pick of the Year" by *USA Today* and reached top-10 bestseller lists in the U.S. and worldwide. His 5 books have been translated into more than 40 languages and published in more than 60 countries.

In 2009, *Time* magazine named Lindstrom one of the World's 100 Most Influential People for his groundbreaking work on neuroscience and branding.